HOW THE
BODY
WORKS

Hearing through a piece
of string

Finding out how flexible your joints are

Building a turbine to test your lung power

Seeing how your kidneys filter wastes from your blood

Finding out about your lung's
inner surface

HOW THE
BODY
WORKS

Steve Parker

Seeing your pupil's reflex action

Following sequences of lights to test your short-term memory

Finding out how
you balance

Dorling Kindersley
London • *New York* • *Stuttgart*

A DORLING KINDERSLEY BOOK

Project Art Editor	Bryn Walls
Project Editor	Roger Tritton
Designer	Christina Betts
Editorial Assistants	Emily Hill, Mukul Patel
Production	Sarah Fuller
Managing Art Editor	Philip Gilderdale
Managing Editor	Ruth Midgley

This Eyewitness ®/™ Science Guide
first published in Great Britain in 1994
by Dorling Kindersley Limited,
9 Henrietta Street, London WC2 8PS

A CIP catalogue record for this book is available
from the British Library

ISBN 0–7513–0081–0

Reproduced by Colourscan, Singapore and printed
by Tien Wah Press, Singapore

Contents

Introduction _____ 6
The home laboratory _____ 8

The body

What makes a body? _____ 12
The body's ingredients _____ 14
Body shapes and sizes _____ 16
Faces and features _____ 18
The body's limits _____ 20
Body systems _____ 22
The body's building blocks _____ 24
Body cells _____ 26
The cell membrane _____ 28

The body's surface

The living barrier _____ 32
The skin _____ 34
Skin changes _____ 36
Fingerprints _____ 38
Hair and nails _____ 40

The body's framework

The flexible frame _____ 44
The skeleton _____ 46
Inside bones _____ 48
Joints and levers _____ 50
Types of joint _____ 52

The moving body

Muscles and movements _____ 56
Muscles _____ 58
Muscle teams _____ 60

Muscle pairs —————————— 62
Muscle stamina and strength —————— 64
The versatile hand —————————— 66

The oxygen supply

The lungs and breathing —————— 70
The respiratory system —————————— 72
Breathing in and out ——————————— 74
Lung power ——————————————— 76

Fuelling the body

Eating and digestion ——————— 80
Diet and energy —————————————— 82
The digestive system ——————————— 84
Teeth —————————————————— 86
Chewing and swallowing ————————— 88
Digestion ————————————————— 90

Transport and maintenance

The circulatory system —————— 94
Circulation ———————————————— 96
The heart ————————————————— 98
The heart-beat ——————————————— 100
Blood —————————————————— 102
The internal environment —————— 104
Hormones ————————————————— 106
Cleaning the blood ———————————— 108
Balancing body fluids ——————————— 110
Body temperature ————————————— 112

The control network

The brain and nerves —————————— 116
The nervous system ——————————— 118
Reflexes ——————————————————— 120
Reactions ——————————————————— 122
Reactions and decisions ————————— 124
The brain ————————————————— 126
Memory —————————————————— 128
Short-term memory ———————————— 130
Learning —————————————————— 132

Sensing the surroundings

The body's senses —————————— 136
The eyes ——————————————————— 138
Seeing —————————————————— 140
The sensitivity of the eyes ————————— 142
Seeing 3-D images ————————————— 144
The eyes and co-ordination ————————— 146
The limits of the eyes ——————————— 148
Tricking the eyes and brain ————————— 150
The ears and hearing ——————————— 152
Judging sounds ——————————————— 154
Balance —————————————————— 156
The nose and smell ———————————— 158
The tongue and taste ——————————— 160
Taste expectations ————————————— 162
Touch —————————————————— 164
The touch picture ————————————— 166

The body's life-cycle

New life and growth —————————— 170
Reproduction ———————————————— 172
Growth and ageing ————————————— 174
Genes and inheritance ——————————— 176

Using a microscope ———————————— 178
Glossary —————————————————— 179
Index —————————————————— 186
Acknowledgments ————————————— 192

INTRODUCTION

WE OFTEN TAKE THINGS FOR GRANTED as we grow more familiar with them. No matter how amazing something may be, we stop noticing it if we encounter it every day. The human body is a perfect example.

Your body is an incredible masterpiece of bioengineering. Under its skin lie hundreds of muscles, bones, blood vessels, glands, and other parts. These work day and night, as blood pulses through the arteries and veins, food passes through the intestines, and electrical signals flash along the nerves.

But do you think very much about the amazing and complex hive of activity that is your body when you look in the mirror each morning and see that familiar face? Probably not.

As you begin to learn about the structure and workings of the body, endless questions occur. How do your muscles move your body? Why do you breathe? What happens to food when you swallow? Why is your blood red? When is the body fully grown? Why do you resemble your parents? This book answers these questions and many, many more in an exciting, visual, and practical way.

The first chapter in this book describes the whole body and its main structures and features. Each of the following chapters is devoted to a major body system. A body system is a set of organs and other body parts that work together to carry out a major function within the whole body – such as making the body move, swallowing and digesting food, delivering and collecting blood, or seeing, hearing, and smelling what is happening in the world around us.

Organs themselves are made of body tissues, which are in turn made of microscopic cells. Every second, even as we sleep, millions of cells are being born and dying as the body maintains and repairs itself. This book includes detailed microscope photographs showing what the cells look like and how they work.

The book is packed with experiments and projects for the whole family. Some of them are safe for young people to carry out. When an adult's help is advised, this is clearly stated at the beginning of the experiment.

Many experiments in the book need only a few everyday items that can be found around the home. Others are more elaborate and call for greater time and effort. But all of the experiments require one vital piece of equipment – *you*. Find out directly about the way you grow and develop, and how your body works inside.

The more that you learn about the body and the way it works, the more fascinating it becomes. Also, the more you know, the better you can look after yourself, stay healthy, and live a long and active life.

The home laboratory

THE EXPERIMENTS in this book do not require specialized equipment. Most of the items can be found in the kitchen and around the house, or obtained easily and inexpensively. Alternatives that work just as well are often given in the list of materials for an experiment. The most important piece of equipment is your own body! You will also need some friends to help you. Shown on these two pages are some items you may find useful to help you to explore the human body.

■ Safety precautions

For some experiments you will need containers that are heat-proof. Always use protective goggles and heat-proof gloves where indicated. NEVER put chemicals in any containers where they might be mistaken for food or drink items.

Glass bowl

Glass jar

Heat-proof gloves

Heat-proof tile

Cutting mat

Noseclip

Plastic-edged mirror

Goggles

Plastic bag

Saucer

Glass jar

Glass

■ Measures

You will need measuring instruments in some of the experiments. All of the measurements in this book are given using two measurement systems. Use one system or the other – do not mix them. Make sure that you use a metal ruler as a cutting edge when you are cutting paper or card.

Protractor

Stop-watch

Metal and plastic rulers

Glue

String

Assorted elastic bands

Paper-clips

Thermometer

■ Materials

Most of the materials you need for the experiments and models are everyday items. You may already have some in your home, such as drinking straws. An assortment of differently coloured sheets of paper and card will be very useful. Other materials, such as wood, dowelling rods, and screws, can be bought from a hardware or modelling shop.

■ Tools and instruments

You will need coloured pens, scissors, pencils, paints, and a good craft knife. Different types of tape are also very useful. You may need to borrow some ordinary household tools, such as saws, pliers, and screwdrivers. Ask an adult for help if these tools or other sharp instruments are required.

A simple light microscope allows you to examine exterior parts of the body in amazing detail, although it is not essential to have one for most of the experiments in this book. Advice on setting up and using a light microscope is given on page 178.

Drinking straws *Candle* *Balloons* *Modelling clay* *Plastic putty* *Plastic tubing*

Assorted pieces of wood *Coloured card*

Paints *Tongs* *Light microscope* *Slides* *Cover slips* *Tenon saw* *Coping saw* *Pliers* *Screwdriver*

Paint-brush *Pen* *Pencil* *Craft knife* *Compasses* *Dropper* *Masking tape* *Insulating tape* *Adhesive tape* *Scissors* *Kitchen knife*

The BODY

Variations on a theme
*From ancient times, people have celebrated the
beauty of the human form in painting and
sculpture. The Ancient Greeks carved an ideal
body shape in stone (above). But every person is
different. The unique shapes and curves of each
body allow us to pick out individuals in a
crowd of thousands (left).*

EACH HUMAN BODY HAS
the same basic design: two
eyes, two ears, a nose, a
mouth, a chest, an
abdomen, two arms, and
two legs. Even so, there is
incredible variation in
body shapes and sizes. All
of our bodies are miracles
of engineering, far more
sophisticated than the
most up-to-date computers.
The body grows and
develops, feeds and
maintains itself, senses the
world around it, and deals
with the countless
challenges of life.

WHAT MAKES A BODY?

THERE ARE MANY POSSIBLE WAYS to approach the question "What makes a body?". The science of biology suggests that humans are relatives of other mammals, and that the human body we know today was made by millions of years of evolution. The science of anatomy shows that the body is made of main parts, called organs, composed of millions of cells. And the science of genetics reveals how, in a sense, the body makes itself – from instructions hidden in its genetic blueprint (pp.176–177).

To understand what makes a human body, we can compare it with other, similar bodies in the world around us. There are many parallels between our bodies and those of other mammals. Just like the four thousand other mammal species, we have warm blood, hairy skin, and a bony skeleton. Also like other mammals, we feed our babies on mother's milk. We belong to the group of mammals called primates, which also includes lemurs, monkeys, and apes. Indeed, the great apes – the orang-utan, gorilla, and chimpanzee – resemble us in incredible detail. Our genetic material, made up of DNA (p.180), is over 98 per cent

The orang-utan (above), chimpanzee, and gorilla – the great apes – are our closest animal relatives.

identical to a chimpanzee's. Therefore it makes scientific sense to view humans as close relatives of the great apes.

Human origins

The philosopher Aristotle (384–322 BC) of Ancient Greece, taught that to understand something thoroughly, we should know its origins (where it comes from). So to understand what makes a body, we must look at the body's origins.

Some people believe that human beings are specially created by a Deity or Supreme Being. Modern biological science sees the human body, like all natural living things, as the result of evolution. It holds that the human body has developed over millions of years, through a long sequence of changes that have made it better adapted to its environment. Since we have most similarities with the apes, it is likely that both we and the apes evolved from a common ape-like ancestor.

In 1859, the English naturalist Charles Darwin (1809–1882) announced his theory of evolution in great detail in his book *On the Origin of Species by Means of Natural Selection*. This book caused a great deal of controversy at the time.

Fossils of human bones and teeth show how the human species may have evolved over several million years. An early human predecessor was the small-brained, chimp-like creature known as *Australopithecus*

The fossil skull of a Neanderthal human (top) is longer from front to back and is made of thicker bone than the skull of a modern person (above).

("Southern Ape"), which walked upright three million years ago in Africa. Almost two million years ago came the bigger-brained, tool-using *Homo habilis* ("Handy Human"). Then, about one million years ago, came the larger, more skilled tool-maker *Homo erectus* ("Upright Human"). People who look like

In their own image, the Aboriginal people of Australia drew "X-ray" pictures of humans, with rods representing limb bones. Australian rock art is thousands of years old.

us, modern *Homo sapiens* ("Wise Human"), probably first appeared about 200,000 years ago.

However, some evolutionary branches came to dead-ends. One such branch was probably the Neanderthal people of what is now Europe and the Middle East. Although Neanderthal people were well adapted to the intense cold of the ice ages, they had died out by about 30,000 years ago.

■ Early anatomy

People have been fascinated by the body's inner structure for thousands of years. Cave art from prehistoric times shows that the artists knew about the inside of the body. In ancient civilizations in Egypt, Greece, China, India, and elsewhere, people studied and wrote about the twin sciences of anatomy (the body's structure) and physiology (how the body works). They did this partly from curiosity, but also to understand how the body became ill, so that they could treat and cure people. These scientists – including the "Father of Medicine", Hippocrates (c.460–c.377 BC) of Ancient Greece – were the first doctors.

The first person to write in great depth about anatomy was Galen (AD 129–c.201) of Ancient Rome. Although he was a doctor, tradition prevented him from dissecting (cutting open) dead people, so many of his descriptions are adapted from animal studies. So great was Galen's authority that people blindly accepted all of his teachings, including the mistaken ones, for over a thousand years.

Galen was physician to the gladiators in the Colosseum in Rome.

In Europe, from about 1300, there was a new interest in the arts and sciences. During this Renaissance period, people began to study the body more thoroughly. They dissected human corpses so that they could see exactly what the body was made of. The major anatomical book of this period was *De Humani Corporis Fabrica* ("The Fabric of the Human Body") by Andreas Vesalius (p.22), professor of anatomy at Padua, Italy. Vesalius drew and described what he actually saw, rather than what tradition taught should be present. His work brought the science of anatomy into the modern world.

■ Micro-anatomy

By about 1600 the body's basic anatomy was understood in detail. But the invention of the microscope opened up a new microscopic world to see and study. Microscope pioneers such as the Dutchman Antony van Leeuwenhoek (p.172) and the Italian Marcello Malpighi (p.104) studied human organs under the microscope and saw that, like other living things, the body is constructed of cells – the "building blocks" of life (pp.24–25).

Each individual cell is a living entity: it uses nutrients and energy, carries out chemical processes, controls its own cellular contents, and reproduces itself. Each cell also has a special role to play in keeping the body running smoothly.

All bodies have the same basic plan, but the variety in physical proportions and features, and in our personality, emotions, and experiences, makes each of us an individual.

■ Genes

Over the last century, we have gained a far more detailed knowledge of what makes a body. A new type of microscope (p.24) – called an electron microscope – can magnify an object a million times or more. It has revealed the structures from which cells are made and even their molecules (p.182).

One of these molecules is deoxyribonucleic acid (DNA), the "blueprint for life". In 1953 the English scientist Francis Crick and the American biologist James Watson unravelled the structure of DNA (p.176). Inside each cell, long strings of DNA

A single body cell (pp.24–25) from the lining of the cheek has a life of only a few hours before it is rubbed away as you chew.

What sets humans apart from other animals is the capacity of our brains (pp.126–127) for abstract thinking, planning, problem-solving, and other aspects of what we term "intelligence".

carry instructions, in a chemical code, for growth from an embryo (p.173) to an adult human, and for running and repairing the body. Each instruction is in the form of a gene. In a single cell there are perhaps more than 100,000 genes, on DNA totalling almost 3 m (10 ft) in length.

When an egg cell is fertilized by a sperm cell (p.172), a new baby is conceived. The egg cell and sperm cell pass on, in the form of genes, the instructions that determine the general shape and size of the new person, and what features he or she will have.

The body's ingredients

HOW YOU STUDY the ingredients of the body depends on which science (type of knowledge) you are interested in. To the biologist, the body is built up from millions and millions of cells that help the body to grow and to maintain itself. To the chemist, the body is an amazingly complicated combination of atoms and molecules – undergoing millions of chemical reactions every second. To the dietary expert, the body is a collection of substances such as proteins, minerals, and carbohydrates, and it needs to take in correctly balanced types of food to keep itself healthy and in good working order. And to a mechanical engineer, the body is an incredibly sophisticated, self-controlling, self-repairing machine.

■ An artificial body?

Many science fiction stories feature robots, androids, or other human-like machines. But the technology needed to build such sophisticated machines is still far in the future, if it will ever exist. Robots have never successfully copied the body's ability to walk in a well-balanced way on two legs, let alone its huge variety of fast-action, precise movements and its range of sight, hearing, touch, and other senses. Even the most advanced computers do not come close to the human brain's capacity for intelligent thought, learning, and creativity.

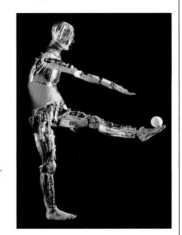

In the human image
Human-shaped robots are built for research purposes. But the balanced, upright, two-legged posture of the human body is very difficult for a robot to mimic.

■ From body to atom

Like all of the matter in the Universe, the body is made of tiny particles called atoms. Collections of atoms make up molecules, molecules make up organelles, organelles make up cells, and so on, in a level-by-level hierarchy (organization) in the body. When early anatomists (p.13) studied the whole body, they were interested mainly in its large structural parts, the organs. Later, microscopists studied the body at a different level of its hierarchy – its micro-structural parts, the cells. Other scientists developed a greater understanding of the body's functions (what it does). These scientists were particularly interested in the nature of body systems and tissues. Only in this century, with the development of the electron microscope, have we been able to view the smallest, most basic units in the body hierarchy – organelles and molecules.

Body
There are more than five billion human bodies on Earth. Each is a unique individual. But all bodies have the same basic outer design, and inside they all have the same main parts in the same places.

System
The body can be thought of as a collection of systems (pp.22–23). Each system has one major role. For the digestive system above, this is to digest food so that it can be absorbed by the body.

Organ
An organ is a distinct body part that carries out one or more main functions. Several organs working together make up a body system. For example, the liver is an organ that is part of the digestive system.

Tissue
Each organ is composed of one or more kinds of tissue. A tissue is a group of similar cells that carry out a specialized job. The liver is mostly made of sheets of hepatocytes – cells that process nutrients.

■ The body's chemical contents

The chemical substances that make up the human body can be divided into different groups, which are similar to the groups of substances – called nutrients – in the food we eat (p.83). The main nutrients in the body are carbohydrates, proteins, lipids (fats and oils), and minerals. If these main nutrients and other substances could be taken from the body and transformed into more familiar forms, they might look something like the collections of ingredients shown here:

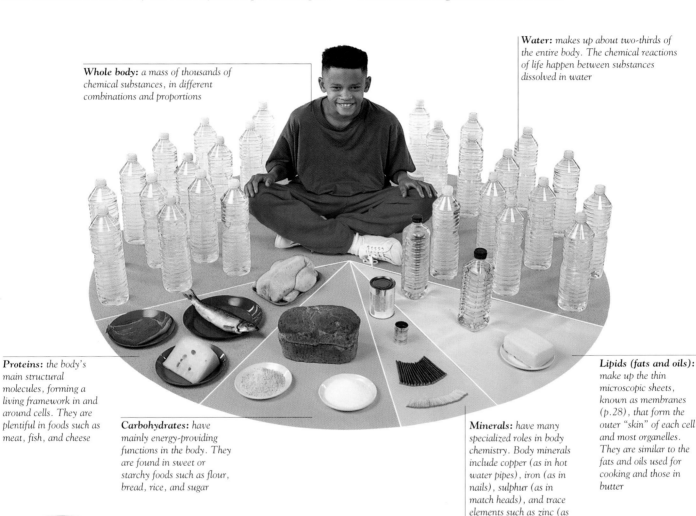

Whole body: *a mass of thousands of chemical substances, in different combinations and proportions*

Water: *makes up about two-thirds of the entire body. The chemical reactions of life happen between substances dissolved in water*

Proteins: *the body's main structural molecules, forming a living framework in and around cells. They are plentiful in foods such as meat, fish, and cheese*

Carbohydrates: *have mainly energy-providing functions in the body. They are found in sweet or starchy foods such as flour, bread, rice, and sugar*

Minerals: *have many specialized roles in body chemistry. Body minerals include copper (as in hot water pipes), iron (as in nails), sulphur (as in match heads), and trace elements such as zinc (as in tin cans)*

Lipids (fats and oils): *make up the thin microscopic sheets, known as membranes (p.28), that form the outer "skin" of each cell and most organelles. They are similar to the fats and oils used for cooking and those in butter*

Cell
The cell (pp.24–25) is the basic unit, or building block, of all living things, plant or animal. A hepatocyte is 0.03 mm ($^1/_{900}$ in) wide and is shaped like a box with rounded corners.

Organelle
The cell contains structures called organelles (p.26). An important example is the sausage-shaped mitochondrion. Inside it, energy is released from nutrients and made available for the cell's use.

Molecule
Each organelle contains thousands or millions of molecules. This molecule is glucose, the body's main energy-rich ingredient. The grey balls in this model of a glucose molecule are carbon atoms (right).

Atom
A molecule is a combination of particles known as atoms. A glucose molecule has 24 atoms (including six carbon atoms like the one above). All life is based on organic (carbon-containing, p.183) molecules.

Body shapes and sizes

HUMAN BODIES COME IN ALL SHAPES, sizes, and proportions. The kind of figure you have depends in part on whether you are a child or an adult, a female or a male. Your figure is mostly the result of the size and shape of the bones of your skeleton. This is especially true for height. Total body height is only about 2.5 cm (1 in) more than the skeleton's height. In an adult, a quarter of this height is taken up by one bone in each thigh, the femur. Body proportions also depend mainly on bone size. For example, some people have broad shoulders; others have narrow ones. Some people have a short torso (trunk) and long limbs; others have a long torso and short limbs. Diet, exercise, and living conditions also affect your shape and size. Excess food is stored as fat that pads out the body, while regular exercise can lead to large, bulging muscles.

Food and conditions

The body's genes play a large part in controlling how it grows and develops. But the amount and quality of food that a person eats are also important. Babies and children who do not get proper nourishment grow more slowly than they would if they had a healthy diet. As adults, they may not be as tall or as well developed as they would have been if they had been well nourished. Cramped, unhealthy living conditions, with a lack of light and fresh air, can also have an effect on growth.

Body measurements

Far back in history, people did not have rulers or tape measures. But they did have body parts, such as hands and arms, which they could use for measuring. The size of the body parts varied from one person to another. But they were an accurate enough guide for the building methods of the day. The ancient civilizations of Egypt (c.3300 to c.1000 BC), Greece (c.900 to c.350 BC), and India (c.2300 to c.1700 BC) all had measuring systems that were based on parts of the body, although they often used different names for the same measurement. The names they used are shown in this table.

Geometric shapes

Great artists and sculptors noted that the head, torso, arms, and legs of the human body are in proportions that please our eyes. "Vitruvius man", by the Italian artist Leonardo da Vinci (1452–1519), showed how the arms and legs of a human body mark points on both a circle and a square.

		EGYPTIAN	GREEK	INDIAN
	Width of finger	Zebo	Daktyloi	Angula
	Width of palm	Shep	Palaste	No equivalent measurement
	Width of outspread fingers	Span	Spithame	Pradesa
	Fingertip to elbow point	Royal cubit	Olympic cubit	Vitasti
	Tip to tip of outstretched arms	No equivalent measurement	Orguia	Vyayama

Poor living conditions
If food is in short supply and conditions poor, as in this 19th-century soup kitchen, people's heights tend to be lower than normal.

EXPERIMENT
Body proportions

Even if you are the same height as a friend, you may have longer legs or shorter arms. Variations like these depend mainly on the sizes of the bones in your skeleton. Using card discs, make a "human graph" to show how body proportions vary. Photograph the line-up so you can study it. Measure distances between different discs with a ruler.

You Will Need
● sets of 6 coloured card discs
● adhesive pads or double-sided adhesive tape

1 Ask a friend to stand up straight, with his or her shoulders square. Press to find the hard, bony points on the shoulder, elbow, wrist, hip, knee, and ankle. Stick a different coloured disc on each of these parts.

2 Stick discs on a whole line of friends. Measure distances between discs on each person. How much of the body height is made up of legs? Is the upper arm longer than the lower arm? Do tall people always have longer arms than shorter people?

Faces and features

HOW EASY IS IT TO RECOGNIZE people you know? You can often identify family and friends from far away by their body sizes and proportions, and the ways they stand and walk. If they are closer, you probably look at their faces. You do this not only to identify people, but also to assess their emotions and what they are thinking. In particular, you concentrate on the eyes and mouth, since these reveal a lot about a person's moods and intentions. It is amazing how easily people can change their appearance – and even become unrecognizable – just by altering the face with spectacles, make-up, or a moustache.

Revealing faces

Which of the face's features helps you to recognize someone most easily? Is it the eyes, the nose, or the mouth? Take photographs of familiar people, or cut out famous faces from magazines. Test your friends by revealing different face features one at a time.

YOU WILL NEED
- *L-shaped cards*
- *camera and film or photographs of faces*

Reveal the parts
Lay the cards over a photograph to reveal only the eyes. Can your friend identify the person pictured? Try again with a new face or a different facial feature. Which feature helps you to recognize people most easily?

Photographing a friend's face
To take a photograph of a face for these experiments, hold the camera directly in front of your friend and level with his or her eyes. Turn the camera so that it is vertical. Make sure your friend's face fills the frame and that she or he is looking into the lens. Then click. You may want to ask an adult to take the picture.

EXPERIMENT
Mirror-image faces

Adult help is advised for this experiment

Is a face exactly symmetrical? In other words, is one side an exact mirror-image of the other? Are your eyes or your ears level with each other? Is your mouth the same shape at both corners? Find out with this experiment, which uses photographs of faces. When you get your film developed, ask for a normal set of prints and a set printed with the image reversed. (Make sure the photographs are taken head-on, as opposite.)

YOU WILL NEED
● *2 sets of photographs of friends' faces, one set printed normally and the other with the image reversed*
● *craft knife* ● *cutting mat* ● *adhesive tape*
● *metal ruler*

1 PLACE THE RULER down the centre of each photograph, exactly through the middle of the eyes, nose, and mouth. Carefully cut along this line.

Right half of face (normal)

Right half of face (reversed)

Left half of face (normal)

Left half of face (reversed)

2 PLACE HALF of one photo next to the reversed version of the same half. Tape together the backs of these two halves. Repeat for the other halves.

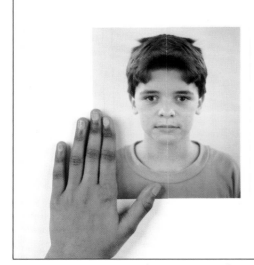

3 YOU HAVE MADE each picture exactly symmetrical. Each picture has one side of the face and its mirror image. See how the two faces look different from each other – often dramatically so! This

experiment shows that people's faces are never exactly symmetrical. One eye or eyebrow is always higher than the other, or one side of the mouth or the nose is shaped differently from the other.

■ Recalling a face

Photo-fits
Human faces like this one can be built up feature by feature using a special computer programme.

Although it may be easy to recognize faces, it can be difficult to describe or draw them. So to recreate the faces of missing people, or to help people to identify suspects in a crime, the police use photo-fits. These are pictures of faces built up from face parts – such as hair, forehead, and eyes – of varying shapes and sizes. The viewer concentrates on recalling each of the suspect's facial features in turn. Then he or she selects the best likeness for each feature from a collection of photographs or a choice of images on a computer screen. These parts are gradually put together to build up a whole face, like the one above.

■ How identical?

Identical twins have exactly the same genes (the "blueprints" of the body, p.181). When they are babies, and even when they are at school, the twins may be very hard to tell apart. But, like two identical cars rolling off a production line, they can never be in precisely the same place all of the time. During their lives, they eat different foods and they are exposed to different types of wear and tear. These different living conditions affect the appearance of their bodies in different ways. Usually, the older the twins become, the more different from each other they look.

The body's limits

Do you think you would win a running race against a cheetah? Or a diving competition against a dolphin? Probably not. But what about a running race against the dolphin? Compared to other animals, humans may not excel at any single event. But we are good at a variety of physical feats and skills. Imagine a well-trained human athlete taking part with various animals in a decathlon competition, comprising ten different events such as running, jumping, throwing, and swimming. The human athlete would almost certainly receive the overall prize – and would definitely win the throwing event, since very few animals are able to throw an object any distance.

Finding your limits

Adult help is advised for this experiment
It is true that "practice makes perfect", especially with such muscle-developing actions as push-ups (opposite). But sometimes we are not aware of what our bodies can do. For example, this experiment shows that your joints may be more flexible than you realize.
Caution: If you feel dizzy, sick, or in any discomfort or pain, stop at once and rest.

■ Animal champions

Here are some of the best performers from the mammal group – but only at their own events. An elephant hardly excels at high jumping! The human is the most capable all-round athlete.

Throwing
A human athlete throws a javelin well over 90 m (295 ft). Few animals could even hold it.

High jump
Big cats such as the puma can clear 4.5 m (15 ft), nearly twice our record.

Weight-lifting
An elephant uses its trunk to lift over 500 kg (1,100 lb), about twice the human record.

Long jump
A kangaroo can leap more than 12 m (39 ft), 3 m (10 ft) more than the human record.

Long-distance running
Wolves can dog-trot on and off at about 8 kph (5 mph) for several days. No human can do this.

Swimming
A sea-lion swims at about 24 kph (15 mph), three times faster than the fastest human.

Place your hands on your knees for better stability

1 SIT ON THE FLOOR, your back upright and legs straight out in front. Slowly move each leg out to the side. Keep moving your legs slowly sideways until you feel you cannot go any farther. Stop moving. Rest and relax in this position.

Move your legs slowly and carefully

2 THIRTY SECONDS LATER, carefully try to move your legs slightly more. You may be surprised at how much farther they go. You can do this because the muscles, tendons, and ligaments in your hip joints have stretched and relaxed into the extended position.

▪ Artificial aids

Through the ages, by ingenuity and inventiveness, humans have created aids to improve and extend the body's physical capabilities. In the Stone Age, rock axes and spears allowed people to hunt bigger, more powerful animals. Today, wearing the latest running shoes saves split-seconds in races.

Webbed feet
Flippers copy the webbed feet of seals and otters. They give swimmers greater speed and power in the water.

▪ A better way

Occasionally, humans develop a completely new way of doing something familiar. For example, US high-jumper Dick Fosbury developed a new leaping technique in the 1960s which was more effective than the old methods. Other high-jumpers took up his technique, and records rose rapidly.

Pre-Fosbury
Most high-jumpers "straddled" the bar, sideways and face down.

The "Fosbury flop"
With his innovative head-first, face-up style, Dick Fosbury won gold at the 1968 Olympics.

EXPERIMENT
Improving your ability

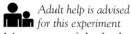 *Adult help is advised for this experiment*

Many parts of the body respond to the demands put on them. For example, regular physical activity increases the strength and stamina of muscles. It also improves the efficiency of the lungs and heart. If you do an activity such as push-ups (press-ups) regularly, you should soon find that you have improved. In a safe place, count how many push-ups you can do without too much strain. For one push-up, bend your arms to lower your chin so that it touches the floor, then straighten your arms and lock your elbows. Repeat the test each day. Does the exercise become any easier? *Caution: If you feel dizzy, sick, or in any discomfort or pain, stop at once and rest.*

Push-ups
When you do push-ups, keep your body as straight as possible.

Body systems

IF YOU LOOK AT THE OWNER'S manual for a car, you will probably find that it is arranged in chapters, each dealing with one particular system – a set of closely connected parts inside the machine. One chapter is about the electrical system, another about the fuel system, another about the brakes, and so on. You could arrange the "owner's manual" of the human body in the same way. Each of the body's main systems has a major job to do, such as getting oxygen, digesting food, or disposing of waste. The systems often work together to make sure that the whole body runs smoothly.

■ DISCOVERY ■
Andreas Vesalius

Until the Renaissance period of the late 14th to mid 17th centuries, people's ideas about the body had changed very little for over a thousand years. In the Renaissance, people began to question the old knowledge. Instead of relying on pictures from books, they wanted to open up bodies and look for themselves. The greatest early anatomist was the Belgian Andreas Vesalius (1514–1564), who became a professor at Padua in Italy. His book of 1543, *De Humani Corporis Fabrica* ("The Fabric of the Human Body"), portrayed the body in amazing detail.

Skin, hair, and nails (integumentary system)
Skin protects the body from wear and harmful rays, keeps in body fluids, and senses touch. Skin and hair also help in the control of body temperature.

Muscles (muscular system)
All body movement is caused by the contraction of muscles. Most of these muscles move bones, for actions such as walking or lifting, but some move other body features, such as the eyebrows.

Bones (skeletal system)
The bones of the skeleton are the supporting framework of the body. Bones also protect some inner parts. The skull shields the brain, and the ribs form a cage around the heart and lungs.

Heart, blood vessels, and blood (circulatory system)
These parts make up the body's transport network. The heart pumps blood, which distributes hundreds of substances, such as life-giving oxygen and body-building nutrients.

Scalp hair

Eyebrow

Area of sensitive skin

Area of tough skin

Thick skin on sole

Nail

Pectoralis (muscle in chest)

Biceps (muscle in arm)

Quadriceps (muscle in thigh)

Skull

Rib

Sternum (breastbone)

Femur (thigh-bone)

Tibia (shin-bone)

Vein

Heart

Artery

Nose, windpipe, and lungs (respiratory system)
Oxygen is vital for life. This system breathes fresh air into the lungs and transfers the oxygen from that air into the blood for distribution.

Kidneys and bladder (urinary or excretory system)
These organs excrete (get rid of) waste substances. The kidneys filter them from the blood as a liquid, urine, that is stored in the bladder.

Male sex organs (reproductive system)
The male organs make microscopic tadpole-shaped sperm. If one of these joins with an egg cell in a female (right), a baby may develop.

Female sex organs (reproductive system)
The female organs are designed to produce egg cells, and nourish a baby as it develops from an egg cell and grows in the womb (uterus).

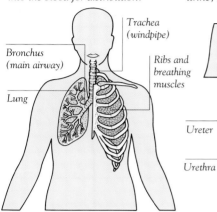

Trachea (windpipe)
Bronchus (main airway)
Ribs and breathing muscles
Lung

Blood supply to kidneys
Kidney
Ureter
Urethra
Bladder

Vas deferens
Epididymis
Penis
Testis

Uterus (womb)
Oviduct
Vagina
Ovary

Brain, nerves, and senses (nervous and sensory systems)
The brain is the body's control centre, "wired in" by the nerves. It receives information from sense organs, such as the eyes and ears, and decides what to do.

Lymph nodes and vessels (lymphatic system)
Lymph is a pale fluid collected from body tissues by a network of tiny vessels. It carries germ-fighting cells and is cleaned in "glands" called lymph nodes.

Mouth, stomach, and intestines (digestive system)
After the teeth cut and chew, this system digests food until the pieces are small enough to be absorbed by the body. Leftover bits of food leave the system as faeces (solid wastes).

Hormonal glands (endocrine or hormonal system)
Hormonal glands, including the male and female sex organs, make hormones – chemicals that control body processes such as growth and blood cell production.

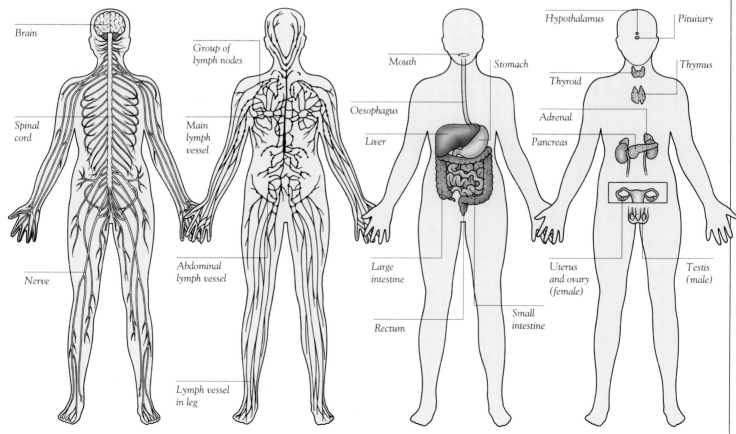

Brain
Spinal cord
Nerve

Group of lymph nodes
Main lymph vessel
Abdominal lymph vessel
Lymph vessel in leg

Mouth
Oesophagus
Liver
Large intestine
Rectum
Stomach
Small intestine

Hypothalamus
Pituitary
Thyroid
Thymus
Adrenal
Pancreas
Uterus and ovary (female)
Testis (male)

THE BODY'S BUILDING BLOCKS

The BODY IS MADE OF UNITS CALLED CELLS. Most of them are tiny – you can see them only through a microscope. Several hundred cells could fit on to this full stop. They are also incredibly numerous. There are about 100 million million cells in a human body, around 20,000 times the number of people in the world today. Cells are enormously varied too. There are dozens of cell types in the body, each with a particular shape and size, and each designed for a special job.

Cells from an onion can easily be studied under a microscope (p.178). They carry out the same basic processes as human body cells.

The cell is often called the "basic unit of life". This is because all living things are made of cells. Indeed, some living things, such as amoebas, consist of only a single cell. Amoebas look like minuscule bags of jelly as they ooze along the bottom of ponds. The amoeba's single cell contains all the amazingly complex chemical machinery that it needs to carry out the basic tasks of life, such as sensing its surroundings, moving about, feeding, disposing of its waste products, and reproducing.

A small worm that is as thin as a hair and as long as a rice grain is built out of many hundreds of cells. Insects such as mosquitoes have tens of thousands of cells. Large living things, from human

Robert Hooke's light microscope used an oil-fuelled flame as a light source. A water-filled globe acted as a lens to focus the light on to the specimen – in this case a small leaf.

bodies to oak trees, are built out of many billions (thousands of millions) of tiny cells.

■ Seeing cells

The technology needed to see what typical cells look like did not exist until the early 1600s, when the light microscope was invented. During the 17th century, pioneering microscopists such as the Dutch cloth dealer Antony van Leeuwenhoek (p.172) observed the huge number and variety of cells in nature. The Italian microscopist Marcello Malpighi (p.104) was one of the first scientists to concentrate on studying the cells in the human body. He described their basic structure and suggested theories about how they might function.

■ Looking closer

The light microscope is still the most common microscope in use today. It can magnify an object about 1,000 times. A simple light microscope (p.178) is used for several experiments in this book.

If you look through a light microscope at body cells, you may be able to see a few vague structures inside them. Each of these structures within a cell is called an organelle ("little organ"). One of the most prominent is a dark blob – the nucleus. This is the control centre of the cell and the site of its genetic instructions (p.176).

For around three centuries, microscopists studied the hazy outlines of organelles, but they

could only guess at what cells look like in detail.

The development of the electron microscope in the 1930s meant that far greater magnifications became possible. Some electron microscopes can

Scientists do not look through glass lenses in an electron microscope, as they do with a light microscope. Instead, an image of the specimen can be focused on a monitor screen.

magnify objects by more than a million times. Instead of rays of light, the electron microscope uses beams of atomic particles called electrons which are fired at the specimen. (These are the same particles that are fired at the inside of a television screen to make it glow.) The specimen is not studied through an eyepiece. Instead, an image of it appears on a visual display screen.

Using an electron microscope, the modern microscopist can see cells and their organelles in amazing detail. Although many mysteries concerning cells remain, we now understand more than ever before about the way they work.

The microtubular network that forms the skeletal framework of a cell shows up in this microscope photograph taken in ultraviolet light.

■ Watery environment

Like amoebas, human cells live in a watery environment. There is water both inside and outside the membrane (the cell's outer barrier). Individual water molecules (p.15) are small enough to pass between the molecules in the cell membrane by osmosis (p.28), a process that the cell cannot control.

Although water can pass in and out of the cell in this uncontrolled way, nutrients, minerals, and other essential items cannot, because their molecules are too large to pass through the membrane. If, as a result, the concentrations of these substances became too low or too high inside or outside the cell, water would flood into or out of the cell by osmosis. Such a flood would destroy the cell and damage the body.

The reason that this does not normally happen is that each cell membrane can regulate the passage of larger molecules through a kind of "door" (p.28) in the membrane. Molecules of

The process of diffusion (p.27) allows cell chemicals to spread through the watery cellular environment.

nutrients and minerals are continually being passed through these "doors" as the cell works to keep a healthy balance of body substances.

■ Chemical factory

Living things are like vast, complex chemical factories. Hundreds of chemical changes and reactions occur every second in each living cell. These changes can take place only if the chemical substances are in the form of a watery solution (dissolved in water). So water is vital for life of any kind. In solution, chemical substances are free to drift around the cell, spreading by processes such as diffusion (p.27).

A cell is not a random collection of chemicals floating about as if they were in a bowl of soup.

Like motor vehicles, from lorries to family cars, cells have different designs for the different jobs that they do.

Instead, just as the interior space of an office building is organized into useful sections by walls, floors, doors, elevator shafts, windows, and stairways, the cell's interior is highly structured too. Membranes are found not only surrounding the cell as a barrier, but also inside the cell. These membranes curve, bend, and fold back on themselves, to create tubes, channels, compartments, organelles, and other structures in which chemicals are organized.

And in the same way that the whole body has a framework of bones to give it shape and strength, a cell also has a

framework. This is made of scaffolding-like microtubules of protein found in the clear fluid of the cytoplasm (p.27).

■ Cell types

If you want to carry a heavy load from one place to another, you might use a lorry. If, however, you need to make a quick trip alone, you might use a small car instead. In the same way there are many different types of body cells for different tasks. For example, nerve cells carry tiny electrical signals around the body, while blood cells carry oxygen from part to part, and epithelial cells form protective coverings or linings. Each different type of cell has a unique design, with a different number of organelles.

The lifespans of the different types of cell vary too. The epithelial cells that line the intestine are rubbed away by digested food squeezing through the intestine tube. These cells die within a few hours of being formed and pass out of the body in faeces.

In contrast, cells called osteocytes make a hard substance around themselves. This substance is bone (pp.44–45). As the bone builds up, it traps the cells that manufactured it. Unable to move, the osteocytes live in their self-built prisons for many years.

A giant chemical factory breaks down substances and builds them up, just like a tiny cell.

Body cells

A CELL IS A HIGHLY ORGANIZED unit. Just as your body as a whole has important organs that carry out specific tasks, each cell also has individual parts – called organelles – for different functions. The most important organelle is the nucleus. This is the control centre for all that goes on in the cell. Another type of organelle, a sausage-shaped structure called a mitochondrion, is like a power station. It transforms nutrients from food into energy that the cell can use. The cell's outer boundary, called the membrane, regulates the flow of substances into and out of the cell by processes such as osmosis (p.28). Inside the cell, many substances move around by a spreading-out process called diffusion (opposite).

▓ Types of cell

This chart shows some of the types of cell in the body. Each type of cell has a specific function. Nerve cells, for instance, have thin, wire-like extensions, called axons (p.119), that carry nerve signals through the body. In some nerve cells in the arms and legs, the axons are over a metre (3 ft) long. Epithelial cells are wide and flat, like paving stones. They form the coverings or linings of many body parts, including the insides of the nose, mouth, lungs, and intestines. In the chart, the sides of each small grid square are just 0.001 mm ($\frac{1}{25,000}$ in) long. On the same scale, one page in this book is as thick as the pinkish-grey strip that runs down the centre of the chart.

White blood cell: *changes shape to squeeze between other cells*

Nerve cell: *long and thin, it carries electrical signals, like a telephone wire*

Red blood cells: *have a large surface area through which they pick up oxygen*

Sperm cell: *swims towards the egg cell by lashing its tail*

Egg cell: *a giant among cells, it contains stored food for the early development of a baby*

Cheek cell: *an epithelial cell that fits like a jigsaw piece with other cheek cells to form a lining*

Muscle cell: *contains fibres that contract, to shorten the whole muscle and make you move*

Intestinal cell: *has a frilly surface to absorb digested food*

▪ Inside a cell

It is hard to see the organelles of a cell through even the most powerful light microscope. But you can see them through an electron microscope (p.24), which magnifies objects a million times or more. Many of the organelles have their own membranes (p.182), which work in similar ways to the main cell membrane. Some organelle membranes are folded many times, like the endoplasmic reticulum here. The organelles form numerous compartments within the cell. Substances can spread from one compartment to another through pores (holes) and "doors" in the membranes.

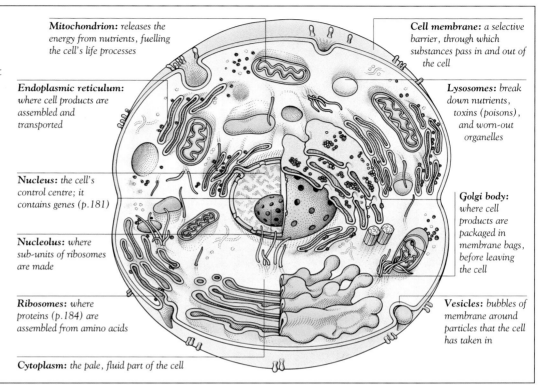

Mitochondrion: *releases the energy from nutrients, fuelling the cell's life processes*

Endoplasmic reticulum: *where cell products are assembled and transported*

Nucleus: *the cell's control centre; it contains genes (p.181)*

Nucleolus: *where sub-units of ribosomes are made*

Ribosomes: *where proteins (p.184) are assembled from amino acids*

Cytoplasm: *the pale, fluid part of the cell*

Cell membrane: *a selective barrier, through which substances pass in and out of the cell*

Lysosomes: *break down nutrients, toxins (poisons), and worn-out organelles*

Golgi body: *where cell products are packaged in membrane bags, before leaving the cell*

Vesicles: *bubbles of membrane around particles that the cell has taken in*

EXPERIMENT
Diffusion in action

Many chemicals move through the fluid inside a cell by "spreading out" in a process known as diffusion. They move from places where they are highly concentrated to places where they are less concentrated. For example, as oxygen is used up in one part of a cell, it becomes less concentrated there. So more oxygen diffuses to that place from the rest of the cell. Carbon dioxide, glucose, and minerals such as calcium move around a cell in the same way. In this experiment you can see diffusion in action – by adding a small amount of water-soluble ink (ink that mixes with water) from a dropper into a jar of water.

You Will Need
● *jar of water* ● *dropper* ● *water-soluble ink*

1 PLACE THE TIP of the dropper into the surface of the ink, and squeeze to fill it. Tap the dropper gently to remove air bubbles from near the tip.

3 LEAVE THE JAR in a safe place, where it will not be knocked or shaken. Examine it the next day. Is the blob of concentrated ink still there?

2 CAREFULLY LOWER the dropper to the bottom of the jar. Slowly squeeze out a large blob of ink. Then lift out the dropper without disturbing the ink.

At first
Molecules (tiny particles) of ink (shown as dots of dark blue) stay in a concentrated blob among the water molecules (light blue).

Later
As diffusion occurs, the ink molecules spread throughout the water. Eventually the ink molecules and the water molecules are evenly spaced.

The cell membrane

LEFT ALONE, THE SPREADING-OUT process of diffusion (p.27) would distribute water, and the substances dissolved in it, evenly throughout the body. But this does not happen, due to the cell membrane, the barrier around each cell. The membrane is semi-permeable. This means that it lets molecules of water permeate (pass through) freely because they are very small, but it does not allow larger molecules to pass freely. The free passage of water molecules through a semi-permeable membrane is called osmosis. Larger molecules, such as proteins and lipids, can pass through the membrane only at certain sites, which are like entrance and exit "doors". By opening and closing these "doors", the cell regulates some of its contents.

■ DISCOVERY ■
Camillo Golgi

The Italian microscope expert Camillo Golgi (1844–1926) was a professor of histology (the study of tissues and cells) at Italy's University of Pavia. Golgi devised new methods of staining cells with chemicals to reveal what their membranes and inner structures look like. In 1898 he showed how certain membranes are folded over many times to form a stack, like a pile of pillows all joined to each other. These stacks are now called Golgi bodies (p.27) in his honour. Golgi also devised a silver-containing stain that revealed nerve cells, and the fibres from which they are made, very clearly. This allowed him to classify nerve cells into types (p.119) and to show the tiny gaps called synapses between these cells. In 1906, Golgi received the Nobel Prize for Physiology or Medicine.

EXPERIMENT
A selective barrier

Adult help is advised for this experiment

Some freezer bags are semi-permeable – like a cell membrane. Gaps between the molecules of the bag let small molecules pass through the bag by osmosis, but not larger ones. Show this using tincture of iodine obtainable from a pharmacist.

YOU WILL NEED
● *large clear jar of water* ● *tincture of iodine*
● *freezer bag* ● *freezer bag tie* ● *cornflour*

At first
The bag is shown as a dashed line. Water molecules are blue, starch molecules yellow, and iodine molecules purple.

Later
Starch molecules are too big to exit the bag, but iodine ones are small enough to enter.

1 PUT TWO tablespoons of cornflour (a type of starch) into the bag. Mix enough water with the starch to make the bag sink. Tie the bag very securely, and lower it into the jar of water.

2 MAKE SURE that the tied part of the bag remains above water, to prevent water leaking in. Add a few drops of iodine to the water. This turns the water pale brown-orange. Leave overnight.

Starch in the freezer bag

3 IODINE MOLECULES are small enough to pass into the bag. They react with the starch, making it blue-black. But starch molecules cannot leave the bag, so the colour outside does not change.

Iodine begins to colour the starch blue-black

Osmosis in action

 Adult help is advised for this experiment

If the solution of chemicals outside a cell is stronger than the chemical solution inside it, water passes out of the cell by osmosis. The cell contents shrink as water is lost. If the shrinkage is too great, it can endanger the life of the cell. In this experiment onion cells are exposed to a very strong salt solution. Onion cells have a different structure from human cells but behave in a similar way.

YOU WILL NEED
● *microscope* ● *slide* ● *cover slip* ● *salt* ● *onion*
● *dropper* ● *toothpick* ● *craft knife* ● *water*

1 ASK AN ADULT to cut a wedge from the onion using the knife. Peel off the dry outer skin. Underneath the dry skin is a very thin see-through layer, which is only one cell thick. Carefully tease off a portion of this layer with the knife, and spread it flat on the slide.

2 PUT A DROP of water on the onion cells on the slide, then gently lay the cover slip on top. Adjust the microscope (p.178) so that you can see rows of onion cells. Next, make a strong salt solution by stirring two teaspoons of salt into one cup of water.

3 LIFT THE COVER slip with the toothpick, and add a drop of the salt solution to the cells. At once, gently replace the cover slip and look through the microscope, adjusting as necessary. Watch the area in the middle of each onion cell, where the cell fluids lie. Does it shrink? Read the captions (right) to find out why. If nothing happens, add stronger salt solution.

Normal red onion cells
Cells from a red onion are especially clear when you look at them through a light microscope. Like all plant cells, they have a stiff outer cell wall and a cell membrane within this. The red cell fluids lie inside the cell membrane.

Shrunken red onion cells
When you add the strong salt solution, this solution is much more concentrated than the solution of chemicals inside the cells. So water passes out through the membrane by osmosis, and the cell fluids shrink.

At first
Water molecules are blue, cell chemicals yellow, and salt grey. Outside the cell, to the right of the membrane (dashed line), the solution is stronger.

Later
Water osmoses out of the cell to try to make the two solutions equal. The cell fluids become more concentrated and the salt solution less so.

The BODY'S SURFACE

Getting a grip
*The ridged skin of the fingers and palm (above),
slightly moistened by sweat, gives the hand its non-
slip grip. Under a microscope the hairs that sprout
from skin over most of the body look like thin yellow
pipes (shown sliced through, left).*

WHEN YOU LOOK AT A
human body, nearly
everything you see on the
surface is dead. The outer
skin, hair, and nails are all
composed of cells that died
weeks ago. Yet just beneath
this outer layer, millions of
cells are multiplying, making
skin one of the body's busiest
parts. Throughout your life,
your skin continues to renew
and repair itself. It protects
the delicate inner parts of
your body from wear and
tear, from excess heat and
cold, and from water and
germs – and it gives you
your sense of touch (p.164).

THE LIVING BARRIER

A LAYER OF SKIN, USUALLY LESS THAN five millimetres (a quarter of an inch) thick, is the only barrier between the body's interior, with its delicate cells and finely balanced fluids, and the harsh, changing conditions of the outside world. Yet we rarely give our skin a second thought – unless it becomes bruised, cut, or otherwise damaged.

Few of the great scientists of the Renaissance period, such as Leonardo da Vinci (1452–1519) and Andreas Vesalius (p.22), took any interest in the workings of the skin. They thought of it as an uninteresting covering that had to be removed in order to study the much more fascinating parts that lay underneath. Perhaps this is not surprising, since there were no microscopes at that time. To the naked eye, the skin and the parts that grow from it, hairs and nails, do not look particularly complex or interesting.

The invention of the microscope in the early 17th century meant that for the first time scientists could see the cells (pp.24–25) that make up the skin. From this point on, people could see how intricate the skin is, and what a vital role it plays. They could see how the epidermis (outer layer) of the skin continually renews itself with new cells, and how tiny sensors in the dermis (inner layer) give the body its sense of touch.

Sweat oozes up this pore (hole) *from the sweat gland (p.34) beneath it. This aerial view of a sweat pore in the skin's surface is seen through an electron microscope.*

■ Skin coat

The skin is the body's heaviest organ. The skin of an average adult weighs around 4 to 7 kg (9 to 15 lb) – about one-twelfth of the body's total weight. If you wore an overcoat that heavy, you would soon appreciate how heavy your skin is.

Your wrap-around coat of skin protects your body from water and from general wear and tear.

Like a showerproof anorak, skin keeps out most of the water and other fluids to which it is exposed, although it is not fully waterproof. Water is repelled by the natural oils and waxes made in the tiny sebaceous glands (p.34) dotted just under the surface of the skin. These sebaceous products also keep the skin flexible and supple.

Skin insulates the body too. When pioneer anatomists cut open the skin, they found a soft, yellowish layer beneath. This layer is called subcutaneous ("under-skin") fat. It works like the padding in a quilted coat to keep the body warm, and also absorbs knocks and bumps.

■ Keratin

One reason that skin is so tough is that skin cells contain a robust body protein called keratin. Sometimes keratin is flexible – for example in epidermal skin cells. But elsewhere it can be much thicker, stiffer, and harder – for example in fingernails and toenails. Keratin is also the material which makes up the human "fur" that we call hair.

Like the cells at the skin's surface, those in hair and nails are dead. The only living parts of hair and nails are the growing points in their roots. Any sensations

you feel through your hair and nails come from sensors wrapped

Fingers are slightly tacky from *natural skin oils and sweat. Use your fingertips to pick up powdered graphite to make fingerprints (p.38).*

around the hair roots or in the skin under the nails.

■ Germ barrier

The world is full of microscopic germs. They float in the air and lie on the things we touch. Even objects that are apparently clean have germs on them or in them.

Skin prevents germs from entering the body. Under a microscope, the skin's surface shows many dead, flattened cells that interlock and overlap tightly, like tiles on a roof. Few germs can penetrate this barrier, which completely covers healthy skin. However, they can enter the body through cuts or breaks in the skin.

The natural waxes and oils on the skin's

Each and every *fingerprint has a special pattern that is unique.*

Like tiles blown from a roof in a gale, hard, dead epidermal cells fall off the skin surface. You can dye cells with blue ink so that they can be seen under a light microscope (p.35).

surface contain germ-killing chemicals. These are the body's own disinfectants, giving added protection against bacteria, yeasts, and other potentially harmful microscopic organisms.

■ Sensitive skin

Before the invention of the microscope, one of the great puzzles for scientists was what role the skin plays in the sense of touch. The microscope showed that in the dermis there are millions of tiny sensors of several different types. These sensors are attached to nerves. The sensors respond to being pressed, squeezed, heated, or cooled, and they send tiny electrical signals along nerves to the brain, where the signals are processed. This gives you the sense of touch (p.164).

Most of the types of microscopic sensor in the

skin are named in honour of the person who first described or studied them. These were mainly the Italian and German microscopists of the 19th century. Pacini's endings are an example. Shaped like tiny onions, these sensors – at most about 1 mm ($\frac{1}{24}$ in) wide – are named after Filippo Pacini (1812–1883), a professor of anatomy at Pisa in Italy. They respond to heavy pressure when the skin is squeezed. Meissner's endings are named after German anatomist Georg Meissner (1829–1903).

Today, scientists know that the skin is a multi-sensitive organ: that is, it can detect light touch, heavy pressure, vibrations, heat, cold, and pain. But they are still not sure how the skin does this.

Early in this century, researchers tried to show that each element of this multiple sense was detected by one kind of microscopic sensor. However, they were not able to prove this. More recently, scientists have suggested that some sensors in the skin respond to more than one type of stimulation, but also that each sensor is particularly sensitive to one or more types of touch. From the billions of nerve signals coming to it every second from the millions of sensors in the skin, the brain assembles an overall picture of the type of touch being experienced.

■ Cooling skin

Skin has other functions too. For example, when the sun shines on it, it produces vitamin D. This vitamin is used by the whole body, particularly the bones. Lots of sunlight stimulates the skin to make more of its dark pigment, called melanin, so that when it is exposed to sun its colour gradually becomes darker (p.36).

Skin also has a vital role

in keeping the temperature of your body stable. If the body becomes too hot, a watery fluid called sweat oozes from tiny coiled tubes (sweat glands) on to the surface of the body, where it evaporates. This evaporation draws heat from the body and so you feel cooler.

We are not as thick-skinned as creatures such as rhinoceroses. Their skin may be more than 2.5 cm (1 in) thick. Rhino horn is made of matted, compacted hair.

■ Lost skin

Did you know that much of the dust in almost any room, from a bedroom to a classroom, is made of tiny fragments of human skin? In one minute, 30,000 to 40,000 microscopic skin cells fall unseen from your body. This shedding is a natural part of the skin's renewal system. Cells are lost continually as skin rubs against clothes, soap and water, sheets, and other objects.

But your skin is not worn away, because while dead cells are being rubbed away, the cells just below the surface of the epidermis are busy reproducing themselves. As soon as they are produced, the new cells begin rising to the surface to replace those that have been lost, like people moving to the front of a queue.

Pacini's endings are the biggest of all the touch sensors in the skin (p.164). Some are just visible to the naked eye.

Human hair is surprisingly strong, considering that it is so thin. *People once used hair for making rope and twine. You can test the strength of hair using marbles (p.41).*

The skin

EACH YEAR UP TO 4 kg (9 lb) of your skin wears away and flakes off your body's surface. The skin that falls from your body collects as dust, which you can find around the house. You do not lose this amount of weight, because your skin is constantly renewing itself. This renewal takes place in the skin's outer layer, the epidermis. Cells in the lower part of the epidermis are always multiplying. Their "offspring" pass upward, gradually becoming filled with a tough fibrous substance called keratin. By the time they reach the surface, the cells are hard, flat, and dead – ready to be worn away. This continual cell sacrifice in the epidermis protects the lower layer, the dermis, which contains delicate blood vessels, nerves, and touch sensors.

Hairy skin
This microscope photograph of skin, sliced horizontally and seen from above, shows the hair shafts and smaller sweat pores.

At the skin's surface

The hard, tough cells in the upper part of the epidermis become wide and flat as they fill with keratin. When they reach the surface, they flake off like tiles blown from a roof in a strong wind. This is due to wear and rubbing, and also to being pushed up by more cells from below.

Microscopic mountain ridges
When seen through an electron microscope, the ridged skin on the palm looks like a range of mountains. The tiny pits are sweat pores.

Under the skin

This diagram shows the numerous touch sensors, blood vessels, and other parts in a piece of skin less than 1 mm (¹⁄₂₅ in) deep. This type of skin is from the back or thigh, where the outer layer, the epidermis, is considerably thinner than the inner layer, the dermis. These layers are fixed firmly together at a line of small bumps, called papillae. Next to each hair is a sebaceous gland, which makes the natural skin oil, sebum. The busily multiplying cells in the lower epidermis have no direct blood supply. They receive nutrients and oxygen by diffusion (p.27) from blood vessels in the dermis.

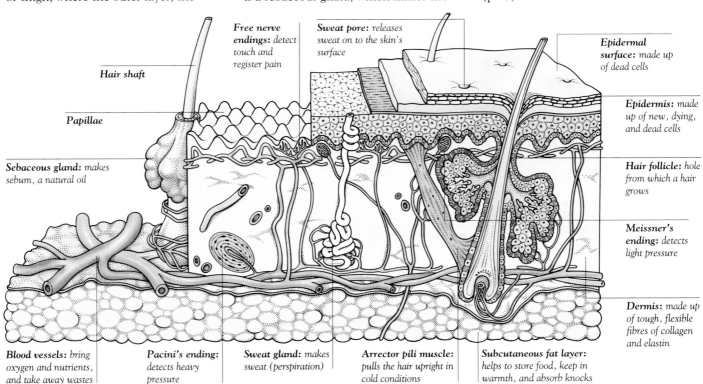

Hair shaft

Papillae

Sebaceous gland: *makes sebum, a natural oil*

Free nerve endings: *detect touch and register pain*

Sweat pore: *releases sweat on to the skin's surface*

Epidermal surface: *made up of dead cells*

Epidermis: *made up of new, dying, and dead cells*

Hair follicle: *hole from which a hair grows*

Meissner's ending: *detects light pressure*

Dermis: *made up of tough, flexible fibres of collagen and elastin*

Blood vessels: *bring oxygen and nutrients, and take away wastes*

Pacini's ending: *detects heavy pressure*

Sweat gland: *makes sweat (perspiration)*

Arrector pili muscle: *pulls the hair upright in cold conditions*

Subcutaneous fat layer: *helps to store food, keep in warmth, and absorb knocks*

EXPERIMENT
Is all skin the same?

Do you know the back of your hand as well as the old saying suggests? What skin looks like varies from one part of the body to another, and from person to person. Look at the skin on the back of your hand through a magnifying lens. Then look at the skin on your palm, fingers, wrist, arm, leg, and sole. Where is the skin smoothest? Which part has the most hairs? Are there any truly hairless areas?

YOU WILL NEED
- *magnifying lens*

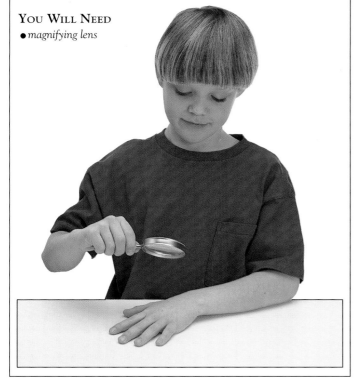

EXPERIMENT
See skin cells

Adult help is advised for this experiment

Use a microscope (p.178) to see some of the dead cells that fall off your skin by the million daily. Lift the cells safely from your hand with adhesive tape. Individual skin cells are almost transparent, so use ink to make them visible. *Caution: Make sure that the ink you use is non-toxic.*

YOU WILL NEED
- *microscope* • *slide* • *scissors*
- *cotton bud* • *non-toxic blue ink*
- *clear adhesive tape*

1 SPREAD A FEW drops of ink on the back of your hand with the cotton bud. Let it dry for a few minutes.

2 PRESS A LENGTH of tape on to the inked area. Peel it off, and place it sticky-side down on the slide.

3 TAKE CARE not to put any fingerprints on the tape. Look at the tape with the cells stuck to it through the microscope. Can you see any blue flakes, like those in the photograph on the left?

■ How hairy are humans?

Our closest cousins in the animal world are the great apes – gorillas and chimpanzees. Their bodies are similar to our own in many ways. One of the most obvious differences, however, is in the skin. Humans seem almost hairless compared with apes (we have been called "naked apes"), except for on the scalp. However, if you examine the skin on your body closely with a magnifying lens, you will find that you have many hairs too. The difference is that human body hairs are small and fine, while the body hairs of apes are long and thick. In fact, a human has just as many hairs as an average great ape – about three to five million.

Human head hairs are long and thick, compared with the rest of the body's hair

A gorilla's hairs are long and thick, and cover most of its head and body

Skin changes

MANY PARTS OF THE BODY can change and adapt, depending on how much they are used. For example, if you exercise your muscles often, they get bigger and stronger. Skin also adapts to the demands made on it. Patches of skin that receive great wear and tear respond by becoming thicker and tougher. This happens on the fingertips of a guitarist, and on the soles of the feet of someone who often walks barefoot. Hard patches called calluses may develop as natural shields to protect the parts beneath. Skin colour also adapts to changing conditions. Skin that is exposed to more sunlight than usual tends to darken in colour. The darker colour helps to filter out the sun's ultraviolet rays. Short-term exposure to these rays can cause sunburn, and the rays are also known to cause skin cancer.

■ Changing texture

The texture of skin (how it feels to the touch) varies from one person to another. Some people have skin that is smoother or more supple than that of other people. Skin texture also changes through the years. Our skin tends to become less supple and more lined with increasing age. These changes are due mainly to the way that elastin fibres in the dermis (p.34) shrink and become less flexible over the years. The changes are also due to the way that, as you get older, the subcutaneous fat layer under the dermis becomes thinner, making the skin's underlayer less supple and less resilient.

EXPERIMENT
Skin colour

You may have noticed that someone who has been indoors for a long time, away from natural sunlight, looks paler than normal. Just as skin may darken when exposed to more sunlight, it may also lighten when exposed to less light. You can investigate this process by using a sticking plaster to prevent light reaching a small patch of skin. For this experiment you need to leave a sticking plaster on your finger for several days. If the plaster becomes dirty, replace it with a new one on the same part of the finger.

YOU WILL NEED
● *sticking plasters (use hypoallergenic ones)*

1 WRAP THE PLASTER around one of your fingers in the usual way. Put it between the knuckle joints, so that it is less likely to fall off.

2 AFTER SEVERAL DAYS, remove the plaster. Has the skin under it changed colour? How long is it before this area returns to its normal colour?

■ Melanin
The skin's colour comes from melanin, a very dark brown, natural pigment (colouring substance). Melanin is made in melanocytes, special cells scattered in the lower epidermis (p.34). The amount of melanin that melanocytes make is controlled chiefly by the body's inherited genes (p.176). Melanocytes are stimulated to make extra melanin by ultraviolet light – particularly from the sun – falling on the skin.

Melanin grains
This microscope photograph shows a piece of cut-through skin viewed from the side. The melanin shows up clearly as dark grains. The melanocytes make the melanin grains, and then pass them out into the cells of the epidermis surrounding them.

Testing texture
The "pinch test" gives an idea of the general texture of someone's skin. Grasp a small fold of skin from the back of the hand. Grip firmly enough to hold the skin away from the hand, but do not pull too hard! Hold for 30 seconds and release. Note how quickly the skin becomes flat again. Test people of widely differing ages. Do you notice any differences?

■ Ancient skin

The skin's proteins – keratin, collagen, and elastin – are tough and durable. Treated with special chemicals, skin becomes even longer-lasting. Ancient Egyptian "mummies" – bodies prepared for burial – were treated with certain chemicals, which have preserved them for thousands of years. The Ancient Egyptians believed that souls could revisit their bodies after death.

Long-lasting face
The preserved skin of this Egyptian mummy is still intact after more than 4,000 years.

EXPERIMENT
The sebum layer

Adult help is advised for this experiment

Sebaceous glands (p.34) make an oily substance called sebum, which mingles with sweat and spreads over the skin, helping it to stay supple and water-repellent. Find out what happens when you remove the sebum layer.

YOU WILL NEED
● *surgical spirit (from a pharmacist)* ● *cotton wool* ● *a weak solution of washing-up liquid in water (a single drop in a beaker of water)* ● *dropper*

1 ASK A FRIEND to place his or her hands on a table. Rub one hand thoroughly with cotton wool soaked in surgical spirit. This dissolves and cleans away the covering of sebum and sweat.

2 ON EACH HAND, place two or three drops of the weak washing-up liquid solution. (This solution will give you a clearer result than water alone.)

3 WATCH WHAT HAPPENS to the drops on each hand. Do they stay as rounded blobs, repelled by the waterproofed skin? Or do they spread out and soak into the skin, because the skin has lost its natural water-repelling properties? In fact, human skin is "showerproof" rather than fully waterproof. After a long soak in the bathtub, the sebum is washed away. Water can then get into the skin and make it soggy and wrinkled.

Fingerprints

WASH AND DRY YOUR HANDS. Now try to pick up a pin. It is difficult because you have washed away the film of sweat and natural skin oils that covers your fingertips. This sticky film coats the swirling ridges on your fingers and palms, helping you to grip objects. The word "fingerprint" means both the pattern on the skin of the finger and the impression left when you touch an object, especially one that is smooth. Each person in the world has a unique pattern of fingerprints. Scientists can help police catch criminals by studying the fingerprints of suspects.

EXPERIMENT
Making fingerprints

Adult help is advised for this experiment
Collect friends' fingerprints on paper, and use them for some simple detective work – to find out which one of your friends secretly picked up an empty glass. Keep the prints on file, and make new ones as you and your friends grow older. The newer fingerprints will be bigger, but the patterns will hardly change.

YOU WILL NEED
- sheets of coloured paper
- wide double-sided adhesive tape
- talcum powder ● magnifying lens
- soft (3B) graphite pencil ● spoon
- felt-tipped pen ● glass ● ruler
- scissors ● soft brush ● craft knife

1 DRAW A GRID of four vertical lines and one horizontal line, so that you have two rows of five spaces.

2 CUT TEN PIECES of tape, each about 2.5 cm (1 in) long. Peel off one side of each and stick it into a space.

3 RUB THE TIP of the pencil on another piece of paper until it leaves a patch of loose, powdery graphite.

4 GET A FRIEND to dab one fingertip into the patch of pencil graphite until it has a light-black coating.

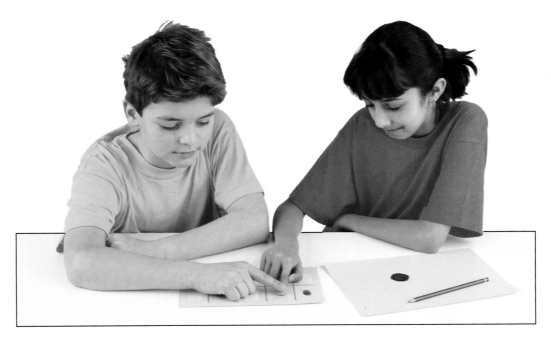

5 PEEL OFF the other side of a piece of tape, and press the finger firmly on the sticky surface to make a fingerprint. Repeat with all fingers and thumbs to make a full set of prints for each hand. Write your friend's name on the back of the piece of paper. Note which prints were taken from the right hand and which from the left hand. Ask your friend to wash his or her hands. Make "fingerprint galleries" like this for other friends. Wait for a few hours, to give time for a new sticky film of sweat and oil to form on your friends' hands.

■ Fingerprint features

The scientific study of fingerprints began in about 1900. Edward Henry of the police headquarters at Scotland Yard, London, devised a system based on three main print patterns called whorls (spirals), arches, and loops. A fourth pattern, called a composite, has combined features of the others. Detectives look for similarities in the fingerprint patterns and the number of ridges. If they find a certain number of similarities between a suspect's prints and prints left at the scene of a crime, they can be sure the suspect was there.

Whorl
Core
Island

Arch
Terminus
Base

Composite
Core
Delta

Loop
Core
Delta

6 NOW YOU ARE READY for the mystery! While you look away, one of your friends picks up the glass, touching the outside.

7 USING THE KNIFE, carefully scrape some more graphite from the tip of a pencil. Using the end of a spoon, mix this with a teaspoon of talcum powder.

8 HOLD THE GLASS from the inside, so as not to disturb the invisible fingerprints. Lightly brush the mixture of graphite and talcum powder on to the outside. This will reveal the prints.

9 PUT A PIECE of dark paper inside the glass, to make the fingerprints easier to see. Now for the detective work! Look at the prints on the glass to see whether they have whorls, arches, or loops, or whether they are composites (above). Then compare them to the fingerprint galleries that you have made. Which friend picked up the glass?

Hair and nails

NEXT TIME YOU STROKE a friendly dog or cat, remember that you too have "fur" and "claws". The hairs on your head are your most obvious "fur", but most of your skin is also covered with hairs – over three million of them, spread over your whole body. The hairs grow out of the skin (pp.32–33) in exactly the same way that animal fur grows. Your fingernails and toenails also grow from the skin, just like dogs' and cats' claws. The main difference is that your nails are broad and blunt while claws are thin and pointed – to help animals run, climb, and hunt. Hair and nails are both made mainly of a tough, hard body protein called keratin. This strong yet light substance is also found in the skin, and it has many uses in the animal world. Horses' hooves and birds' feathers are made of keratin.

Root of the hair
Hairs grow from pits in the skin called hair follicles. A hair grows by adding new cells at its root. Under a microscope these cells appear as a grey bulge in the hair base. The hair shaft (the pink area) is dead.

■ Hair raising

In furry animals, a tiny muscle in the skin – the arrector pili muscle – is attached to the base of each hair. It can pull the hair base to make the hair stand on end. This happens when the animal wants to look big and fierce. It also happens when it is cold. Air becomes trapped between the erect hairs, creating an air blanket to keep in body heat. Our hairs are smaller than animal hairs, but they stand on end in exactly the same way when we are scared or cold.

Normal skin
The arrector pili muscles attached to your hair roots are relaxed, so your body hairs lie fairly flat.

Hairs on end
If you are cold or frightened, your arrector pili muscles contract and pull your skin hairs upright.

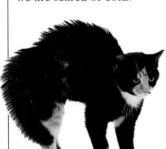

Scared cat
A cat's fur stands on end when it is scared, to make it look bigger.

EXPERIMENT
How thick is hair?

You can measure how wide a hair is using a microscope (p.178). Ask an adult to cut a strand of hair. Put the hair on the slide, and place a cover slip over the hair to hold it still. Now lay a transparent plastic ruler over the cover slip. Look at the hair and the markings on the ruler through the microscope, and judge how wide the hair is. How much do the hair widths vary on one head, and how much do they vary from person to person?

YOU WILL NEED
● *hair* ● *microscope* ● *slide* ● *cover slip* ● *ruler*

EXPERIMENT
How fast do your nails grow?

Nails grow faster on some people than others. They may also grow faster when warm – in summer rather than winter. Nails on the hand you use most may grow faster than those on your other hand, because the greater activity of that hand keeps them warmer. How fast do your own fingernails grow?

YOU WILL NEED
● *ruler with 1 mm or 1/16 in divisions* ● *graph paper* ● *pen*

1 MEASURE the nail length of each finger. Include all of the nail, from base to tip.

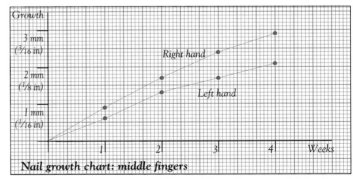

2 A WEEK LATER, measure the nail lengths again. Make five charts (one for each finger and the thumb, on both hands) to see how much your nails grow each week. Do not bite your nails! Is there a difference between the growth rates in different seasons or between your left and right hands?

EXPERIMENT
How strong is hair?

Adult help is advised
for this experiment

Is hair as strong as other materials, such as cotton? Use marbles to test hair strength. Find out also whether some colours of hair are stronger than others.

You Will Need

● tools (file, saw) to make a wooden stand ● for the stand supports: 2 wooden strips 30 cm (1 ft) long ● for the base: wood 25 cm x 10 cm (10 in x 4 in) ● 4 small triangular blocks ● dowel rod ● pin ● small plastic bag ● paper-clip ● pliers ● adhesive tape ● ruler ● pencil ● marbles ● wood glue ● protractor ● notepad ● scissors ● hammer ● hair

Assembling the stand
File a large groove in the top of each stand support. Glue the supports to the base and strengthen the joints by gluing on the triangular blocks. Lay the dowel rod in the grooves in the supports, with the pin resting against one groove.

Dowel rod — Pin — Stand support — Triangular block — Base

1 ASK AN ADULT to cut some strands of hair using the scissors. You need long strands for this experiment.

3 TAPE THE HAIR to the rod again. Carefully tap a pin into one end of the rod with the hammer, so that the rod will not spin in the stand (left).

2 ATTACH ONE END of the hair to the rod with adhesive tape. Wrap the hair around the rod twice.

4 USE THE PLIERS to bend the paper-clip into a U shape, and tape it to the plastic bag. Loop the hair around the clip, and tape it together securely.

5 LAY THE ROD in the grooves in the stand. Support the bag with your hand, and add one marble. Then slowly take your hand away. Repeat by adding another marble, then another. How many marbles can you add before the hair breaks? Now test hair of different colours, and from different parts of the head. Try cotton and other fibres too. Measure the thickness of the strands of hair and the other fibres (opposite). Is hair stronger than other materials of similar width?

The BODY'S FRAMEWORK

A head case

Bones support and protect. The large dome of the skull (above) is actually made from eight separate bones. They grow and fuse together during early childhood to form a rigid case, the cranium, which shields the brain. The interior of a rib (left) is shown magnified many times. The jelly-like bone marrow has been removed, leaving the hard, honeycomb-like scaffolding of proteins and minerals.

YOUR MUSCLES, GUTS, BLOOD vessels, and other body parts would collapse into a soggy heap if it were not for the body's supporting framework – the skeleton. In an adult, this consists of 206 bones, linked at flexible joints, which allow movement. Bones also contain the marrow that makes millions of new blood cells each second, and they act as reservoirs of minerals, which other parts of the body can call upon when deprived of nourishment.

THE FLEXIBLE FRAME

THE BONES AND JOINTS TOGETHER form the inner framework of the body. This highly flexible, constantly moving, internal scaffolding is designed to work non-stop for your whole lifetime. Unlike most structures built by humans, the body's framework can adapt to the demands placed on it. For example, reasonable amounts of activity and exercise help to make the bones stronger and more resilient, and encourage the joints to stay supple and healthy for longer.

Have you seen animal or human bones in a museum? They are usually pale, dry, and brittle-looking. They show the shapes and sizes of the bones, but they do not give a true picture of the many active roles fulfilled by living bones.

Bones were probably the first parts of the human body to be studied in detail by anatomists. Although the flesh and other soft parts of the body soon rot away after death, bones are hard and tough, and can last for hundreds of years without decaying. So early anatomists had no problem in finding a supply of skeletons to study. Bones were among the earliest parts of the body to be given formal scientific names, many of which are still used nearly 2,000 years later (p.46).

With enough practice, most people could increase the flexibility of their joints and become as supple as this yoga expert.

Living parts
In studies by early anatomists, bones were likened to the stone columns and wooden beams in a building. They were thought of as lifeless internal supports that held up the nerves, muscles, vessels, and other soft, floppy parts of the body.

However, as the science of anatomy advanced during the Renaissance period, this view of bones gradually changed. Anatomists realized that bones in the body are not dry and brittle. They discovered instead that up to one-third of a bone is water, that bones are slightly soft and flexible, and that they have their own blood vessels and nerves, like any other organ. In other words, a bone is alive, it uses energy and nutrients, and it can detect sensations.

Physiologists realized that bones also store extra mineral reserves for the body. If the body runs short of food, essential minerals can be transported from the bones to places where they are needed more urgently, such as the blood or the nerves.

Strength by design
Anatomists discovered that the construction of bones can take different forms. A typical bone consists of a hard, dense outer shell containing a "filler", which resembles a honeycomb. The outer shell is

Bone is formed of bundles of microscopic tubes, which are themselves arranged in tubes. A simple model shows how the design of bone makes it very strong (p.48).

called compact bone, and the inner type is known as spongy, trabecular, or cancellous bone.

The strength of bone comes from its design. The Italian astronomer and physicist Galileo Galilei (1564–1642) knew that if hollow tubes and solid

Inside a thigh-bone is a chamber called the marrow cavity. This cavity contains the pale, jelly-like tissue called bone marrow.

rods are both made from the same weight of material, the hollow tube is stronger. Following the same principle, the long, slim bones in the body's limbs, such as the femur (thigh-bone) are not solid rods but tubes, with hollow chambers along their shafts. This makes them both light and strong.

The spongy centres of other bones, such as the breastbone and ribs, do not have to be as strong as the femur, but it is important that they too are light.

Bone-making cells
The invention of the microscope in the 1600s had a great impact on osteology (the study of bones). Microscopists discovered that bone is built from hundreds of tiny, cylindrical units called Haversian systems (p.48), which are also known as osteons. Haversian systems are constructed from cells, like all other body parts.

A modern medical scanning machine can produce a computerized three-dimensional image from X-rays of the skull of a living person.

Bone-making cells are called osteocytes. These cells, which look like tiny spiders, produce a complex substance known as bone matrix. This has two main components. One component is a mixture of microscopic crystals containing minerals such as calcium, phosphorus, magnesium, and sodium. The other component is bundles of fibres, made from the body protein collagen, which is also found in the skin and muscle tendons. The minerals make the bone hard and fairly rigid, but the collagen gives it some elasticity and resilience. As a result, bones are slightly flexible, and under a small amount of stress they tend to bend rather than snap.

Bone marrow
In the body, the centres of bones are filled with a soft, jelly-like substance called bone marrow, of which there are two main types.

The first is red marrow, which makes nearly all of the body's new blood cells (p.103). When you are young, red marrow occurs in all the bones of your skeleton. Red marrow is found in the spaces in the spongy interiors of bones and in the large marrow cavity of long limb bones.

From the time you are about five years old, the red marrow in your limb bones is gradually replaced by the second type, called yellow marrow. This consists mainly of fibrous connective tissue and fat, and it produces far fewer blood cells than red marrow.

By the time you are about 25 years old, the production of blood cells takes place in only a few bones – mainly the spine, sternum, collar-bones, hip-bones, and skull.

Mechanical devices
Giorgio Baglivi (1668–1707), an Italian physician, held the opinion that the human body was a collection of mechanical devices. He thought that the lungs were bellows, the teeth were scissors, and the bones were a variety of beams, girders, rods, and plates. Baglivi's "mechanical body" ideas brought him into conflict with those colleagues who argued correctly that the body could not possibly be made from non-living machines.

However, then and now, both anatomists and engineers could see many parallels between the body's bones and the structural frameworks and mechanical joints of various machines.

One principle of engineering is that a system of levers gives an

Unlike humans, insects such as beetles wear their skeletons on the outside of their bodies, as hard protective cases.

object a mechanical advantage (p.50). Mechanics recognize that there are three orders (types) of lever, which can be used for various purposes. The human body has examples of each of these orders (p.51) for lifting objects and moving itself around.

Where bones meet
You can nod your head, walk, run, and reach out and grasp objects, because your bones are linked together by moveable joints (p.182). Human joints are very similar to mechanical joints, from door hinges to computer joysticks. In a well-designed joint there are special smooth, hard-wearing substances where the two parts come into contact. In the body this is cartilage. This shiny, hard substance is made by cells called chondrocytes. Also, in the same way that a machine bearing needs grease or oil to keep its parts moving smoothly, the human joint has its own "oil", which is called synovial fluid (p.51).

Together the body's joints work as a smooth unit, constantly maintaining – and occasionally repairing – themselves, to give the body a lifetime of service.

Bones and muscles work together using the lever-based principle of mechanical advantage. Make a model joint to see mechanical advantage in action (p.50).

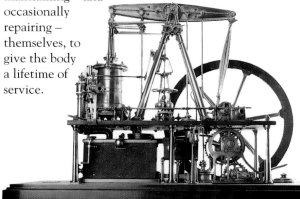

A 19th-century steam-powered engine for pumping water has many of the same mechanical features as a skeleton, including systems of levers and lubricated joints.

The skeleton

IF A BABY HAS A FALL, it is much less likely to break the bones of its skeleton than an adult. This is partly because a baby is lighter than an adult, but more importantly, it is because a newborn baby's skeleton is very different from the skeleton of an adult. The newborn baby has more than 300 parts that we call bones, yet some of these contain very little true bone at all. They are made mainly of the slightly softer, more flexible cartilage (gristle). In a fall, cartilage bends rather than breaking. During childhood, true bone gradually replaces nearly all of the cartilage. Some of the separate bones fuse together, as in the skull, reducing the total number of parts. The skeleton continues to get larger and harder in the teenage years. By the age of 20 to 25 years it has the final number of 206 fully mature, hardened bones.

■ Rebuilding from the bones

Bones hold many clues to the size, age, and features of a person. For example, the shape of the mandible (lower jawbone) gives a face its characteristic jawline. Using clay, experts are able to rebuild the muscles and the exterior features of a person from clues given by a skull and other bones. This work helps scientists to reconstruct the faces and bodies of people long dead, like the owner of the skull below.

The bones
First, plaster casts are made of the bones to avoid damaging the originals, which may be fragile. Cracks, chips, and missing fragments can be filled in at this stage.

The muscles
Using their knowledge of anatomy, the experts reconstruct the muscles of the neck and jaw. Roughened patches on the bones indicate where the muscles joined them.

The skin
The shape and size of the skeleton and the changes in bone due to ageing show how old the subject is. Skin of a suitable texture is added to complete the reconstruction.

■ Naming the bones

Every bone has its own anatomical name, usually in Latin. Some names are given here. Most of these names were introduced by anatomists of ancient times, especially the Roman physician Rufus of Ephesus, in his book *The Names of Different Parts of the Human Body* (about AD 100), and Galen (p.13). Many bones also have everyday names.

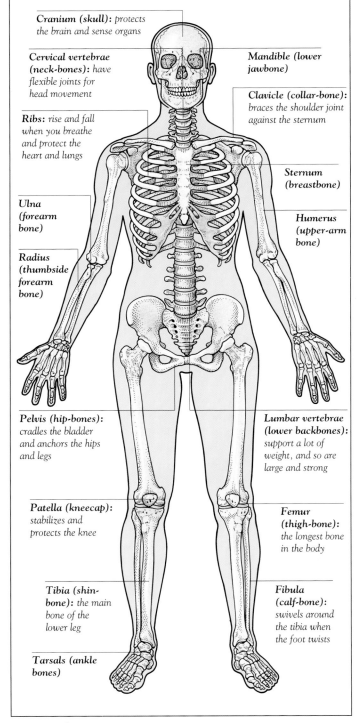

Cranium (skull): protects the brain and sense organs

Cervical vertebrae (neck-bones): have flexible joints for head movement

Ribs: rise and fall when you breathe and protect the heart and lungs

Ulna (forearm bone)

Radius (thumbside forearm bone)

Mandible (lower jawbone)

Clavicle (collar-bone): braces the shoulder joint against the sternum

Sternum (breastbone)

Humerus (upper-arm bone)

Pelvis (hip-bones): cradles the bladder and anchors the hips and legs

Patella (kneecap): stabilizes and protects the knee

Tibia (shin-bone): the main bone of the lower leg

Tarsals (ankle bones)

Lumbar vertebrae (lower backbones): support a lot of weight, and so are large and strong

Femur (thigh-bone): the longest bone in the body

Fibula (calf-bone): swivels around the tibia when the foot twists

■ Bone growth

This sequence of X-rays shows how bones grow and develop during childhood.

■ DISCOVERY ■
Wilhelm Röntgen

X-rays were discovered in 1895 by the German physicist Wilhelm Röntgen. He detected mysterious electromagnetic rays created by streams of high-speed electrons. He found that the rays, although invisible, could "shine" through living flesh and form an image on a photographic plate on the other side. X-rays pass easily through soft body parts, such as muscles and nerves. But they cannot pass through hard, dense bones. So an X-ray photograph, called a radiograph, shows bones as distinct shapes against a contrasting background. However, X-rays can damage living tissues, so their use is carefully controlled.

X for unknown
Röntgen, a 1901 Nobel Prize recipient, called the rays "X" due to their mysterious nature.

Hand of a 2-year-old
The skeleton is formed, but much of it is made of cartilage, which does not show on the X-ray.

■ Hands and feet

According to the theory of evolution (p.12), our distant ancestors of millions of years ago walked on four legs, like other mammals. Early humans started to walk on two legs 5 to 10 million years ago, leaving their arms free for carrying and manipulating objects. But the bones of our arms and hands are still similar to those of our legs and feet. The upper arm and thigh each have one long bone. The forearm has two bones, like the shin. On the hand and foot there are five fingers and five toes respectively, each with the same pattern of bones inside. The main difference is that the wrist has eight bones, but the ankle has only seven.

Hand of a 3-year-old
The cartilage is gradually being replaced by bone. Note that the wrist is still mostly cartilage.

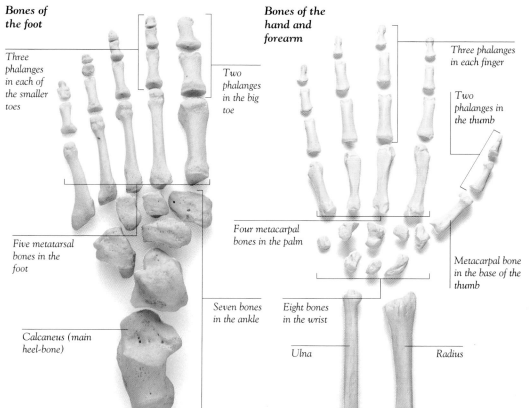

Bones of the foot

Three phalanges in each of the smaller toes

Two phalanges in the big toe

Bones of the hand and forearm

Three phalanges in each finger

Two phalanges in the thumb

Four metacarpal bones in the palm

Metacarpal bone in the base of the thumb

Five metatarsal bones in the foot

Seven bones in the ankle

Eight bones in the wrist

Calcaneus (main heel-bone)

Ulna

Radius

Hand of a 14-year-old
The skeleton of the wrist and hand is now made of mature, hard bone (see also the bones on the left).

Inside bones

STRUCTURAL ENGINEERS have long acknowledged the combination of strength and lightness given by bone. Weight for weight, bone is stronger than wood, concrete, or steel. If the human skeleton were made of enough steel to equal the strength of bone, it would weigh five times as much. The strength of bone comes mainly from its inner structure. It is built up from thousands of compactly arranged, tube-shaped units, each called a Haversian system (p.44). The units are named after the English physician Clopton Havers (1650–1701), who published his bone studies in 1691. The bone tissue in the walls of these tubes is made of fibres of the protein collagen, which give it elasticity, and mineral crystals, which make it hard. Haversian systems lie in the direction of the greatest stresses on the bone. In a long bone, such as the femur (thigh-bone), the tubes lie lengthwise in the bone shaft, so the bone resists buckling.

Haversian systems

A Haversian system is only 0.25 mm ($\frac{1}{100}$ in) in diameter. It is made from thousands of fibres of collagen, embedded in mineral salts of calcium and phosphorus. The fibres are laid in circular layers known as lamellae, like the growth rings you see in a sliced-through tree-trunk.

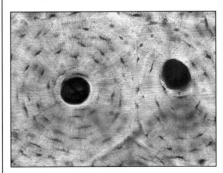

Lamellae, blood vessels, and nerves
This microscope photograph shows a cross-section through two Haversian systems with their lamellae. The central dark areas are canals for blood vessels and nerves. The spots that ring the canals are bone cells (p.44).

Tower of strength

Adult help is advised for this experiment

When engineers work on the design for a large structure, such as a skyscraper or big crane, they know that the strength of the building material to be used is only one consideration. Other factors are the size, shape, and arrangement of the main supporting parts, such as steel girders or concrete pillars. This experiment shows how you can arrange structural parts in different ways: some arrangements may be weak, but others can have surprising strength. A structure may have a good supporting capacity even if its individual structural parts – in this case drinking straws – are quite weak. The ring-of-straws design that you build here is similar to the way that Haversian systems (left) are arranged in bone.

YOU WILL NEED
- *wooden board or book* ● *plastic beaker*
- *2 egg-sized lumps of modelling clay*
- *about 50 plastic drinking straws*

1 FLATTEN EACH LUMP of modelling clay into a disc just larger than the beaker mouth. Press the beaker rim into one disc, to make a slight indentation.

2 MAKE A TOWER of straws pointing in all directions. Then make a second tower with the same number of straws, placed upright around the indentation.

3 TEST THE STRENGTH of each tower by pressing the board or book on it. The random arrangement soon collapses. The ring-of-straws design is much stronger.

EXPERIMENT
A tube of tubes

 *Adult help is advised
for this experiment*

The arrangement of Haversian systems is only part of bone's structural strength. These tube-shaped units are also stuck firmly to each other by the bone matrix, which acts as a "living glue". Extend the experiment opposite by sticking the straws together – in this case using a paper tube as a container. See how a very strong structure can be built from lightweight materials. Real bones are covered by a kind of flexible "skin" – like the paper tube. This is called the periosteum.

YOU WILL NEED
● *wooden board or book* ● *stiff paper* ● *modelling clay* ● *scissors* ● *single- and double-sided adhesive tape* ● *drinking straws*

1 TRIM THE PAPER so that its width equals the straws' length. Cover one side of the paper completely with double-sided adhesive tape.

2 ROLL THE PAPER into a tube with the tape inside. Tape its edges together. Stick a closely packed layer of straws around the inside.

3 STICK MORE double-sided tape to the inward-facing parts of the straws. Now stick more straws to this tape to make a second layer.

4 THIS TUBE of tubes is a simple model of the shaft of a long bone. The paper represents the periosteum; the straws are Haversian systems; and the space in the middle is the bone marrow cavity (p.45). Flatten the modelling clay to make a non-slip base, and push the tube into it. Now press on the tube with the board or the book to test its supporting strength. Is it stronger than the circle of loose tubes in the experiment opposite? (Be very careful not to trap your hands under the board or book.)

▨ How bones heal

Bone has a great advantage over structural materials such as steel and concrete. If it breaks, it can mend itself. The self-healing process is more effective if the bone's broken ends are brought back into their natural alignment, a process doctors call "reducing a fracture".

Within an hour
Healing of a fracture (break) begins almost at once. Leaking blood from the broken bone ends forms a clot.

After a few days
Cells called fibroblasts and osteoblasts make an open network of spongy bone (p.44) in the gap.

A week or two later
The spongy bone gradually fills in and becomes harder. Blood vessels have regrown and healed.

After two or three months
The bone is almost mended. The bulge at the break shrinks away, a process called bone remodelling.

Joints and levers

MANY OF YOUR BONES work as levers. They tilt to lift and move various parts of the body. The bones are connected by flexible joints, which allow them to move freely. To make body movements, your muscles pull on certain parts of the bones. The muscles, bones, and joints in the body work according to the same principles as those used by engineers who design lifting and moving machines, such as cranes and mechanical diggers.

1 WITH THE PENCIL, draw a line along the middle of each cardboard strip. On one strip, make marks on this centre line at 1 cm (½ in) and 15 cm (6 in) from one end. Put marks on the other card at 1 cm (½ in) and 2.5 cm (1 in) from one end.

2 SCREW ONE EYE into each of the four marks that you have made. At the other end of each strip, make a new pencil mark 2.5 cm (1 in) from the end. This will be the site of the joint that is the "elbow" between two cardboard "arm bones".

3 PLACE THE STRIPS, with the new pencil marks on top of each other, to form an L-shape. Carefully push the pin through the marks. Place a blob of clay on the sharp pin end, to cover the point and make it safe. Check that the "arm bones" move easily.

Fold and glue paper squares to make triangle pointers

4 TIE A PIECE of string to each of the widely spaced eyes. Feed the strings through the corresponding eyes on the other strip. With the strips at right angles, glue a paper triangle pointer to the string of the same colour, at a point just past the closely set eyes.

Living levers

Adult help is advised for this experiment

Like all levers, many bones work by mechanical advantage; that is, when your muscles pull part of a long bone near a joint a small distance, the other end of the bone moves a much greater distance. A small movement is turned into a large one, so an advantage is gained. In this experiment you see the mechanical advantage of the biceps muscle, which moves the elbow.

YOU WILL NEED
- 2 strips of thick cardboard 25 cm x 5 cm (10 in x 2 in)
- cutting mat • craft knife • ruler
- pencil • scissors • 2 lengths of string in 2 colours • small squares of paper coloured to match the strings • 4 small metal screw eyes
- pin • modelling clay • glue

Hold the upper arm, and pull each string in turn to raise the forearm by 45°

The true biceps joins the forearm bone here

The alternative biceps joins the forearm bone here

Upper arm

Elbow

Forearm

5 ONE STRING (yellow in the photograph above) represents the biceps (p.59), which pulls on the forearm when you lift things. The other string (red) represents an alternative muscle, which does not exist in the body. This muscle would also pull on the forearm, but at a point nearer the hand. Lift the forearm half way, using each string in turn. Which pointer travels the shortest distance? This shows which string "muscle" raises the arm with the least amount of contraction, and so has the greatest mechanical advantage.

EXPERIMENT
Smooth-moving joints

Adult help is advised for this experiment

If the ends of bone pressed directly on each other in a joint, their rough surfaces would grate together and wear away. So inside a typical joint, the bone ends are covered with a smooth, glossy substance called cartilage. There is also a slippery "oil" called synovial fluid. These features greatly reduce friction (resistance or rubbing) in your joints, as this experiment shows.

YOU WILL NEED
● tray ● wooden board ● wooden block with natural sanded finish (not varnished or polished) ● adhesive tape ● plastic bag or plastic sheet ● cooking oil ● scissors

1 THE BOARD and block represent two bone ends in a joint. Press them together hard, and slide one against the other. Feel the friction.

2 WRAP THE BOARD and block in plastic, taped in place. The plastic is smooth like cartilage. Feel how the "bone ends" slide more easily.

3 SMEAR SOME COOKING OIL on the plastic. Now feel how easy it is to slide the block over the board. The cooking oil works like the synovial fluid in the body's joints. It lubricates the cartilage surfaces to help them slide past each other, with little effort or wear.

■ Orders of lever

A lever is a rigid bar or rod that turns on a certain point, called the fulcrum. The lever moves a weight called the load, using a moving force known as the effort. There are three main orders (types) of lever – and the body has examples of all of them. In the body, the lever is a bone, the effort is supplied by a muscle, and the load is the weight of the body parts supported by the bone. Gently move your various body parts around, and see if you can identify which types of lever are involved in the movements you make.

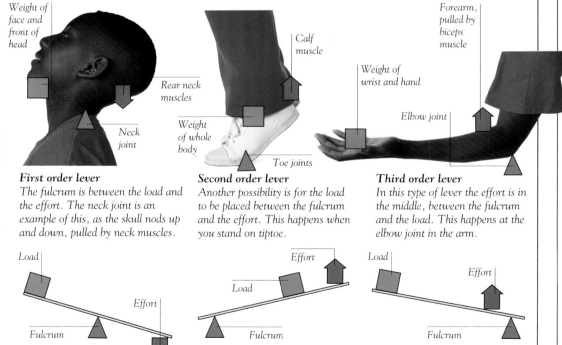

Weight of face and front of head

Rear neck muscles

Neck joint

First order lever
The fulcrum is between the load and the effort. The neck joint is an example of this, as the skull nods up and down, pulled by neck muscles.

Load

Effort

Fulcrum

Calf muscle

Weight of whole body

Toe joints

Second order lever
Another possibility is for the load to be placed between the fulcrum and the effort. This happens when you stand on tiptoe.

Effort

Load

Fulcrum

Forearm, pulled by biceps muscle

Weight of wrist and hand

Elbow joint

Third order lever
In this type of lever the effort is in the middle, between the fulcrum and the load. This happens at the elbow joint in the arm.

Load

Effort

Fulcrum

Types of joint

PEOPLE DESIGN different mechanical joints for different types of job. The hinge-joint on a door, for example, could not replace the ball-joint on a computer joystick. The body has many joints, and each is designed for a special job too. Your shoulder can move in almost any direction, like a joystick. Your elbow is less flexible, moving only to and fro, like a hinge. A joint that has high mobility usually has low stability. For example, a shoulder is more likely to be dislocated (put "out of joint") than an elbow.

EXPERIMENT
Knee joints

Adult help is advised for this experiment

The knee joint is the body's largest single joint. It is a hinge, which allows the leg to swing backward. The bottom of the femur (the main bone in your upper leg) and the top of the tibia (the main bone in your lower leg) are shaped so that, as the knee straightens, the femur slips into and sits in the tibia, "locking" the joint (below). Make a knee joint out of card that shows how the leg locks.

YOU WILL NEED
● *cutting mat* ● *metal ruler* ● *glue* ● *plastic ruler* ● *pencil* ● *compasses* ● *craft knife* ● *paper-clip* ● *thick card about 40 cm x 20 cm (16 in x 8 in) for cutting into 7 pieces: lower leg and foot (A), upper leg (B), 2 knee sides (C), and 3 foot supports (D)*

■ Shoulder and arm joints

There are many types of joint in your shoulder and arm. A bone often has more than one joint type. For example, the humerus has a ball and socket at the shoulder and a hinge at the elbow. The main joints have been colour-coded below, with simplified representations showing their range of movement.

Scapula (shoulder blade)

Humerus (upper arm bone)

Radius (thumbside forearm bone)

Ulna (forearm bone)

Carpals (wrist bones)

First metacarpal (bone in base of thumb)

Ball and socket
The top of the humerus (orange) has a ball-shaped head that fits into a shallow, cup-shaped socket formed by the scapula (red). This gives good all-round mobility.

Hinge
The humerus (yellow) and the ulna (green) move to and fro in one plane only, like a door hinge. Other elbow movements are made by twisting the shoulder or forearm.

Pivot
As the wrist twists, a C-shaped notch in the end of the radius (green) pivots around the rounded end of the ulna (red). This joint is also called a swivel joint.

Plane
There are about 20 joints between the eight carpal bones. The plane joint between the bones coloured light blue and violet allows small amounts of sideways movement.

Saddle
Wiggle your thumb at its joint with the wrist. It can tilt in all directions. The bone ends (dark blue and maroon) are shaped like saddles and slide smoothly over each other.

■ Stable positions

Each joint has a position in which its bones fit together most securely. For example, when you stand upright, your knee joints are "locked" and your muscles do not have to use up valuable energy to prevent your body from collapsing to the floor.

Knees straight
In their locked position, little muscle power is required.

Knees bent
Muscles take the strain. How long can you stand like this?

1 Draw an upside-down "T", 3 cm (1½ in) wide, 35 cm (14 in) tall, with a base of 18 cm (7 in). Draw three slots in the base and a line halfway up the upright. Below this line, against the left edge, draw a half-circle of radius 1 cm (½ in). Draw a short line from the lowest point on the half-circle to the left edge.

2 Cut across the short line, around half of the half-circle, and along the long horizontal line to the other side of the "T". This divides the "T" into a lower leg (A) and an upper leg (B). For B, trim the rest of the half-circle to leave a knob as above. Cut off excess card and cut out the slots in the base.

3 Draw two shapes for the knee sides (C). Each is a square with 3-cm (1½-in) sides, and a 3 cm x 1 cm (1½ in x ½ in) rectangle set 0.5 cm (¼ in) from a corner of the square. These shapes must be mirror images of each other.

4 Carefully cut out each knee side. In the model they keep the upper leg from collapsing sideways. In the real knee this job is done by ligaments – bundles of taut fibres attached to bone or cartilage (p.179).

5 Carefully make a hole in each knee side, using the compasses. Make it in the mid-line of the projecting rectangle, 1 cm (½ in) from the square. Now make a hole in the centre of the knob on the upper leg (B).

6 Glue the knee sides to A, so the holes are in line with the top of A, at the centre of the cutaway half-circle. Cut out supports (D), each 5 cm x 3 cm (2 in x 1½ in), with a small slot. Unbend the paper-clip.

7 Slot the upper leg between the knee sides, so that the three holes line up. Push the paper-clip through the holes, and bend it to secure the joint. Slot in the supports (D). Now stand your model knee upright. See how the upper leg balances on the lower leg. The flat part of the top of the upper leg (on a real femur this is a knuckle-like part called a condyle) prevents the body from falling forward. Now push the upper leg backward. The upper leg collapses. There is no "lock" there.

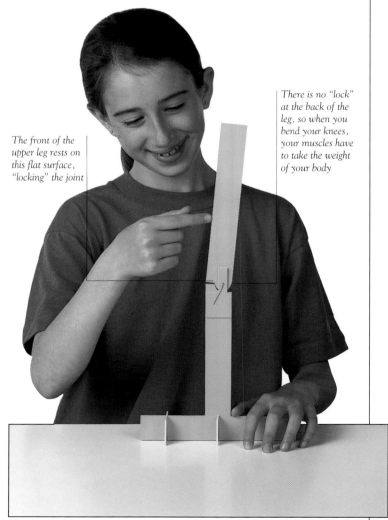

The front of the upper leg rests on this flat surface, "locking" the joint

There is no "lock" at the back of the leg, so when you bend your knees, your muscles have to take the weight of your body

The MOVING BODY

Teaming up

Many body muscles are arranged in partnerships. In the arm (above), one muscle makes the elbow bend, while its partner makes it straighten. Even simple body movements rely on large teams of muscles. The canoeists (left) use more than 50 muscles in each arm, together with dozens more muscles in the chest and abdomen, to propel their craft.

The human body is moved by muscles. There are about 640 skeletal (body-moving) muscles, most of which are attached to the bones of your skeleton. Muscles can only pull, not push. They pull on the bones to shift them into new positions. Muscles are controlled in teams, by your brain and nerves, and enable you to perform a huge range of movements – running and jumping, pulling and pushing, bending almost double, and threading cotton through the eye of a needle.

MUSCLES AND MOVEMENTS

MUSCLES ARE RESPONSIBLE FOR all of the body's movements, from kicking a ball and writing a letter to squeezing digested food through the intestines and making the heart beat. The body's biggest single muscle is the huge gluteus maximus in the buttock, which drives your climbing, running, and leaping movements. The smallest muscle is the stapedius in the ear, which looks like a tiny piece of cotton. It reduces the vibrations of sounds that are too loud.

The leaping flea can jump more than 100 times its own height. The burst of muscle power in its back legs is boosted by energy stored near the joints in blocks of a special elastic-like substance called resilin.

Muscle tissue very similar to our own is found in all kinds of animals, from worms and insects to cows and whales. Animal muscle is what we think of as "flesh" or "meat", from the red meat of cattle and pigs to the white meat of poultry and fish. Ancient peoples knew a great deal about the muscle layouts of many different kinds of animal because, like many people now, they consumed animal muscle as food.

Animal spirit

In ancient times, the anatomists of Egypt, Greece, and Rome all studied the shapes of muscles and how they work. Some of the first studies were made by Erasistratus (c.300–250 BC), who belonged to the great medical school in Alexandria, Egypt.

Erasistratus recognized that muscles cause movement by becoming shorter and pulling on the body's bones. But he also believed, wrongly, that muscles were made to shorten and bulge out when an invisible "animal spirit" flowed along the nerves to the muscles.

Myology

Galen (p.13) of Ancient Rome made some excellent descriptions of muscles in various animals. In particular, he studied the muscle layouts of the Rhesus monkey – the same animal in which the Rhesus blood system was discovered earlier this century (p.102). Galen noted how a typical muscle's wide, fleshy main part, the body or belly, is attached to a bone at either end by a strong, cord-like part known as a tendon or sinew.

During the Renaissance period, myology (the study of muscles) progressed significantly. Leonardo da Vinci (1452–1519) and Andreas Vesalius (p.22) both drew in great detail the 640 or so individual muscles in the body. (We do not all have exactly the same number of muscles. In certain people some muscles – such as the platysma in the neck – may be much reduced in size or even absent.)

It was not just Renaissance anatomists who looked at the design of muscles in great detail. Renaissance artists studied muscles too, so that they could draw and paint the body's bulges and ripples as accurately as possible.

The way that muscles work has been studied by engineers as well as

Facial expressions are made by the actions of over 40 facial muscles (p.61).

by scientists and artists. Engineers wanted to copy the way that muscles work in teams (p.60), so that they could apply the same principles to machines.

Most muscles are arranged in opposing pairs around the body. This is because a muscle can only pull – it cannot push. One muscle, or set of muscles, pulls

The bulging muscles visible just under the skin are only the outermost of three or four layers of skeletal muscles.

part of the body one way, and an opposing muscle or set pulls it back again.

Working in these so-called antagonistic pairs (p.62), muscles can produce a huge range of movements.

Inside muscles

By the 1600s, scientists understood the body's muscle layout in detail. But people still had little idea of how the insides of each individual muscle work.

With the invention of the microscope, there was a great deal of progress. Niels Stensen (1638–1686) from Copenhagen, Denmark, was a physician, anatomist, geologist, and later a bishop. In 1664 he described how, at a microscopic level, a muscle is made of hundreds of tiny muscle fibres (p.181). Stensen realized that different combinations of these fibres contract (shorten) and then relax as the body makes different movements. The greater the number of fibres that shorten, the

The faint vertical stripes in these rod-like muscle cells give skeletal muscle (p.58) the alternative names of "striped" or "striated" muscle.

more the whole muscle contracts. When the fibres relax, the whole muscle relaxes too.

▦ Muscle contraction

From the time of Erasistratus, it was thought that muscles increased in volume when they contracted. But in the 17th century this notion was shown to be wrong. In a famous experiment the Dutch microscope expert Jan Swammerdam (1637–1680) immersed the leg muscle of a frog in a measuring-bath of water.

A whole muscle consists of bundles of muscle fibres. In turn, each of these consists of bundles of myofibrils.

When the muscle was stimulated to contract by pinching the nerve connected to it, the water level stayed the same. This showed that contraction does not change the volume of a muscle, but is instead a result of changes within the muscle fibres.

A muscle fibre, which is thinner than a hair, can be up to 30 cm (1 ft) long in a large muscle. Yet it is a single giant cell (pp.26–27). Each muscle fibre is made of collections of even thinner fibres called myofibrils. These consist of long strands of two proteins, actin and myosin. When the muscle is stimulated, the actin pulls the myosin along past it, like a line of people hauling on a rope. This slide-past mechanism makes the myofibril shorten, causing the muscle fibre to contract, and the whole muscle becomes shorter.

▦ Energy and control

In the 17th century physiologists discovered that muscles use the sugar glucose as their main source of energy. The glucose energy is released by cellular respiration (pp.70–71), using oxygen which is brought to the cells by blood. When a muscle is active, blood vessels to it and within it widen to increase the blood supply.

Another 17th century discovery was that muscles are controlled by the nerves, called motor nerves (p.118), connecting them to the brain.

▦ Types of muscle

The microscope shows that there are three types of muscle (p.59). Each type has a different function and is made of a different kind of tissue (p.185).

To lower your hand, the triceps (p.59) in the back of your upper arm contracts and straightens the elbow, aided by gravity.

To raise your hand, the biceps in the front of your upper arm contracts and pulls up the bones of your forearm.

Muscles attached to the bones are called skeletal muscles. The cells of these muscles are arranged in parallel bundles, and within these bundles each cell has a striped pattern. Skeletal muscle is therefore also called striped or striated muscle. As we can control the actions of our own skeletal muscles, they are known as voluntary muscles too.

The muscle layers of internal organs, such as the stomach and the intestines, are a second type of muscle called smooth muscle. This muscle type contracts more slowly than skeletal muscle, but uses much less energy. It is responsible for automatic (autonomic) muscle actions such as peristalsis (p.89).

The walls of the heart are the third type of muscle, called cardiac muscle. This muscle sends blood pulsing around the whole body. Because you cannot consciously control the actions of smooth and cardiac muscles, these types are also known as involuntary muscles.

See how your forefingers move mysteriously and return to their relaxed state, unless you hold the muscles that work them under tension (p.58).

Muscles

ABOUT TWO-FIFTHS of your body weight is muscle. There are three types of muscle: skeletal, smooth, and cardiac (opposite). Most of the muscles shown on the following pages are skeletal muscles. Skeletal muscles are designed to contract

Nerve to muscle
This microscope photograph shows muscle fibres as huge pink rods. The yellow finger-like parts are the end branches of a nerve. They form a structure called a motor end plate. This is where nerve signals pass from the nerve into the muscle.

(get shorter). By doing so, they pull your bones to make you move. They are also known as voluntary muscles, since you can control them voluntarily (at will), unlike the involuntary muscles in parts such as the stomach. Muscles are controlled by electrical signals from the brain. The more signals that arrive, the more the muscle contracts, until it reaches its minimum length – about three-fifths of its relaxed length.

■ Achilles' heel

In Ancient Greek mythology, Achilles was a hero of the siege of Troy. When he was a baby, his mother dipped him in the magical River Styx to make him invulnerable. But Achilles was slain when an arrow pierced his one weak point – the heel where his mother had held him. The large tendon in the heel is named the Achilles tendon (opposite) after the myth.

The Greek hero Achilles
This engraving shows the fatal arrow piercing Achilles' heel.

EXPERIMENT
Relaxing fingers

When they are not active, muscles and tendons have natural relaxed positions, in which they use minimal energy. In the resting hand, for example, the fingers are slightly bent under tension from the muscles and tendons. Show this by clasping your hands with your fingers interlocked. Hold your forefingers straight and parallel. Do your forefingers stay parallel when you let your muscles relax, or do they move together?

Moving fingers
Hold your forefingers up like this and see what happens when you relax your muscles.

EXPERIMENT
Tightening tendons

A typical muscle has a wide fleshy part, called the body or belly, which shortens when you move. The narrow, rope-like ends of the muscle, called tendons, anchor the muscle to bones. As you move parts of your body, you should feel the tendons tightening as they pull on the bones. Feel how they stand out under your skin, like taut ropes.

Tendon points
Tendons show up particularly well in the elbows, neck, and other areas shaded in grey. As you tighten your muscles, feel for their taut tendons under your skin.

▨ Muscle maps

These charts show the main muscles at the front and back of your body. However, the muscles shown here are only the superficial muscles – those just under the skin. Beneath them is a middle layer and under that a deep layer. Most muscles have Latin names derived from the movements they produce or the names of nearby bones.

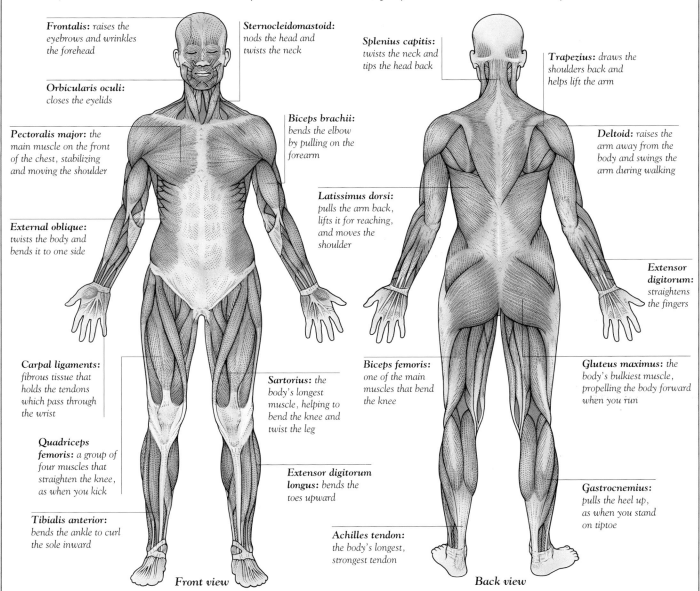

Frontalis: raises the eyebrows and wrinkles the forehead

Orbicularis oculi: closes the eyelids

Pectoralis major: the main muscle on the front of the chest, stabilizing and moving the shoulder

External oblique: twists the body and bends it to one side

Carpal ligaments: fibrous tissue that holds the tendons which pass through the wrist

Quadriceps femoris: a group of four muscles that straighten the knee, as when you kick

Tibialis anterior: bends the ankle to curl the sole inward

Sternocleidomastoid: nods the head and twists the neck

Biceps brachii: bends the elbow by pulling on the forearm

Latissimus dorsi: pulls the arm back, lifts it for reaching, and moves the shoulder

Sartorius: the body's longest muscle, helping to bend the knee and twist the leg

Extensor digitorum longus: bends the toes upward

Achilles tendon: the body's longest, strongest tendon

Front view

Splenius capitis: twists the neck and tips the head back

Biceps femoris: one of the main muscles that bend the knee

Trapezius: draws the shoulders back and helps lift the arm

Deltoid: raises the arm away from the body and swings the arm during walking

Extensor digitorum: straightens the fingers

Gluteus maximus: the body's bulkiest muscle, propelling the body forward when you run

Gastrocnemius: pulls the heel up, as when you stand on tiptoe

Back view

▨ Types of muscle

When magnified, the three types of muscle tissue (p.57) look different. Skeletal muscle cells are rod-like and line up parallel to each other. Smooth muscle cells are thinner and spindle-like. Cardiac muscle has Y-shaped interwoven cells.

Skeletal (voluntary)
Found throughout the body. It can contract powerfully, but tires easily.

Smooth (involuntary)
Found in internal organs. It can stay contracted for long periods.

Cardiac (involuntary)
Found in the heart. It contracts every second or faster, yet never tires.

Muscle teams

HOLD YOUR ARM straight out to the side, then bend your elbow. You will feel your biceps, the main muscle on the front of your upper arm, tense as it contracts and pulls on your forearm. But a single muscle hardly ever works on its own. As you bend your elbow, the other muscles in your shoulder, upper arm, and forearm adjust to cope with the new positions of the arm bones. Some of these muscles contract, since they have to take up the strain, while others relax, as the strain has been shifted away from them. Whole teams of muscles around the body adjust and shift even for small movements of one body part. You make most of these minor changes almost without thinking. Your brain learned how to control muscle teams, and how to keep your balance and posture, during the first years of your life.

EXPERIMENT
Muscle links

In some body parts, one muscle can cause several movements, because the muscle is linked by different tendons to several bones. An example is the muscle in your forearm that curls your fingers. Bend your middle finger, and see how your other fingers curl up too.

1 PLACE YOUR HAND palm up, flat on a table. Raise your middle finger slowly, keeping it as straight as possible.

2 WHAT HAPPENS to your ring (fourth) finger? Keep raising the middle finger. Does your forefinger move?

EXPERIMENT
The stuck finger

Each of your fingers has its own tendons attached to the finger-pulling muscles in your forearm. On the back of the hand there is an "inter-tendon connection" linking the tendons that run to the middle finger and the ring (fourth) finger. Curl up your middle finger on a table-top, stretch out your other fingers, and see how this inter-tendon connection makes your ring finger completely immoveable.

Extensor digitorum (finger-pulling muscle in the back of the arm)

Inter-tendon connection between middle finger and ring finger

Tendons to each finger

Trying to lift your ring finger
Place your hand fingertips down on a table, with your middle finger curled under. Try to lift your other fingers, one by one. You will be able to lift all of your fingers – except the ring finger.

Tendon connections
Tendons to the forefinger and middle finger are not linked, but those to the middle finger and ring finger have an inter-tendon connection. This restricts their ability to move on their own.

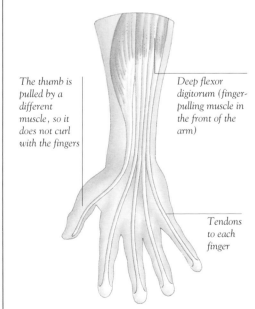

The thumb is pulled by a different muscle, so it does not curl with the fingers

Deep flexor digitorum (finger-pulling muscle in the front of the arm)

Tendons to each finger

Multiple tendons
The finger-pulling muscle has four main tendons. Each is attached to a finger bone. As the muscle shortens to pull on the middle finger, it also pulls on the other three fingers and lifts them too.

Face muscles

Many of the muscles in the face are attached not to bones, but to each other, or to the skin. We use these muscles to make the huge variety of facial expressions that convey our thoughts, moods, and emotions. We also use these muscles for such activities as eating, speaking, and blinking.

Frontalis

Orbicularis oculi

Temporalis

Corrugator supercilii

Levator labii

Orbicularis oris

Zygomaticus

Masseter

Depressor anguli oris

Mentalis

Depressor labii

Disapproval
Corrugator supercilii wrinkles the brow in a frown.

Happiness
Zygomaticus pulls the mouth corners up and out in a smile.

Surprise
Frontalis raises the eyebrows and exposes more of the eyes.

Disgust
Depressor anguli oris lowers and widens the corners of the mouth.

Changing muscle teams

See how the muscle teams in your body change and are replaced by other teams as you move. Choose a movement – such as taking a drink of water – and do it slowly, stage by stage. Feel for the tensed muscles and their taut tendons at each step. Which muscles are involved at each of the stages?

YOU WILL NEED
● *cup of water*

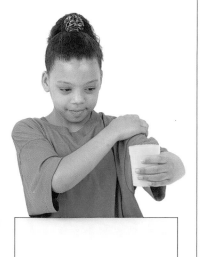

1 PUT YOUR forearm on the table, and grip a cup. Feel the muscles and tendons on the inside of your forearm and wrist, bending your fingers.

2 SLOWLY RAISE your arm. Press gently around your shoulder to feel muscles such as the deltoid and trapezius, which help to move the arm.

3 BEND YOUR elbow to bring the cup near your mouth. Feel the biceps, the main elbow-flexing muscle, on the front of your upper arm.

4 TWIST YOUR forearm and wrist to tilt the cup, as if to drink. See how the muscle on the inside of your elbow tightens as you tilt the cup.

Muscle pairs

AN INDIVIDUAL muscle moves its part of the body by contracting (getting shorter) and pulling on the bone that it is attached to. To let the whole body push, pull, and make all its other movements, muscles are usually arranged in pairs, one on each side of a bone. This means that the bone can be pulled in one direction or the other. Muscles that produce opposing pulling forces in this way are called antagonistic pairs.

EXPERIMENT
Making a model of an arm

Adult help is advised for this experiment

In an antagonistic pair of muscles, one muscle pulls a bone in one direction. The other muscle is sited on the other side of the bone. When this muscle contracts, it pulls the bone the other way. As this happens, the first muscle relaxes and is passively stretched. You can make a model of an arm with an antagonistic pair of muscles – the biceps and the triceps – in its upper part. One of these muscles contracts to bend the elbow; the other contracts to straighten it. Working alternately, they can make your arm wave its hand. You can stick "bones" made of card to your model arm to make it look more realistic.

Rear bracket (**D**)

Top bracket (**E**)

Main support (**C**)

Upper arm (**F**)

Support bracket (**B**)

Base (**A**)

Arm stand
*This is an exploded view of parts for the stand. Bolt the lower arm (**G** – see below) to the upper arm (**F**) with the washers, so that it can move up and down easily.*

1 CLAMP THE lower arm (**G**) to the drilling board. With adult help, carefully drill a hole on the centre line, 6 cm (2¼ in) from its "elbow" end. The bolt will pass through this hole.

2 SCREW IN the four small eyes: one on each side of the "wrist", where hand and arm join; one at the outside corner of the elbow; and one 12 cm (5 in) from the elbow on the inside.

3 DRILL A hole in the upper arm (**F**), on the centre line, 3 cm (1½ in) from the elbow end. Bolt **G** and **F** together, with washers under the bolt head and nut, and between the arm parts.

4 GLUE THE ends of the straws into the holes in one strip of corrugated plastic. Space the straws out, so that you use about 12 to 15 straws along the 20-cm (8-in) length of the strip.

5 GLUE THE other ends of the straws into another corrugated strip. Allow to dry. Then, with the metal ruler, press on the straws halfway along and crease them, so that they will bend easily.

6 ROLL THE strips and straws to make a cylinder-shaped cage, and tape with insulating tape. Make sure the creases let the straws bend outward when the ends of the cage are pushed together.

7 CUT AN elastic band. Loop one end around a corrugated strip, and tape it down. Loop and tape the other end of the elastic band to the opposite side of the same corrugated strip circle.

8 REPEAT STEPS 4 to 7 to make a second straw cage. Now cut the plastic tube in half. Tape the mouth of a balloon very firmly to one end of each piece of tube, making sure the seal is airtight.

YOU WILL NEED
● *pieces of plywood: for* **A**, *25 cm x 12 cm x 1 cm (10 in x 5 in x ¹/₂ in)*; *for* **B**, *12 cm x 3 cm x 3 cm (5 in x 1¹/₂ in x 1¹/₂ in)*; *for* **C**, *60 cm x 12 cm x 0.5 cm (24 in x 5 in x ¹/₈ in)*; *for* **D**, *30 cm x 8 cm x 1 cm (12 in x 3 in x ¹/₂ in) with a 1-cm (¹/₂-in) notch*; *for* **E**, *10 cm x 1 cm x 1 cm (4 in x ¹/₂ in x ¹/₂ in)*; *for* **F** *(upper arm)*, *33 cm x 5 cm x 0.5 cm (13 in x 2 in x ¹/₄ in)*; *for* **G** *(lower arm)*, *40 cm x 8 cm x 0.5 cm (16 in x 3 in x ¹/₈ in) with hand shape* ● *2 large screw eyes* ● *4 small screw eyes* ● *bolt 3 cm (1¹/₂ in) long and 5 mm (³/₁₆ in) diameter with 3 washers and a nut* ● *double-sided adhesive tape* ● *4 strips of corrugated plastic 20 cm x 2 cm (8 in x 1 in)* ● *30 plastic drinking straws* ● *2 large elastic bands* ● *glue* ● *2 balloons* ● *insulating tape* ● *2 drawing pins* ● *string* ● *2 m (6 ft) of 1-cm (¹/₂-in) diameter plastic tube with 2 taps to fit (or 2 clamps)* ● *cutting mat* ● *drilling board* ● *drill with 6-mm (¹/₄-in) bit* ● *metal ruler* ● *craft knife* ● *pencil* ● *scissors* ● *G-clamp* ● *tenon saw* ● *coping saw*

9 ASSEMBLE THE arm stand (opposite) with the double-sided tape. Drill two holes in the top of the rear bracket (**D**) and screw in the large eyes. Stick the whole arm (**F** and **G**) to the top and rear brackets (**E** and **D**) with the double-sided tape, making sure the hand of **G** has its thumb uppermost.

10 HANG ONE straw cage on the left end of the top bracket (**E**) and secure it with a drawing pin. Tie a loop of string around the lower corrugated strip. With the hand propped up, tie a piece of string to this loop, thread it through the eye on the inside elbow, and tie it to the eye on the upper wrist.

Triceps

Biceps

11 PIN THE other cage to the bracket's right end, with a string loop on its lower strip. Tie string to this, thread it through the outside corner eye, adjust its length so there is an equal pull on each cage, and tie to the lower wrist eye.

12 DAB SOME glue on all knots, so that they do not unravel. Let it dry. Insert a balloon into each cage as a "muscle". Push the attached tubes through the large eyes. Fix a tap or clamp to the free end of each tube.

13 YOUR MODEL ARM is now ready. The muscle at the front of the arm is the biceps, that at the back is the triceps. Blow through the tube into the biceps. The inflating balloon shortens the cage, like a contracting muscle. It pulls the strings (the muscle's tendons). These pull on the wooden lower arm, representing the forearm bones (radius and ulna), which pivots at the bolt (the elbow's hinge joint). Make the hand move up with the biceps, and down with its antagonistic pair, the triceps. Use the taps or clamps to hold the muscles in position.

Muscle stamina and strength

YOUR BODY IS LIKE a well-crafted machine. It has moving parts that are perfectly designed for your everyday movements, such as breathing, eating, walking, and running. But, unlike any machine, your body's muscles can adjust themselves, becoming tuned to your regular actions and movements. If a muscle is used more and for longer periods, it becomes larger and more powerful. The blood vessels that supply it widen to bring it more energy-giving food for its activities. Its stamina – how long it works without becoming tired – increases too. In contrast, muscles that are used little become small and weak. Because muscles become accustomed to certain repeated movements, you can trick them into acting in unusual ways (below).

Tired muscles

Finger muscles grip well, but are not designed to have great stamina. Clench your fingers and open them, once a second, for as long as you can. How long can you continue?

Fingers closed ...

... fingers open, and so on.

Tricking muscles

Sometimes you can trick your muscles. If, when you try to lift your arm, a friend stops you, your brain and muscles soon adapt to this situation. When your friend lets go, the nerves and muscles stay adjusted to the old situation for a few seconds, with strange effects.

1 STAND next to a friend. Try to raise your arm, while your friend holds it down by your side. Continue trying to lift your arm for 20 to 30 seconds.

2 ASK YOUR friend to release your arm, and at the same time let it relax. Your arm will try to lift itself. See how it rises upwards.

■ Fast and slow muscles

Some skeletal muscles (p.58) are called fast-twitch muscles and others slow-twitch muscles. The fast-twitch type works rapidly and powerfully. It gives explosive force in sports like weight-lifting (below right), but has little staying power. The slow-twitch type contracts slowly, using little energy, so it tires less quickly. It gives stamina in endurance sports, such as long-distance running (below left).

EXPERIMENT
Test the strengths of different muscles

Adult help is advised
for this experiment

Each team of body muscles has its own special features, to carry out the jobs that it needs to do. Some teams are more powerful than others. You can compare the strengths of the muscle teams in your body using a set of bathroom scales.

YOU WILL NEED
● *bathroom scales* ● *notepad* ● *pencil*

2 TRY OTHER positions, such as pressing the scales between your palms or your elbows. Draw an outline of your body, and note the results on the drawing. Which parts of the body squeeze with most power?

1 HOLD the scales between your knees, and squeeze as hard as you can. This measures the strength of the adductor magnus and other muscles in your inner thighs. Ask a friend to note the highest reading.

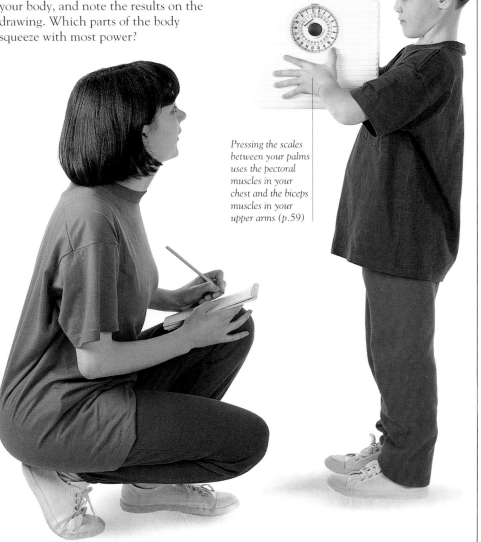

Pressing the scales between your palms uses the pectoral muscles in your chest and the biceps muscles in your upper arms (p.59)

EXPERIMENT
Muscle habits

Habitual movements make the muscles that perform them strong and agile. Tapping your fingers on the table, palm-down, is an example of this. Unusual movements, like tapping your fingers palm-up, use weak, less co-ordinated muscles.

Force of habit
Fingers are more used to bending forwards – the position they adopt when relaxed – than to straightening out. So you can probably tap palm-down for longer than you can palm-up.

The versatile hand

HOW DID YOU tie your shoe-laces this morning? How did you open the pages of this book? How do you carry out hundreds of similar, very precise actions every day? Look at your hand to see why it is such a marvellous device. It combines all of the body structures described so far in this book. The touch-sensitive covering of skin is wrapped around numerous sets of muscles and tendons, joints and ligaments, which are in turn attached to a framework of strong, light bones. The human hand is powerful yet delicate, adaptable yet precise. There is no device in the whole world of animals or of machines that is quite so versatile.

(p.58)

EXPERIMENT
Make a model hand

Adult help is advised for this experiment

When you grip, long muscles on the inside of your forearm contract. They pull their tendons (p.58), which are attached to the jointed sets of bones in your fingers. The tendons and muscles are kept in place by ligaments and other fibrous tissue. Make a model hand to show, in a simplified way, how your own hand works.

YOU WILL NEED
- coping saw
- about 80 small metal screw eyes
- 5 elastic bands
- pen
- string
- carpet tape
- ruler
- wood strip 30 cm x 12 mm x 12 mm (12 in x ½ in x ½ in)
- wood block 10 cm x 10 cm x 12 mm (4 in x 4 in x ½ in)
- vice
- scissors

EXPERIMENT
Precise work

Bones, joints, and muscles in your arm and hand are smaller and finer the farther down your arm they are – from your shoulder to your fingertips. So the movements you can achieve with the fingertips are more precise than those with the shoulder.

YOU WILL NEED
- felt-tipped pen
- paper
- ribbon

■ Robot "hands"
Engineers have tried for years to build machines that mimic the human hand. But none of these devices has come close to our range of movements. It is hard for scientists to match the control systems of the body. Your eyes, and the hand's muscles and skin, give your brain sophisticated feedback about your hand's position.

Extra hands
Robot machines on assembly lines carry out certain simple, repetitive tasks in a tireless fashion. But a robot welder-arm cannot spray paint, and a robot suction-grab cannot tighten screws. Each device is designed to do only one or a few of the multiple tasks that our hands can do.

1 WRITE THE numbers 1 to 9 on the paper in the usual way. Then ask a friend to tie the pen to the middle section of your forefinger. Try again – it is still not too difficult.

2 USE ONE less joint by tying the pen to the base section of your forefinger, and write 1 to 9 again. The bigger bone, joint, and less practised muscles make it awkward.

3 ASK YOUR friend to tie the pen to the back of your hand. Now you are using only your shoulder, elbow, and wrist. Is neat writing more difficult?

4 ASK YOUR friend to tie the pen to the inside of your wrist. Now you can use only your shoulder and elbow. These are big joints, not designed for precision.

1 DRAW A palm shape on the wood block. The palm top should be about 6.5 cm (2½ in) wide. Ask an adult to cut out the shape, holding the wood in a vice. Next, study your fingers. Is each of their sections the same length?

2 LAY YOUR fingers in turn against the side of the wood strip. Mark the length of each finger and thumb section on the strip. Ask an adult to cut off the 14 pieces you have marked (three for each finger, two for the thumb).

3 TAPE THE pieces together on one side (call this the front), and attach them to the block. Attach an eye to each fingertip and to each side of each knuckle. Fix five eyes in the wrist too. The thumb is slightly different (below left).

4 FLIP THE hand. Fix eyes in the same pattern (but only four at the wrist). Snip the elastic bands. Tie each to a fingertip eye, and thread it through the others. Tie it at the wrist with slight tension. For the thumb, see below left.

5 FLIP THE hand, so that it is front-up again. Tie a length of string to a fingertip eye, and thread it through the other eyes, including those in the wrist. Leave some string free below the wrist. Repeat for all fingers. For the thumb, see below.

6 YOUR "HAND" is now ready. Hold the block with one hand and all of the strings with the other. When you pull the strings, you mimic the action of the tendons that connect the muscles in your forearm to the ends of your fingers (p.60). The strings run through the screw eyes, which represent loops of ligament and fibrous material in the wrist and knuckles. The elastic bands give the "hand" tension, like the muscles on the back of the hand. The "thumb" twists inward to give a realistic grabbing action. Can you make your model hand drum its fingers on a table?

Screw-eye ligament

Carpet-tape knuckle

Elastic-band muscle

String tendon

Pull the tendons to mimic the action of the forearm muscles

Twisting thumb

Tape the knuckle between the upper and lower thumb sections on the inside. But for the knuckle between lower thumb section and block, tape at the front. Fix four eyes in the sides of the upper thumb section, one on the outside below the knuckle between upper and lower sections, one on the front of the lower section, and two on the side of the block. Feed the thumb's elastic band from the fingertip eye down the outside of the block. Feed the string through the eyes on the inside of the upper section, then through the eye on the front of the lower section, and then through the one free wrist eye.

Insert screw eyes in the sides of the upper thumb section

Feed the string from the side of the thumbtip to the front of the block

Screw an eye into the front of the lower thumb section

Tie the thumb's elastic band at the lower eye on the side of the block

The OXYGEN SUPPLY

Air travel
A branching system of air tubes known as bronchi (above) carries air deep into the spongy honeycomb of the lungs. The bronchi become narrower and turn into bronchioles. Bronchioles themselves end in microscopic air bags called alveoli. Through a microscope, alveoli appear as cave-like holes (left). The "fluffy balls" are white blood cells, scavenging for bits of dust or germs.

LIFE DEPENDS ON OXYGEN. This substance plays a vital role in the chemical reactions inside every body cell, releasing energy from food to power life processes. The parts of the body designed to obtain continuing supplies of oxygen – the nose, airways, lungs, and breathing muscles – are collectively known as the respiratory system. In the lungs, fresh air is brought into almost direct contact with blood, so that the oxygen in the air can easily pass into the blood, and be carried to every body part.

THE LUNGS AND BREATHING

THE BODY CAN STORE many of the substances it needs. For example, the liver holds reserves of vitamins, the bones store minerals, and body fat acts as an energy stockpile. But the body cannot store more than a few minutes' worth of its essential supply of oxygen, so it must continually take in fresh stocks. It does this by a process called respiration. The two lungs are the organs that obtain oxygen from the air and pass it to the blood, and the blood distributes this oxygen to cells around the body.

The word "respiration" actually has two meanings.

In one sense the word is another term for "breathing". When you respire, you breathe in and out. Your body takes in fresh air, absorbs oxygen from it, adds carbon dioxide to it, and then expels this now-stale air.

The other meaning is concerned with cell chemistry. A cell needs energy from substances such as the sugar glucose. To release this energy in a form that the cell can use easily, the glucose must be broken up by a series of chemical reactions. Oxygen is a vital ingredient in these chemical reactions, and carbon dioxide is a waste product of them. The process of obtaining energy by these chemical reactions is called cellular respiration.

Cellular respiration is found in almost all living things, from amoebas and worms to trees and mushrooms. They all need oxygen to survive. Only a few microbes, called anaerobic bacteria, do not need oxygen. They live in places, such as the mud at the bottom of the oceans, where no oxygen is available.

Early anatomists did not know about cellular respiration. This was partly because it is essentially a chemical process, and cannot be observed with the naked eye.

The lungs are filled with air as the chest expands. You can show this with balloon "lungs" in a plastic-bottle "chest" (p.72).

It was also because the central substance in the respiratory process, the gas oxygen, is invisible. There was little progress in our knowledge of how the lungs work until the 17th century, when the microscope was invented, and chemistry began to advance as a science.

■ The pneuma

The great philosophers of Ancient Greece, such as Plato (c.428–c.347 BC) and Aristotle (384–322 BC), believed that life was based on a type of fire, a "vital flame" that burned within the heart. Nourishment from food supposedly stoked up the flame, while breathing brought in

The "Father of Chemistry", Antoine Lavoisier, carried out many experiments on the gases in air. He first gave the name "oxygen" to the part of air that supports life.

Amphibians such as salamanders can take in oxygen through their moist skin, as well as through their lungs.

air to damp it down and keep it from burning out of control. These philosophers thought that if the flame went out, the body became cold and life ended.

Galen (p.13) of Ancient Rome also had strong views on the roles of the airways and lungs. He believed that a mysterious substance in air, called the pneuma (p.94), passed into the mouth, down the throat, and through the trachea (windpipe) into the branching, tree-like system of airways deep inside the lungs. He thought that the pneuma then passed into the blood, which carried it to the heart. There the pneuma "vitalized" the blood, bringing life and taking away waste substances.

Although Galen's notion of the pneuma has now been proved wrong, his descriptions of the routes taken by air in the respiratory system paved the way for later discoveries.

■ Dogs and frogs

In 1660, the Italian microscopist Marcello Malpighi (p.104) described how lungs work at a microscopic level – in this case, in a dog. In the following years, he found out more about lung structure. The big airways, the bronchi, divide many times, to become smaller bronchioles, and then even smaller, when they are called terminal bronchioles. Each of these terminal bronchioles ends in a group of tiny air sacs, called alveoli. There are more than 600 million alveoli in a pair of human lungs (p.72).

When he studied a frog's lungs, Malpighi saw the tiny blood vessels, called capillaries, that pass close to the alveoli. However, the function of this meeting of the alveoli and capillaries was not understood until the 18th century.

Breathing and fire

The British scientists Robert Boyle (1627–1691) and Robert Hooke (p.26) were interested in the nature of air. Boyle and Hooke found that all animals need to breathe fresh air to stay alive. This may seem obvious today, but at the time it was a very important discovery.

Another British scientist, Joseph Priestley (1733–1804),

Fish and other water creatures take in oxygen dissolved in water through their gills. Air-breathers like us need oxygen in its gas form. So divers must carry air tanks.

placed a burning candle in a sealed jar with normal air. Priestley knew that this air contained a gas, which he called "dephlogisticated air". (This gas later came to be known as oxygen.) He also placed a second burning candle in a jar with air from which he had removed this gas. He found that the first candle burned for some time, whereas the second went out almost immediately. Priestley also carried out experiments on animals and discovered that they must breathe "dephlogisticated air" in order to survive.

It was the French chemist Antoine Lavoisier (1743–1794) who named this vital gas oxygen. He realized that the body uses oxygen and produces carbon dioxide in the same way as a fire, although the process in the body is much slower.

Lavoisier's discoveries finally made clear the reason for the internal design of the lungs. Blood flowing through the capillaries that pass next to the alveoli comes very close to the air inside the alveoli. So the

This view down the throat shows closed vocal cords. The cords are vibrated by air passing between them, making sounds.

oxygen in breathed-in air travels the short distance from the alveoli to the blood. Once in the blood, the oxygen is delivered all around the body so that cellular respiration can take place. Carbon dioxide is carried in the other direction – from the blood to the air in the lungs, and it is then breathed out.

If the alveoli in human lungs were spread out flat, they would cover a surface as large as a tennis court. This huge surface area (p.185) within the lungs ensures that enough oxygen can be absorbed, from the alveoli into the blood, to keep the body working efficiently.

Speech

Vocal communication is a useful "by-product" of the respiratory system. Air flowing in and out of the lungs along the trachea passes between two tough, pearly-pink ridges in the larynx (voice-box). These are the vocal cords.

The air flow makes the cords vibrate, which produces sounds. Stretching the cords by varying amounts produces vibrations of varying pitch (high or low sound). If the cords are stretched tight, they vibrate faster and produce a high pitch. If they are loose, the pitch is low. Sounds are louder when air flows faster and in greater amounts over the vocal cords.

As you speak, these sounds are altered by the positions of your tongue, teeth, cheeks, and lips. The result is the immense range of words, whispers, shouts, screams, laughs, and other kinds of sound we use to communicate.

When breathing is normal, the vocal cords are apart, so there is usually no sound.

To breathe out, your lungs spring back from their large, inflated size to their normal smaller volume, like a balloon deflating. To blow hard, your abdominal muscles squeeze to give added push.

The respiratory system

THE RESPIRATORY SYSTEM gets oxygen from the air into the blood via the lungs. It consists of the nose, throat, trachea (windpipe), and lungs. As you inhale (breathe in) you draw in fresh air. As you exhale (breathe out) you expel stale air from the lungs. Deep in the lungs, in air pockets called alveoli, the air is brought into very close contact with blood passing through tiny blood vessels. This process allows oxygen, which is vital for cellular respiration (p.70), to pass from the lungs into the blood. It also allows the waste product carbon dioxide to pass from the blood to the lungs, and then out into the air. If carbon dioxide were allowed to accumulate in the body, it would be poisonous. Listen to your own breathing, and see how your chest movements suck in and blow out air.

(p.70)

EXPERIMENT
Model lungs

Adult help is advised for this experiment

When you inhale, muscles cause the chest to expand (opposite), making the lungs do the same. When this happens, air is sucked into the lungs. Make a model to demonstrate this.

YOU WILL NEED
● large clear-plastic bottle ● three-way hosepipe connector ● modelling clay ● 2 elastic bands ● plastic tube ● 3 small balloons ● scissors

1 PUSH THE plastic tube into one opening of the hosepipe connector. Use modelling clay, if necessary, to make an airtight seal. Fix the balloons tightly on to the other openings with elastic bands, making sure that the joins between the connector and the balloons are airtight.

■ Inside the chest

Air passes to and from the lungs through the trachea (windpipe). The top of the trachea opens into the pharynx (throat). The lower end divides into two main bronchi (air tubes), one of which enters each lung. The bronchi branch again and again inside the lung, becoming smaller and smaller until they are as thin as hairs. Now called terminal bronchioles, they end at the microscopic, bubble-shaped alveoli. There are about 300 million alveoli in each lung. Each alveolus is surrounded by capillaries (p.179). Oxygen in the air inside the alveolus passes the short distance to the blood in the capillary, and the blood carries it around the body.

(p.179)

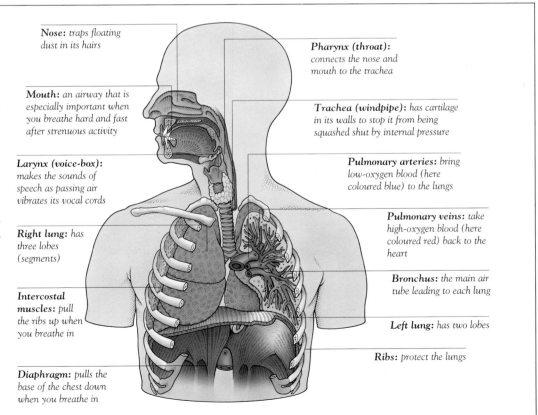

Nose: traps floating dust in its hairs

Mouth: an airway that is especially important when you breathe hard and fast after strenuous activity

Larynx (voice-box): makes the sounds of speech as passing air vibrates its vocal cords

Right lung: has three lobes (segments)

Intercostal muscles: pull the ribs up when you breathe in

Diaphragm: pulls the base of the chest down when you breathe in

Pharynx (throat): connects the nose and mouth to the trachea

Trachea (windpipe): has cartilage in its walls to stop it from being squashed shut by internal pressure

Pulmonary arteries: bring low-oxygen blood (here coloured blue) to the lungs

Pulmonary veins: take high-oxygen blood (here coloured red) back to the heart

Bronchus: the main air tube leading to each lung

Left lung: has two lobes

Ribs: protect the lungs

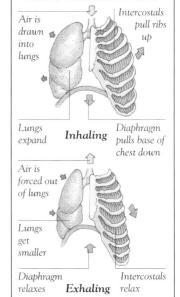

Breathing

When you inhale, the lungs become bigger and draw in air. When you exhale, the lungs spring back to their smaller size.

Air is drawn into lungs

Intercostals pull ribs up

Lungs expand   **Inhaling**   *Diaphragm pulls base of chest down*

Air is forced out of lungs

Lungs get smaller

Diaphragm relaxes   **Exhaling**   *Intercostals relax*

2 CAREFULLY cut off the bottom 2.5 cm (1 in) from the bottle, using the scissors. Make sure the cut edge of the bottle is smooth. Place the balloons and connector inside. Seal the plastic tube into the neck of the bottle with the modelling clay to make an airtight fit.

3 TIE A KNOT in the neck of the third balloon. Then carefully cut it in half, crossways. Gently stretch the knotted part of the balloon over the lower end of the bottle, and pull it around the sides. Make the balloon as taut as you can – like a drum skin. Now hold it by its knot.

4 THE LOWER balloon represents the diaphragm, the main breathing muscle (right). Pull it down, as though you were inhaling. This lowers the air pressure in the bottle. Air from outside rushes in and makes the two balloons expand, just like the real lungs in your chest.

EXPERIMENT
Lung surface

Adult help is advised for this experiment

The millions of alveoli in a lung expose its insides to air. They make the lung's surface area (p.185) much greater than if the lung were one hollow chamber, so the lungs can absorb lots of oxygen. Make your own "alveoli" out of card.

YOU WILL NEED
- adhesive tape • scissors • thin sheet of blue card 45 cm x 15 cm (18 in x 6 in)
- lots of thin sheets of yellow card • ruler

1 BEND THE large blue sheet into a cylinder. Tape its edges. This represents the outside of a lung. Now you are ready to make tubes representing the alveoli for the inside of the "lung".

2 CUT THE yellow card into pieces 15 cm x 10 cm (6 in x 4 in). Roll into tubes, to represent alveoli, and tape their edges. Place the tubes inside the large blue "lung" until it is full.

3 NOW UNRAVEL the alveoli tubes, and spread them out flat. You have increased the surface area of your "lung" greatly by adding just a few alveoli tubes. Imagine how great the oxygen-absorbing surface area of a real lung is, with millions of alveoli packed inside.

Breathing in and out

NEXT TIME YOU are outside on a dry winter morning, exhale (breathe out) slowly. Your breath looks like steam from a kettle. Exhaled air contains more water vapour than the air you inhale (breathe in). Its moistness comes from moisture in the lining of the respiratory system. In cold air the vapour condenses (turns into tiny water droplets). In warm air the vapour does not condense, but it is still there. Exhaled air is different from inhaled air in other ways. Because it has been in the body, it is warm. And it contains less oxygen, as well as more waste carbon dioxide, than breathed-in air.

Using up oxygen

Adult help is advised for this experiment

Accurate measurements show that the normal air you inhale contains about 21 per cent oxygen, but the air that you exhale has only 17 per cent oxygen. The missing four per cent is used by the body to help it stay alive and work properly. Show how breathing removes oxygen from the air by exposing a candle flame to a jar of fresh air and then to a jar of exhaled air. A candle flame only burns in air that contains enough oxygen. For this experiment, you must use a large heat-proof jar and a short, wide candle that will not topple over. Make sure you wear the heat-proof gloves because the jar will become hot.

YOU WILL NEED
● bowl ● water ● stop-watch ● plastic tube
● large heat-proof jar ● matches ● short, wide
candle ● saucers ● heat-proof gloves

1 LIGHT THE CANDLE. Put on the gloves and carefully cover the candle with the jar so that the mouth of the jar rests fully on the saucer. Time how long the flame burns before it goes out (uses up all of the oxygen in the jar). Now fill the jar and bowl with water.

2 TIP THE JAR upside-down in the bowl of water. Put the end of the tube under its rim. Inhale, wait a few seconds, then put the tube to your mouth and exhale down it into the jar. Steady the jar with your hand. Repeat until the jar is full of exhaled air.

3 DO THIS STEP quickly. Lift out the jar, keeping it upside down. Cover the mouth of the jar with the second saucer, so your breath is trapped inside.

4 LIGHT THE CANDLE, and put on the heat-proof gloves again. Quickly remove the second saucer and place the jar over the lit candle. How long does the flame burn in exhaled air? Does this air have more oxygen than normal air or less? *Caution: Remember that the jar will become hot.*

EXPERIMENT
Moist breath

The air that you breathe out contains water vapour. Show this by turning the vapour back into liquid water on the surface of a mirror.

YOU WILL NEED
● *small plastic-edged mirror*

Condensing breath
Put the mirror in the fridge for an hour. Wipe it, hold it in front of your mouth, and breathe on it. The vapour in your breath condenses as a fog of droplets on the cold mirror surface.

EXPERIMENT
Breath temperature

 Adult help is advised for this experiment

Exhaled air carries heat from the warm inner core of your body – from the vital organs such as your heart. In this experiment, you use a thermometer to find out how much warmer exhaled air is, compared to the air around you. *Caution: If the thermometer cracks, do not touch it. Get help from an adult.*

YOU WILL NEED
● *plastic tube* ● *cotton wool*
● *small jar* ● *standard scientific thermometer*

■ Altered breathing

Breathing muscles respond automatically to everyday hazards. If your diaphragm is irritated, you may hiccup; if there is too little oxygen in your blood, you may yawn; and if dirt finds its way into your air passages, you may cough or sneeze.

Hiccups
In normal breathing, the diaphragm muscle at the base of your chest (p.72) works smoothly. But if you eat or drink too much, your stomach stretches and irritates the diaphragm, which contracts jerkily. As a result, you hiccup.

Yawns
If you breathe slowly at rest, the lungs do not get rid of enough carbon dioxide, and it builds up in the blood. So the brain triggers an extra-deep breath, called a yawn. This "blows off" the excess carbon dioxide and brings in more oxygen.

Coughs
A cough gets rid of mucus and dirt in the trachea (p.72) or the air passages to the lungs. You breathe in deeply, close the top of the trachea, build up lung pressure, and let out the air with an explosive rush that rattles the vocal cords.

Sneezes
Sometimes mucus or dirt irritates the linings of the air spaces in your nose. So you take a deep breath, and blast the air through your nose at more than 160 km per hour (100 miles per hour) to blow out the irritation.

1 PUT THE tube and the bulb end of the thermometer carefully into the jar. Pack the cotton wool in the neck of the jar quite firmly, making sure that the thermometer is held securely.

2 PUT THE other end of the tube in your mouth, and breathe in deeply. Then breathe out away from the tube. Do this ten times and note the temperature. This is the temperature of the air you breathe in. Then breathe in from the air and out through the tube ten times. Note the temperature. This is the temperature of your breath. How much warmer is it?

Lung power

WHEN YOU EXERCISE or play a sport, you sometimes find yourself breathless and panting. This is because your hard-working muscles need more oxygen and energy-rich nutrients to fuel their movements. The heart rate increases so that more of the oxygen and energy carried in the blood can reach the muscles. You breathe faster and deeper to get the extra oxygen from the air into your blood. With regular exercise, your breathing muscles and lungs become better at taking in more air, more quickly. Breathing rate and lung power are two good indicators of fitness and health.

EXPERIMENT
Fast breaths

To measure your breathing rate, see how many breaths you take in one minute. The rate depends mainly on how active you have just been. Sit still for five minutes and measure the rate. Then do two minutes of vigorous exercise, such as running on the spot. Check your breathing rate every minute after this. How long does it take to return to the resting rate? *Caution: If you feel dizzy or sick when exercising, stop at once and rest.*

Counting and timing
Breathing in and then out again counts as one breath. To time the number of times you breathe in one minute, use a stop-watch.

EXPERIMENT
Blowing power

Adult help is advised for this experiment

This experiment tests lung power – how hard you can blow, and for how long. Make a fan-shaped turbine that pulls a car up a ramp to see how much lung power you have. *Caution: If you feel dizzy or sick, stop blowing at once and rest.*

YOU WILL NEED
●*cutting mat* ●*cutting edge* ●*ruler* ●*30 cm (1 ft) stiff wire* ●*drinking straw* ●*compasses* ●*toothpick* ●*adhesive tape* ●*double-sided adhesive tape* ●*craft knife* ●*for the ramp top: stiff card 60 cm x 20 cm (24 in x 8 in), shaped as* **A** ●*for the ramp sides: 2 pieces stiff card 75 cm x 18 cm (30 in x 7 in), shaped as* **B** ●*for the ramp crosspiece: stiff card 28 cm x 7 cm (11 in x 2½ in), shaped as* **C** ●*scissors* ●*plastic bottle* ●*glue* ●*small card discs* ●*cotton reel* ●*cotton thread* ●*large cork* ●*toy car* ●*notepad* ●*pen*

1 CUT 12 SLOTS around the cork. Be sure to cut away from the hand that holds the cork. Make the slots slightly angled and equally spaced. Ask an adult to drill a hole – the right size for the straw to fit tightly – through the cork.

2 CAREFULLY cut 12 vertical strips, each about 10 cm x 2 cm (4 in x 1 in), from the bottle. Trim the ends of the strips into V shapes. Push these into the cork's slots. Make sure that the curves in the strips all face in the same direction.

3 CUT SINGLE holes in the centres of the card discs. Slide one disc on to the straw, followed by the cotton reel, then the other disc, and finally the cork. Glue these parts together so that no part moves on its own. This is the turbine.

4 DRAW MARKER lines at regular intervals – say 2 cm (1 in) – along one edge of the ramp-top card. Number each marker, beginning with number 1 at the lower end of the ramp. This is the lung-power scale.

EXPERIMENT
Deep breaths

To breathe in very deeply, your rib and chest muscles pull your ribs up and out (p.73). Your whole chest gets bigger and sucks in more air than with an average breath. Measure this chest expansion using a flexible measuring tape. Compare results with your friends. How much your chest expands is one indication of your lung efficiency. In athletes, chest expansion is usually greater than normal.

Breathing out
A friend holds the tape around the widest part of your chest, usually just above the lowest of your ribs. Breathe out as far as you can. Your friend quickly takes the measurement around your chest.

Breathing in
Take the deepest breath that you can. The friend now measures around your fully expanded chest. The difference between the two measurements gives your chest expansion.

Pierce a small hole here

Ramp pieces joined by slits

Trim the straw so that it fits closely between the ramp sides, but without rubbing

Feed the wire through the small hole

5 JOIN THE sides and the crosspiece (**B** and **C** opposite) by the slits you have cut into the card. Glue or tape the ramp top (**A**) to the top edges of the ramp sides. Use the toothpick to carefully pierce a small hole in the upper part of each ramp side.

7 TAKE A DEEP breath, and, from 5 cm (2 in) away, blow hard and steadily at the turbine until your air runs out. Get a friend to see how far the car has travelled up the ramp. Practise aiming your breath. (If the car moves too easily, or not easily enough, try a heavier or lighter one.) Now test the lung power of your friends. *Remember to stop at once if anyone feels dizzy or sick.*

6 HOLD THE turbine in place and push the wire through the hole that you have pierced in one ramp side, along the inside of the straw, and then out and through the other hole. Check that the turbine spins freely. Tape one end of the cotton to the toy car. Cut the cotton to the length of the ramp, and tape the other end firmly to the cotton reel.

FUELLING the BODY

An absorbing business
Even seemingly simple foods usually contain a variety of nourishing substances. Wheat (above), for example, contains starch, fibre, vitamins, and minerals. These are absorbed into the body in the small intestine, which has many tiny folds and fingers known as villi (left).

ALL MACHINES, FROM A flashlight to a jetliner, need energy to make them go. That energy comes from fuel. The body "machine" is no exception. Its fuel is food, which contains energy to power life processes, and raw materials for body growth and maintenance. Food gets into the body through the digestive system, which includes the stomach, intestines, liver, and pancreas. Their task is to break down and process food into simple parts, small enough to be absorbed by the cells of the body.

EATING AND DIGESTION

THE OLD SAYING IS VERY TRUE: "You are what you eat." Your body is built up from the food you take in. The conversion of food into body substances takes place in two stages. Stage one involves eating (getting food to the stomach) and digestion (breaking it down into sub-units). The sub-units are absorbed by the body and distributed to cells. Stage two takes place in the cells, where the sub-units are reassembled to make body parts. Food also provides energy to carry out these processes.

Your teeth have different shapes for different jobs. You can use mirrors to study the shapes of your own teeth (p.86).

To an observer, the digestive system might seem one of the easier body systems to understand. Food goes in one end. Parts of it come out the other end, usually in a changed form. The early anatomists opened the body and traced a long tube through it. They called this tube the digestive tract. They found that the digestive tract is wide at some points, such as the stomach and the large intestine, and narrow at others, such as the oesophagus and the small intestine.

However, there was little interest in the study of digestion for many centuries. Galen of Ancient Rome (p.13) realized that nutrients in food are absorbed by the intestines and that they go mainly to the liver, along a blood vessel called the hepatic portal vein. But Galen wrongly believed that the liver converted the digested food into blood, and that it gave the blood "animal spirit". In fact blood is not made out of digested food. It is simply a liquid carrier, which transports nutrients around the whole of the body.

Food bricks

Not until the 19th century was the chemistry of the digestive process understood in detail. We now know that digestion starts when the food is bitten off and chewed by the teeth in the mouth. It continues in the stomach, and is completed in the small and large intestines.

There are two main reasons why we eat. Firstly, food is fuel for our bodies, providing the energy for living. Secondly, food provides the nutrients that are the "spare parts" required for the body's growth, maintenance, and repair processes.

The whole process of digestion is like dismantling a building brick by brick – including the doors, windows, floorboards, and roof tiles – and then putting these parts back together according to another set of plans, to make a completely different building. In this comparison, the first building is your food, while the second building is your body tissue.

The tiny shrew, the smallest of mammals, uses so much energy that it must eat its own weight in food every day.

Food groups

To stay healthy, a body needs enough of the right kinds of food. This means eating a range of foods that provide a good balance of the main dietary components.

The first group of components is proteins (p.15). These are the main body-building nutrients. Proteins form the bulk of the structures in every body cell, including parts of the cell membranes (p.28). The tough keratin in the upper skin, the fibres of collagen in the lower skin and in bones, the actin and myosin in muscles, and the haemoglobin in red blood cells are all proteins. The dozens of different enzymes in the body that help to digest food (opposite) are also proteins.

The second dietary group is carbohydrates (p.15), which are the main energy-containing nutrients. In most foods, these take the form of starches. In the body, carbohydrates are mostly broken down into their sub-unit sugars such as glucose.

The third group is lipids (fats and oils, p.15). They are made mostly of sub-units formed from fatty acids. Lipids provide structural building blocks for cells, and they also contain

Chewing mixes food with saliva, beginning the breakdown of food substances (p.90).

With a ball and a stocking,
demonstrate how waves of muscle
contraction propel lumps of food through
the digestive tract (p.85).

energy. Together with proteins, they form the membrane around each cell, and the membranes of the organelles within the cells. The body's stores of fat are also a long-term reservoir of energy. This can be used if the body runs low on the short-term energy that it gets from sugars. In addition, the myelin sheaths around the axons of many nerve cells (p.119) are made from lipids.

The fourth dietary group is vitamins. Compared with the quantities of proteins, carbohydrates, and lipids that the body requires, the amount of vitamins that it needs is very small. Vitamins take part in many chemical processes inside body cells. The body can make some vitamins of its own, such as vitamin D, which is produced in the skin by the action of sunlight. However, it must take in ready-made supplies of other vitamins in food.

Fifth are minerals (p.15). These contribute mainly to the structural upkeep of cells. Calcium is an important mineral for strong bones and teeth. Iron is

essential for haemoglobin (p.95). And sodium in the nerves is vital for the nerve signals that constantly flash around the body.

The sixth dietary component is fibre (roughage). This is found only in plant foods, especially fresh fruit and vegetables, unrefined flour, and pulses such as lentils. Fibre is made up of huge molecules of cellulose, which the body cannot break down or absorb. So it passes right through the digestive tract and is expelled in faeces. Fibre helps the digestive process because it gives food "bulk" and allows the intestines to massage the food on its way, providing enough time for thorough digestion.

Sub-units

The huge molecules of carbohydrates, proteins, and lipids are too big to pass through the lining of the intestines and become absorbed into the body. Digestion breaks these large food substances into their sub-units, so that they are small enough to pass through. With digestion, proteins are split into amino acids, carbohydrates into sugars, and lipids into fatty acids and other sub-units.

These sub-units are carried around the body in both blood and lymph (p.182) and supplied to the cells. In each cell, the nutrients are used according to the cell's needs – perhaps to provide energy or to make new substances.

The stomach does not only
digest food. It can also absorb
certain substances, such as
sugars and alcohol, directly into
its network of blood vessels.

Enzymes

The chemical splitting of food substances into sub-units is aided by enzymes. These are special proteins that control the rate of chemical changes but are not

changed themselves. Digestive enzymes are made by the salivary glands, stomach, pancreas, and small intestine. Hundreds of other types of enzyme are found all over the body, regulating cell chemistry. In digestion, enzyme action is particularly intense in the stomach.

Grains of potato starch, shown in
this microscope photograph, are massive
lumps of molecules that are broken
down by digestion into sugar sub-units.

By-products

In addition to enzymes, the stomach lining makes hydrochloric acid. This eats away at the food and helps to kill germs that have entered the body in food. To stop itself from being digested by its own enzymes and acid, the stomach lining produces a thick layer of slimy mucus.

As the stomach contents ooze into the small intestine, they meet more enzymes – from the intestine lining and in juices made by the pancreas. The pancreatic juices also contain an alkali. This counteracts the stomach acid, so that it does not harm the rest of the digestive tract.

These by-products of digestion, together with undigested food left-overs, move through the large intestine, where minerals and water are removed and recycled by the body. Finally the remains are expelled from the body as faeces.

Like this recycling factory, the
large intestine reabsorbs into the body
valuable left-overs of the digestive
process, such as minerals from the
digestive juices and water.

Diet and energy

JUST AS WE put petrol in a car or coal on a fire, so we must put food into our bodies. Food contains energy that drives the body's many chemical processes. But it differs from such fuels as petrol or coal in one very important way. Food contains not only energy but also the raw materials needed for the body's growth, maintenance, and repair. It is as if you put petrol into a car's tank and then watched the car change the petrol into replacement bearings, nuts and bolts, and new tyres for itself! To carry out its maintenance and repair processes, the body needs a selection of nutrients, such as proteins, carbohydrates, fats and oils, minerals, and vitamins (pp.80–81). It must get these from food. Your diet (the food and drink you take in) should contain enough of each type of nutrient, as well as a good balance of them.

■ Energy units and equivalents

Like fuels such as coal, food contains energy in chemical form. How does the energy content in food compare with that of other fuels? The modern international unit for energy is the joule (J). A meal of chicken with salad in a roll, a pot of fruit yoghurt, and an orange totals about 2,300 kJ (1 kJ, or kilojoule = 1,000 J). This is equivalent to the energy in a lump of a coal about half the size of the yoghurt pot. Another energy unit is the calorie (cal). But since 1 cal, like 1 J, is a small unit, the more common measure is the kilocalorie, also called kcal or Cal (with a capital "C"), which is 1,000 cals. To convert calories to joules, 1 cal = 4.2 J, and 1 kcal (1 Cal) = 4.2 kJ. The number of kcals or kJ in food products is often indicated on their packaging.

Picnic lunch
This meal, which gives 2,300 kJ of energy, weighs 530 g (19 oz). Most of the energy is in the bread and chicken.

Coal comparison
When it is burned, this piece of coal gives the same amount of energy as the meal, but it weighs only 80 g (3 oz).

EXPERIMENT
Energy in a peanut

👥 *This is an adult demonstration and should not be attempted by children*
Measure the energy content of a peanut by making your own simple calorimeter (heat-measuring device) with a tin can. Compare the peanut's energy to that of an ordinary type of fuel, wood.

YOU WILL NEED
● saucer ● short, wide candle ● notepad ● pencil ● metal tongs ● wire cooling rack ● bowl of water ● fresh (uncooked) peanuts ● piece of wood of the same weight as a peanut ● ceramic tile wrapped in aluminium cooking foil ● standard scientific thermometer ● matches ● metal soft-drink can ● goggles ● heat-proof gloves

Peanuts burn well for this experiment, as they have a high oil content and so are packed with energy

Wear goggles and heat-proof gloves for this experiment

1 FILL HALF the can with water, and place it on the rack. Hold a peanut in a candle flame with the tongs.

Check the temperature of the water before you heat it with the peanut

2 AS THE PEANUT catches fire, place it on the foil-covered tile. Slide the tile under the can on the wire rack.

Your energy needs

Even when you sleep, your body uses energy to keep warm and make your heart beat. The more active you are, the more energy your muscles use. The blood brings energy to the muscles in the form of glucose (a sugar). Your daily energy needs depend on various factors, such as your age and lifestyle.

At rest
Basic energy use is about 3–4 kJ per minute for a 12-year-old.

Mild activity
Brisk walking raises the energy use rate to 10–15 kJ per minute.

Strenuous activity
When jogging or playing sports, the body uses 30–40 kJ per minute.

Energy and nutrients

Each type of food has a typical energy value. But energy alone is not always desirable. You could run all day on the energy in chocolate bars. But chocolate is made almost solely of high-energy sugar, with few other nutrients.

Nuts
Nuts are high in fats, carbohydrates, and proteins. 50 g (nearly 2 oz) of peanuts contain 1,200 kJ.

Fruits
These contain fibre, vitamins, and some carbohydrates. Bananas have more energy than most fruits, at 250 kJ.

Vegetables
Leafy vegetables are high in fibre, minerals, and vitamins, but low in energy. A cabbage leaf contains 25 kJ.

Breads
These starchy, high-carbohydrate foods are packed with energy for their weight, about 250 kJ per slice.

Fish
Fish is rich in protein, but has few carbohydrates. A portion gives up to 1,000 kJ.

Meats
Like fish, meat is high in protein. A chicken leg gives 600 kJ, and a serving of steak 1,700 kJ.

3 KEEP TWISTING the peanut with the tongs to make sure it burns all over. The peanut's chemical energy converts to heat energy, which warms the water. Keep your eye on the thermometer scale, and make a note of its highest reading. Now repeat the process with the wood. Before burning the wood, cool the tongs in water. Add fresh water up to the same level in the can as before, and make sure that the water is the same temperature as at the start of the first test. Check that the burned peanut and wood are cold before you dispose of them. Which fuel gives the highest thermometer reading, indicating that it contains the most energy?

The digestive system

WHEN YOU SWALLOW FOOD, it enters a long tube, called the digestive tract (gut). This tract has several main sections – the mouth, pharynx (throat), oesophagus, stomach, and intestines – each of which has a special role in digestion. When food reaches the small intestine, it passes through the intestine lining into the body. This process is called absorption. The lining of the small intestine has thousands of tiny finger- or tongue-shaped parts called villi, which are themselves covered by thousands of microvilli (opposite). The villi absorb digested food into the blood, to be distributed to the body tissues. The digestive system as a whole also includes the pancreas, liver, and gall bladder (opposite), which make and distribute different digestive juices.

■ The digestive tract

The basic parts of the digestive system are common to all but the smallest, simplest animals. Food enters at the mouth and is swallowed through the pharynx. However, there are differences between the digestive systems of humans and of animals like the worm shown here. Unlike humans, worms do not have teeth, so their digestive tube includes a muscular chamber called a gizzard, which crushes and mashes the food. Also, worms eat bulk food that is low in nutrients. They store this in a chamber called a crop, which expands to hold as much food as possible.

The worm's digestive tract
The basic design of the digestive tract, and the specialized parts of the system that carry out particular jobs, can be seen clearly in a relatively simple creature such as the earthworm. Its intestine is not looped and folded as in the human body, but is a straight tube.

Straight gut
This hosepipe represents the full length of the digestive tract, as if it were pulled out straight. The real tract has a folded, compact design within the body.

■ The digestive journey

A piece of food that disappears into a child's mouth is starting a journey that is about 6.5 m (20 ft) long. The typical length of each region of the digestive tract is shown below. Exactly how long digestion takes depends on the types and amounts of food that you have eaten. Foods with plenty of carbohydrates are digested faster than those containing large amounts of fats. Also, like most body processes, digestion tends to be slightly slower during the night. The approximate amount of time that has passed by the end of each stage of digestion is shown on the clocks below.

Mouth (8 cm, 3 in)
It takes a few seconds to chew a mouthful of food and mix it with saliva, to make an easy-to-swallow bolus (p.88).

Eating: for 5 to 30 seconds

Pharynx and oesophagus (25 cm, 10 in)
The back of the tongue pushes food down the pharynx, and waves of muscle action thrust it through the oesophagus.

Swallowing: for 10 seconds

Stomach (15 cm, 6 in)
The stomach expands during the meal to hold all of the food that it receives. About two to three hours after eating, semi-digested foods are passed from the stomach on to the intestines.

In the stomach: for 3 hours

■ Parts of the system

Each section of the digestive system has its own role. The oesophagus is a transfer tube; the stomach is a food-squasher and chemical bath; the small intestine finishes food breakdown and carries out absorption; and the large intestine recycles body substances by absorbing water, minerals, and other useful items into the body. The appendix is a mysterious, finger-sized part that seems to lack a major function. It may be an evolutionary remnant from our distant ancestors.

Huge surface area
Microvilli like these cover the tiny villi in the small intestine. The villi and microvilli create a huge surface area – ten times greater than your whole skin area – for absorbing food.

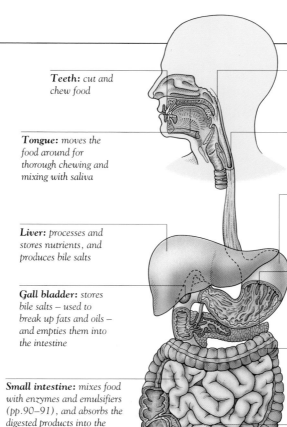

Teeth: *cut and chew food*

Tongue: *moves the food around for thorough chewing and mixing with saliva*

Liver: *processes and stores nutrients, and produces bile salts*

Gall bladder: *stores bile salts – used to break up fats and oils – and empties them into the intestine*

Small intestine: *mixes food with enzymes and emulsifiers (pp.90–91), and absorbs the digested products into the body. It has three parts: the duodenum, jejunum, and ileum*

Appendix

Pharynx (throat): *the muscular passage between the mouth and the oesophagus*

Oesophagus (gullet): *transports food from the pharynx to the stomach*

Stomach: *squashes food and mixes it with acid and its own digestive enzymes plus enzymes from the pancreas*

Pancreas: *makes pancreatic juices containing digestive enzymes*

Colon: *the part of the large intestine that absorbs water and minerals from the digestive leftovers back into the body*

Rectum: *the part of the large intestine that forms left-overs into faeces, and stores them*

Anus: *opens to allow the faeces to be expelled*

Small intestine (4 to 5 m, 13 to 16 ft)
Some six hours after eating, the partly digested food is like a thick milk-shake. It oozes along the three parts of the small intestine: from the duodenum to the jejunum and then to the ileum.

In the small intestine: for 3 hours

Large intestine (1.2 m, 4 ft)
Water and minerals are absorbed into the body by the colon. Faeces (solid wastes) accumulate in the last part of the large intestine, the rectum, where they remain until a convenient moment, when they exit through the anus.

In the large intestine: for up to 2 days

Teeth

TEETH ARE THE FIRST STOP for the fuel entering your body. They have several jobs. First, they bite and chop mouth-size lumps out of large food items, like bread or an apple. The chisel-shaped front teeth, called incisors, do this best. The pointed canine teeth just beside them may tear and rip at the food. The teeth then squash, crush, and chew the food into a pulp. They mix it with saliva into a soft, squishy lump – ready to swallow. The broad, flat-topped rear teeth, the premolars and molars, are best at doing this. They are near the hinge of the jaw joint, where the powerful jaw-closing muscles allow them to exert tremendous pressure.

Your second set of teeth – 32 adult (permanent) teeth – is designed to last from childhood into old age. These teeth are covered by white or yellow enamel, the hardest substance in your body. Enamel can stand years of physical wear as the teeth bite and chew hard foods. But it may be worn down in a chemical way. If old food and bacteria build up in the mouth, they can decay the enamel, cause toothache, and destroy the whole tooth.

■ How teeth grow

You are born with all the teeth you will ever have. At birth, they are tiny tooth buds, deep inside the jawbone. As you grow, your teeth grow too. Your initial teeth enlarge and appear through the gums between the ages of six months and three years. They are called milk or deciduous teeth, and there are 20 in the full set. Milk teeth start to fall out when you are about six years old. By the age of

Look at your teeth

Study your teeth using small mirrors. How many do you have?

YOU WILL NEED
● *2 small plastic-edged mirrors*

Getting a good view
For your lower teeth, open your mouth wide, and angle the mirror to reflect them. For the upper set, hold one mirror just inside your mouth, facing upwards. Adjust the second mirror to reflect the teeth in the first one.

20, most people have all of their adult teeth. There are 32 in total, although not all of these appear in everybody. Some adults never grow their back four molars, which are called wisdom teeth.

Teeth at birth (milk teeth in grey)

Teeth at three years (adult teeth in blue)

Teeth at nine years

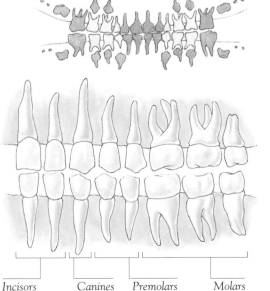

Full set of adult teeth (with the right-hand side of the mouth separated into tooth types)

3 pairs of molars chew and crush | *2 pairs of premolars chew and cut* | *1 pair of canines rip and tear* | *2 pairs of incisors cut and chop*

Incisors | Canines | Premolars | Molars

■ Inside a tooth

This cutaway diagram shows the main parts of a human molar. The outer layer is enamel, which resists years of wear. Under it is dentine, which is softer than enamel. The pulp cavity in the centre of the tooth is filled with blood vessels and nerves. (Blood vessels are shown in one root of the tooth and nerves in the other, but in reality all roots have both.) The roots of the tooth are fixed into their sockets in the jawbone by cementum, a kind of living glue. The soft gum covers the jawbone.

Crown: *the part of the tooth that shows above the gum*

Root: *the part of the tooth embedded in the gum*

Blood vessels: *feed the tooth with oxygen and nutrients*

Jawbone: *anchors the tooth*

Enamel: *forms a hard, protective surface*

Dentine: *forms a shock-absorbing layer*

Pulp cavity: *contains nerves and blood vessels*

Gum: *seals the neck of the tooth into the jawbone*

Nerves: *sense touch, pressure, and temperature*

Cementum: *fixes the tooth into its socket*

Root canal: *allows nerves and blood vessels into the tooth*

Specialized teeth
Animal teeth are designed to chew particular types of food. An elephant molar is as big as a fist and has sharp ridges for munching plants.

■ Plaque on teeth

Teeth are good places for bacteria to grow. The bacteria feed on leftover particles of food, and they make waste products, such as acids, which then attack the teeth. On uncleaned teeth the dead bacteria, their wastes, old food, and saliva build up into a sticky, tooth-decaying layer called dental plaque.

Microscopic attackers
Rod-shaped bacteria find food on the smooth surface of teeth.

EXPERIMENT

How clean are your teeth?

Disclosing tablets show whether your teeth are clean or not, by colouring plaque and bits of old food. Use the tablets to check how effective your tooth-cleaning is, and see if you can improve it.

YOU WILL NEED
●*disclosing tablets (from a dentist or pharmacist)* ●*toothbrush and toothpaste* ●*mirror* ●*water to rinse*

Using disclosing tablets
Follow the instructions on the tablet package. Look at your mouth in the mirror. Can you see the coloured patches where plaque and old food lurk? Brush your teeth well, then try the tablets again. How much plaque remains?

Chewing and swallowing

ONCE YOU HAVE bitten off a piece of food, using your sharp front teeth, the second stage in the digestive process is to chew it, using your big, broad back teeth (p.86). Chewing crushes and mashes the food, mixing it with watery saliva (spit). The saliva comes from three pairs of salivary glands – one pair at the back of the mouth close to each ear, one pair under each side of the lower jaw, and one pair under the tongue. Saliva is mainly water, which turns foods into a pulp. This makes it easier to carry out the third stage of digestion, swallowing the food down the oesophagus, the muscular tube that connects the throat with the stomach.

EXPERIMENT
Chewing and leverage

 Adult help is advised for this experiment

Next time you eat an apple, feel how your mouth and teeth work. After you bite off a mouthful, your lips seal to prevent food from falling out, and your tongue moves the food around. The main chewing power comes from your premolar and molar teeth. They are nearest to the hinge joint (p.52) of your jaw, where the leverage is greatest, as this experiment shows.

YOU WILL NEED
● *sheet of medium or thick card* ● *strong scissors*

1 TRY TO cut the card with the tips of the scissors, which are furthest from the fulcrum (p.51). This is like chewing with your front teeth. Feel how much pressure you need to slice the card.

2 CUT THE same card with the part of the scissors nearest the fulcrum. You have more leverage here, and cutting should be easier. This is like crushing food with your back teeth.

EXPERIMENT
Mouth-watering food

As soon as you put food in your mouth, or even just smell it, your salivary glands release saliva. You can feel the saliva collecting in your mouth as the sensation we call mouth-watering. Study this by encouraging salivation with strong-tasting juice from fresh fruit. Does it matter where on the tongue you drop the fruit juice?

Using the dropper
Collect some fruit juice in the dropper. Carefully place a few drops on different parts of your tongue, and feel the saliva flow.

YOU WILL NEED
● *dropper* ● *strong-tasting fruit juice such as lemon or lime*

■ Swallowing

When you swallow, a small lump of food, called a bolus, passes from your mouth, through your pharynx, into the upper oesophagus. You can control only the first part of this process. When the bolus reaches the back of the pharynx, reflex actions seal off the trachea (windpipe) by closing a flap, the epiglottis. This stops food from going the wrong way. Peristalsis (opposite) takes over to force food through the oesophagus.

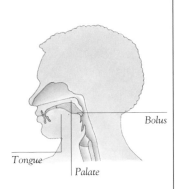

1. To the back of the mouth
The tongue feels for and shapes a suitable-sized lump of food and pushes it to the back of the mouth.

2. Through the pharynx
As the back of the tongue lifts and pushes back, the food is squeezed into the upper part of the pharynx.

3. Into the oesophagus
The epiglottis covers the trachea, the food slides into the top of the oesophagus, and peristalsis begins.

EXPERIMENT
Peristalsis

Food is pushed through the oesophagus and intestine tubes by a process called peristalsis. In this process, two layers of smooth muscle (p.59) in the tube wall – one circular layer, and another lying lengthways – contract and relax in a co-ordinated wave.

YOU WILL NEED
- *small ball such as a tennis ball or baseball*
- *old stocking, long sock, or similar*

1 TO SHOW the principle of peristalsis, imagine that the stocking is the oesophagus and the ball is a just-swallowed lump of food. Place the ball in the stocking, and make a small ring with your fingers, as shown, to represent the circular layer of smooth muscle.

2 HOLD THE end of the stocking firmly with your other hand. Squeeze and push the ball so that it slides along in the stocking. In swallowing, muscles in the oesophagus wall contract, massaging food along in a similar way (below).

■ Moving food
Peristaltic waves of muscle contraction travel along the oesophagus at a speed of 2.5 to 5 cm (1 to 2 in) each second. As the oesophagus is about 25 cm (10 in) long, it takes several seconds for the food to reach the stomach.

Muscles contract here

1. Upper oesophagus
The lump of food is set in motion by a wave of peristaltic muscle contraction behind it.

Muscles relax in front of food lump

2. On the move
The muscles in the wall just in front of the food relax, so the lump can slide forward more easily.

Wave of contraction is now here

3. Toward the stomach
The peristaltic wave moves along the oesophagus. Subsequent waves push along any food left behind.

EXPERIMENT
Feel how you swallow

Swallow slowly, and feel the movements in your neck. When you swallow, the epiglottis forms a tight seal over the trachea (opposite). As it does so, you can feel the "Adam's apple" – part of your larynx (voice-box) – rise up to get out of its way.

"Down the hatch"
Lightly feel for your "Adam's apple" with your fingers.

■ Swallowing upward
When you swallow, food does not "fall" through your oesophagus under the force of gravity. The oesophagus is normally pressed almost flat by the internal pressure in the chest. This is why you need peristalsis to push food into the stomach. The movements are so strong that they can force food and drink upward. So you could swallow food while standing on your head! But do not try this – you might choke.

Drinking upward
When tall animals like giraffes bend down to drink, they use muscles in their throat and oesophagus to swallow the water upward.

Digestion

FOOD CONTAINS MOLECULES of many different nutrients (pp.80–81). The main ones are proteins, carbohydrates (starches and sugars), and fats and oils (also known as lipids). Most of these molecules are too big to pass through the lining of the small intestine, which is the main area where food is absorbed into the body itself. Digestion is a combination of physical and chemical processes that break the big molecules into small ones. Teeth cut and mash the food (pp.86–87). Then the stomach churns and squashes it (pp.88–89). The salivary glands, stomach, small intestine, and pancreas make body substances called enzymes, which attack the chemicals in the nutrient molecules and speed their breakdown. There are different digestive enzymes for each type of nutrient. For example, proteases split proteins into amino acids, the building blocks that they were constructed from. In addition, the stomach lining makes strong hydrochloric acid to dissolve the food. This "acid bath" also helps to kill germs found in food.

Starches to sugars
Note the taste of the bread as you first bite it, then again after chewing for a minute or so. At first it will taste bland, because starches have little flavour. But can you taste the sweet sugars after a minute or two? Try this experiment with non-starchy foods. Do they have the same effect?

EXPERIMENT
Digesting starches

You start to digest starches in food while the food is still in your mouth. Saliva has an enzyme, amylase, that splits big starch molecules into smaller sugar ones. You can taste this for yourself by chewing a starchy food such as bread. Try other starchy foods and compare results.

YOU WILL NEED
● *slice of bread, cooked potato, spoon of cooked rice, or similar starchy food*

How enzymes attack starches

At first
Starch molecules in the bread (blue) and the molecules of the amylase enzyme (pink) are separate. Their shapes have been simplified for clarity.

After a short time
Starch and enzyme fit together like a lock and key. The enzyme begins to break the starch molecule into smaller sugar ones (light and dark blue).

Later
The enzyme detaches, leaving the starch split into different types of sugar molecule. The enzyme is now ready to repeat this action on other starch molecules.

EXPERIMENT
Digesting proteins

Like the human body, "biological" washing powders contain enzymes. These split big molecules into smaller ones, to remove stains such as egg or tomato from cloth. In this experiment, you use washing powder to break down the protein parts of the pigment that makes tomatoes red, destroying the pigment colour. Check the label of the washing powder packet to make sure that the powder includes enzymes.

YOU WILL NEED
● *2 glasses* ● *warm water* ● *rubber gloves* ● *washing powder containing enzymes* ● *ordinary washing powder* ● *scraps of cotton material* ● *tomato ketchup with no artificial colouring*

Splitting the proteins
Smear ketchup on two pieces of cotton material. Allow it to dry. Mix one of the powders with warm water in one glass. Do the same with the other powder in the other glass. Lay a piece of cotton in each glass. Which tomato colour fades first?

EXPERIMENT
Digesting fats

Fats and oils are awkward to digest. Their molecules do not dissolve in water. Instead, they clump into blobs, which makes it difficult for enzymes to work on them. Fats and oils must be emulsified (broken into tiny droplets), so that their molecules are more exposed to the enzymes. In the body, fats and oils are emulsified in the small intestine by bile fluids (p.179). You can imitate this digestive action with washing-up liquid.

YOU WILL NEED
● *2 glasses* ● *warm water* ● *washing-up liquid* ● *cooking oil* ● *tablespoon* ● *teaspoon*

Breaking up the oil
Fill the glasses with warm water. Add a tablespoon of cooking oil to each. Now add a teaspoon of washing-up liquid to one glass. Stir both. The washing-up liquid emulsifies the oil, forming a milky fluid of tiny oil drops in water. Does the oil in the other glass change?

■ DISCOVERY ■
Captain William Beaumont

US Army surgeon William Beaumont (1785–1853) had a unique opportunity to study digestion in action. In June 1822 he attended a patient, Alexis St. Martin, who had been accidentally shot in the stomach. The wound healed, but left a hole leading right into the stomach. St. Martin had to plug this with a bandage to stop the contents from leaking out. With the co-operation of the patient, Beaumont watched the stomach's movements and did tests on the foods and stomach juices. He discovered and published many facts about digestion – for example, the fact that the stomach produces a strong acid.

■ Intestine images

Modern X-ray techniques allow doctors to see the stomach and intestines in great detail. One technique involves swallowing barium sulphate, a substance that shows up clearly on X-rays. The "barium meal" spreads through the digestive tract, making the shape of the tract appear on X-rays. Using barium allows blockages and other problems to be identified.

Coloured colon
This X-ray shows the colon containing barium.

■ How emulsifiers attack fats and oils

At first
Oil molecules have a "head" (yellow) and a "tail", and they clump together in blobs. The emulsifiers (red) begin to attack the oil molecules.

After a short time
The emulsifiers split the oil blobs and turn them into smaller droplets. In the body this exposes the oil to lipase (fat-splitting) enzymes (blue).

Later
The lipase enzymes can now get to work on the oil molecules, breaking the heads from the tails, and allowing further digestion to occur.

TRANSPORT and MAINTENANCE

Red for go
Blood's red colour is due to the oxygen-carrying substance known as haemoglobin. Nearly 300 million molecules of haemoglobin cram into each doughnut-shaped red blood cell (above). Billions of red cells hurtle through the body's blood vessels, which are shown in this special X-ray of the head and brain (left).

WITHOUT ITS NETWORK OF roads, railways, and waterways, a country would grind to a halt. Your body has its own highways and byways – the blood vessels of the circulatory system. Through them flows red blood, pumped non-stop by the heart. Blood carries innumerable substances from one part of the body to another. It also distributes nutrients and collects wastes, in the never-ending task of keeping every body part fuelled and serviced.

THE CIRCULATORY SYSTEM

I T IS ESTIMATED THAT if all the blood vessels in the body's transport system were laid end to end, the total length would be more than 100,000 km (60,000 miles). In reality the blood vessels form an immense, branching network. They fan out from the heart and eventually converge back there. The shortest return trip that blood makes from the heart – to the heart's own muscle – takes only a few seconds. The longest – to the toes – takes over a minute.

The heart lies *between the two lungs, almost in the centre of the chest. It is tilted slightly to the left side.*

The first people to investigate the body did not know of the circulatory system. They did not realize that the heart pumps blood round and round the circular network of blood vessels, carrying oxygen and nutrients to all the cells and collecting wastes. They did notice, however, that when a person feels deep emotions, such as fear or anger, the heart produces strong physical sensations, such as heavy pounding or skipping a beat. This led to the belief that emotions were based in the heart. We now know that it is not the heart but the brain that is the centre of emotions. The brain sends signals to the heart, by way of nerve messages and hormones (p.106), to make the heart beat harder and faster in certain situations. As a result, more blood is supplied to the muscle. This is particularly important in reactions such as the "fight or flight" response (p.105).

■ Ebb and flow

The role of the blood as the body's main transport fluid has long been accepted. But how and where blood flows was not understood until the 17th century. Before the invention of the microscope, anatomists believed that blood ebbed and flowed to and from the heart.

In reality blood moves through the vessels in one direction – from arteries to capillaries to veins. Arteries branch out many times, finally becoming tiny vessels called capillaries, whose walls may be only one cell thick. These capillaries then join together to make small veins, which merge to form larger veins.

The arteries carry blood away from the heart. They have muscular, elastic walls, which expand to cope with the high-pressure surge of blood from each heart-beat (p.100). The veins return blood to the heart. They have thinner and slacker walls because the blood that oozes sluggishly through them is under almost no pressure.

Early anatomists believed that only veins carried blood, and that arteries had another purpose. This was a natural assumption, because after death, when the heart stops, blood is quickly squeezed out of the arteries by their muscular walls and drained into the

veins. So each time an anatomist examined the arteries of a corpse, they were found empty.

■ Four humours

Hippocrates (c.460–c.377 BC) of Ancient Greece, the "Father of Medicine", believed, like many of his colleagues, that the body was made of four substances called

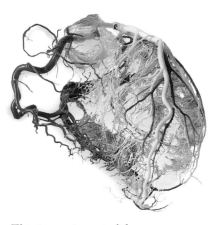

This is a resin cast of the coronary *vessels, which supply the heart muscle (not shown) with blood.*

humours – blood, yellow bile, phlegm (mucus), and black bile. He thought that if the humours lost their natural balance, people would become ill.

It was thought that a mysterious life force, the pneuma (p.70), "vitalized" humours into action. Galen of Ancient Rome (p.13) believed wrongly that blood seeped from one of the heart's ventricles (p.98) to the other through pores in the septum – the dividing wall of the heart. He thought that at this point it mixed with the pneuma from the

This computer model of a haemoglobin molecule *shows proteins in yellow and blue, and haem pigments as red discs. Oxygen molecules link with each disc. In this way oxygen is carried round the body in the blood.*

Where arteries come near the skin, *you can feel your pulse – pressure surges* *of blood from the heart. Count the beats* *to find your heart rate (p.101).*

air to create a "vital spirit" that flowed along the arteries.

Many of Galen's theories were accepted right up to the time of the Renaissance. In their anatomical studies both Leonardo da Vinci (1452–1519) and Andreas Vesalius (p.22) drew pores in the heart's septum.

Harvey's discovery

By the late 16th century scientists had still not worked out the way that the heart pumped blood. Several Italian anatomists made important advances but could not work out an overall system. Realdo Columbus (1516–1559) suggested correctly that there is a separate system of blood vessels to the lungs in addition to the supply to the whole body. Hieronymus Fabricius (1537–1619) studied one-way valves in the main veins, but he thought that their function was to slow

Blood flowing the *right way pushes open the* *flaps of valves in the* *heart and main veins.*

After each heart-beat, *the valves are pressed* *shut, preventing blood* *from flowing backward.*

down the blood flow. Andrea Cesalpino (1519–1603) came close to realizing that blood travels around the body, rather than swishing to and fro within the blood vessels. He even used the word "circulation". But Cesalpino thought that blood flowed from the heart along both the arteries and the veins.

In 1628 a student of Fabricius, the English physician William Harvey (p.96), proposed that the function of the heart is to pump blood in a continuous circuit through the system of vessels. Once this discovery had been made, it became obvious that the valves in the heart (p.98) and veins (p.96) are to keep blood flowing in one direction only.

Although Harvey understood that blood flows in one direction only, he did not know how it passes from the arteries to the veins. The answer was found by Marcello Malpighi (p.104) who discovered connecting capillaries through his microscope.

Two pumps

We now know that the heart is two separate pumps (p.98). The right pump sends low-oxygen blood along the pulmonary artery to the lungs. There the blood gets rid of carbon dioxide and picks up oxygen. The oxygen-rich blood returns to the heart's left pump via the pulmonary vein. This pump then sends the blood along the aorta (main artery) and other arteries, out to the whole body. The blood delivers its oxygen to the body's cells, collects carbon

dioxide, and returns along the main veins to the heart's right pump again.

The one-way valves in the heart sometimes become stiff and leaky, allowing a backflow of blood. Surgeons can then replace them with artificial ones.

Red blood

The heart is muscle. Like any other muscle, it needs a blood supply to provide it with oxygen and nutrients. So the heart has a system of blood vessels that bring it oxygen. These vessels are called coronary arteries and veins, because they surround and permeate the upper heart muscle like a crown ("corona" in Latin).

By the 1860s, physiologists discovered that the red cells in blood are packed with the protein haemoglobin. This links easily with oxygen, with the result that it carries oxygen around the circulatory system. In the lungs, where a lot of oxygen is available, haemoglobin becomes bright red. In lower-oxygen surroundings in the body tissues, haemoglobin releases its oxygen and becomes darker in colour.

An X-ray image reveals *three artificial heart valves. They* *show up clearly because they are* *made of dense metal.*

Not all blood is red. A lobster's *blood is blue, because it contains* *copper-based haemocyanin instead of* *iron-based haemoglobin.*

Circulation

BLOOD FLOWS round and round through blood vessels. This is called circulation. From the heart's left side blood passes into the aorta (main artery), then into other arteries. Each artery branches 15 or 20 times, becoming smaller and smaller. The smallest arteries lead into a network of minute capillaries. The thin walls of these capillaries allow oxygen and nutrients to diffuse (p.27) through them from the blood into the body tissues. In due course, the capillaries join other capillaries, eventually forming veins. These take blood back to the heart's right side. This side pumps it to the lungs to collect more oxygen, and from there it returns to the heart's left side. So blood makes a double circuit: around the body (systemic circulation), then to the lungs and back (pulmonary circulation).

■ DISCOVERY ■
William Harvey

Since ancient times, there have been many explanations for the roles of the heart and blood vessels. One theory was that blood ebbed and flowed in the vessels, like the tide. The English physician William Harvey (1578–1657) did many experiments on blood flow. In 1628 he published the results in his book *De Motu Cordis et Sanguinis* ("On the Motion of the Heart and Blood"). He showed that blood flows around the body in a circular route, pumped by the heart.

Studying veins
These illustrations from Harvey's book show how blood flows along veins back to the heart, and how valves in the veins stop blood from flowing the wrong way (below).

EXPERIMENT
Blood flow and gravity

Adult help is advised for this experiment

In some parts of the body, blood has to flow against gravity. To see the effect of this, hold one arm up high and one down by your side for a minute. Then compare hands.

Contrast in colour
From the hand held high, blood drains easily to the heart, speeded by the force of gravity. In the lower hand, blood struggles to rise against gravity. The blood collects in this hand, making it darker.

EXPERIMENT
Vein valves

Adult help is advised for this experiment

William Harvey realized that vein valves (p.95) stop blood from flowing backward. You can recreate a version of one of Harvey's experiments. Before starting, ask an adult with prominent veins on his or her hands to let one hand hang low for a minute, so that its veins stand out.

1 NOW ASK the adult to put his or her hand on a table, palm down. Find an unbranched vein on the back of the hand and, firmly but gently, place your finger on it.

2 PLACE A second finger next to your first finger, then stroke the vein in the direction of blood flow – toward the heart. This empties the vein of blood.

3 NOW LIFT your second finger. The vein should not refill. The vein's valve stops the blood from flowing backward. Lift your first finger to allow more blood to arrive.

■ Arteries and veins

Arteries carry blood away from the heart, and veins carry blood toward the heart. Most arteries contain bright red, high-oxygen blood (red in the illustration below). But the pulmonary arteries, which run from the heart to the lungs, contain dark reddish-blue blood, which is low in oxygen and needs new supplies. Most veins contain blood that is low in oxygen (blue in the illustration), except for the pulmonary veins, from the lungs to the heart, which contain oxygen-rich blood. At any instant, three-quarters of your blood is in veins, one-fifth in arteries, and one-twentieth in capillaries.

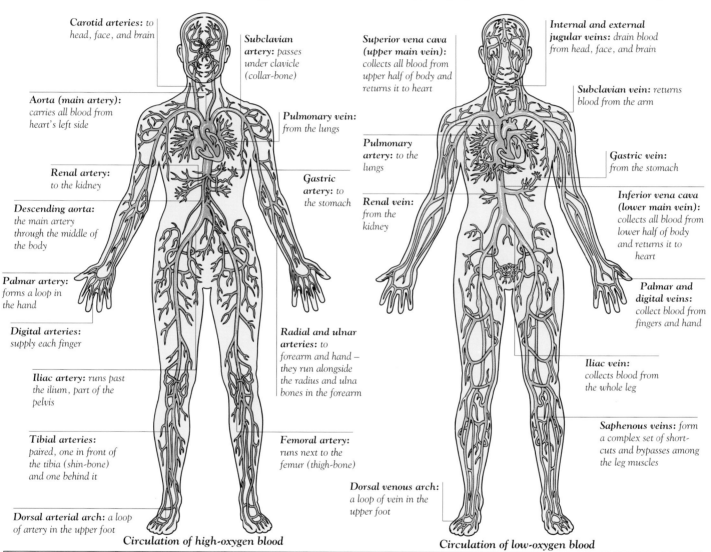

Carotid arteries: *to head, face, and brain*

Aorta (main artery): *carries all blood from heart's left side*

Renal artery: *to the kidney*

Descending aorta: *the main artery through the middle of the body*

Palmar artery: *forms a loop in the hand*

Digital arteries: *supply each finger*

Iliac artery: *runs past the ilium, part of the pelvis*

Tibial arteries: *paired, one in front of the tibia (shin-bone) and one behind it*

Dorsal arterial arch: *a loop of artery in the upper foot*

Subclavian artery: *passes under clavicle (collar-bone)*

Pulmonary vein: *from the lungs*

Gastric artery: *to the stomach*

Radial and ulnar arteries: *to forearm and hand – they run alongside the radius and ulna bones in the forearm*

Femoral artery: *runs next to the femur (thigh-bone)*

Circulation of high-oxygen blood

Superior vena cava (upper main vein): *collects all blood from upper half of body and returns it to heart*

Pulmonary artery: *to the lungs*

Renal vein: *from the kidney*

Dorsal venous arch: *a loop of vein in the upper foot*

Internal and external jugular veins: *drain blood from head, face, and brain*

Subclavian vein: *returns blood from the arm*

Gastric vein: *from the stomach*

Inferior vena cava (lower main vein): *collects all blood from lower half of body and returns it to heart*

Palmar and digital veins: *collect blood from fingers and hand*

Iliac vein: *collects blood from the whole leg*

Saphenous veins: *form a complex set of short-cuts and bypasses among the leg muscles*

Circulation of low-oxygen blood

■ Blood vessel structure

Each of the three major types of blood vessel is designed for a specific job. An artery has a thick, muscular wall to cope with the high-pressure surges of blood from the heart. A capillary has a wall only one cell thick. Oxygen and nutrients can easily diffuse through these cells to the surrounding tissues. A vein has a loose, slack wall, since the blood in it is under very little pressure.

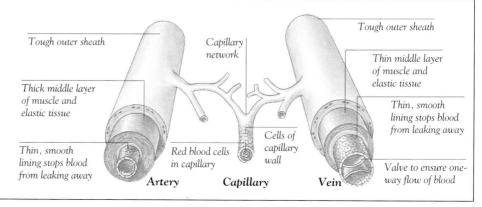

Tough outer sheath

Thick middle layer of muscle and elastic tissue

Thin, smooth lining stops blood from leaking away

Capillary network

Red blood cells in capillary

Cells of capillary wall

Tough outer sheath

Thin middle layer of muscle and elastic tissue

Thin, smooth lining stops blood from leaking away

Valve to ensure one-way flow of blood

Artery   **Capillary**   **Vein**

The heart

AT ONE TIME, people thought that the heart was the seat of love, desire, courage, and bravery. Today we know that these feelings are based in the brain. The heart is simply a bag of muscle that – about once every second – squeezes itself to send blood flowing through the body's network of blood vessels. The heart has two pumps, working side by side. The left one sends blood out along arteries to the whole body, from head to toes. This blood gives up oxygen (p.71) and returns along veins to the right pump. From here it is sent on a much shorter trip – to the lungs to gather more oxygen. Two special features make the heart incredibly hard-working and versatile. The first is the muscle in the heart's walls. It is called cardiac muscle and, unlike normal muscle, it never tires. The second is the heart's ability to change its pumping speed and force to match the body's needs. Nerve signals from the brain (p.118) and hormones in the blood (p.106) help to control these changes.

■ The ECG

This wavy line is part of an ECG (electrocardiogram). It shows a pattern of tiny electrical signals. These signals pass through the heart as it pumps. They are detected by metal sensors placed on the skin, and the line is shown on a monitor. This ECG section shows the signals from one complete heart-beat. Doctors study ECGs to see if a heart is healthy.

Signal produced to make the atria squeeze

Signal produced to make the ventricles squeeze

Signal produced as the ventricles relax

■ Inside the heart

Look inside the heart, and you see its two pumps side by side. Each pump has a small upper chamber known as the atrium (plural: atria). Blood flows into this from the vena cava (main vein) or the pulmonary vein. Below the atrium is a larger chamber, the ventricle. This provides the heart's main pumping power. The cardiac muscle of the ventricles squeezes hard during each heart-beat, forcing the blood inside them into the aorta (main artery) or the pulmonary artery. From there the blood is distributed around the body and to the lungs. Blood is kept flowing the right way through the heart by four one-way valves. On the right of the heart (the left side in the illustration) is the tricuspid valve, and on the left is the mitral valve. When the ventricles squeeze, blood presses on the flaps of these valves and closes them. This means that the blood cannot flow back into the atria. The other two valves are the aortic and pulmonary valves at the entrances to the arteries. After the ventricles have squeezed the blood out into the arteries, these valves close to stop it flowing back into the ventricles.

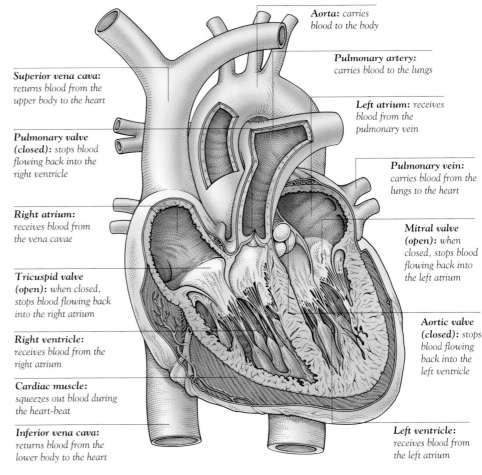

Superior vena cava: *returns blood from the upper body to the heart*

Pulmonary valve (closed): *stops blood flowing back into the right ventricle*

Right atrium: *receives blood from the vena cavae*

Tricuspid valve (open): *when closed, stops blood flowing back into the right atrium*

Right ventricle: *receives blood from the right atrium*

Cardiac muscle: *squeezes out blood during the heart-beat*

Inferior vena cava: *returns blood from the lower body to the heart*

Aorta: *carries blood to the body*

Pulmonary artery: *carries blood to the lungs*

Left atrium: *receives blood from the pulmonary vein*

Pulmonary vein: *carries blood from the lungs to the heart*

Mitral valve (open): *when closed, stops blood flowing back into the left atrium*

Aortic valve (closed): *stops blood flowing back into the left ventricle*

Left ventricle: *receives blood from the left atrium*

The heart-beat

A heart-beat can be shown in three stages, though in reality these stages merge into each other and into the next beat. When the body is resting, each ventricle pumps out about 70 millilitres (an eighth of a pint) of blood with each beat. When the body is active, the muscles need extra oxygen and nutrients from the blood. So the heart pumps harder and faster to keep up the supply.

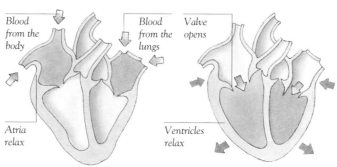

Blood from the body · Blood from the lungs · Valve opens · Blood out · Blood out · Valve closes · Atria relax · Ventricles relax · Ventricles contract

Atria fill
The aortic and pulmonary valves are shut. The right atrium fills with low-oxygen blood (blue) from the body, and the left atrium with high-oxygen blood (red) from the lungs.

Ventricles fill
The muscles in the walls of the atria squeeze gently. Blood flows from each atrium into the ventricle below, through the one-way valves. The ventricle walls bulge.

Ventricles empty
The ventricles contract. The mitral and tricuspid valves close, and blood is ejected into the arteries. Then the aortic and pulmonary valves close.

EXPERIMENT
Hearing the heart

Adult help is advised for this experiment

Each time the heart pumps, both pairs of valves close suddenly with a snap-shut sound. Doctors use a device called a stethoscope to listen to this sound. Make your own stethoscope to listen to your heart, and find out how exercise changes your heart rate. *Caution: If you feel dizzy or sick when exercising, stop at once and rest.*

You Will Need
● *scissors* ● *small plastic funnel* ● *plastic tubing* ● *three-way hose connector* ● *adhesive tape* ● *stop-watch* ● *notepad* ● *pen*

2 Ask a friend to do something active, such as running, for one minute. Now ask your friend to hold the funnel over his or her chest (as right), and hold the tube ends to your ears. (Do not push them in.) Count the number of heart-beats in one minute. This is the heart rate. Now ask your friend to run around for two minutes. Count and note the rate again. Is it faster and louder after more exercise?

1 Carefully cut three lengths of tubing, each about 30 cm (1 ft) long. Tape the funnel to the end of one of the tubes. Push the other end of this tube and one end of each of the other tubes into the hose connector. Use tape to make sure that they fit snugly.

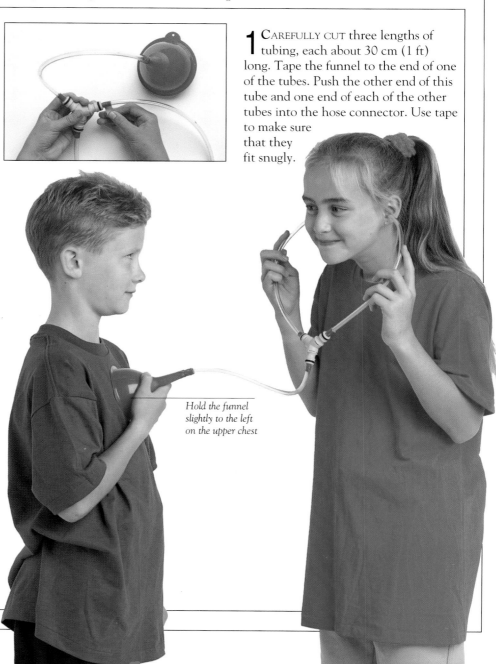

Hold the funnel slightly to the left on the upper chest

The heart-beat

EACH POWERFUL heart-beat sends a high-pressure surge of blood, like a miniature tidal wave, racing into the elastic-walled arteries. As the surge travels out through the body, it loses force and becomes lost in the vast network of microscopic capillaries – only to be followed, a second or less later, by another surge of pressure from the next heart-beat. You can feel these pressure surges – your pulse – at various places in the body. Your pulse can be most easily felt where an artery lies near the surface of the body, such as at the inside of the wrist. The pulse rate is the same as the heart rate, and it allows a convenient check on how hard and how quickly your heart is pumping.

EXPERIMENT
The pulsing leg

If you sit with your legs crossed in a certain position, the bulging surges of blood through the arteries in the upper leg make it rock slightly on the lower one. This turns your leg into a pulse meter that measures your heart rate.

The leg pulse meter
Sit upright in a chair. Cross your legs so that the knobbly part of the knee of the lower leg fits snugly into the hollow behind the knee of the upper leg. Relax and let your muscles loosen. Your upper leg should kick up very slightly with each heart-beat, as a pressure bulge passes through the large popliteal artery inside the back of the knee. Experiment by shifting your legs to different positions. The movement may be very small, but you should be able to notice it.

EXPERIMENT
Hard-working heart

When you are at rest, each heart-beat sends about 150 ml (⅓ pint) of blood into the arteries. In an average adult, this happens between 60 and 80 times each minute. See how hard the heart works by getting your hand and arm to work at the same rate as your heart.

YOU WILL NEED
● *plastic beaker that holds about 150 ml (⅓ pint)* ● *2 bowls* ● *water* ● *stop-watch*

Pumping like the heart
With a friend to time you, use the beaker to try to bale water from one bowl to another, at 70 beakerfuls per minute – the same speed as a normal heart rate. Can you do it? If you can, how long can you keep baling water at this rate? Your arm muscles soon get tired. The heart is made from a special muscle called cardiac muscle (p.98). It keeps pumping, without getting tired, for an entire lifetime.

EXPERIMENT
Seeing your pulse

At a medical check-up, the doctor will probably take your pulse. Your pulse rate gives a rough guide to the general health of your heart and body. You can take your pulse in the standard way at the radial artery (below) in the wrist (as in Step 1, right). But in this experiment you can actually see your pulse by making a simple visual pulse meter with a drinking straw and a piece of plastic putty or modelling clay.

YOU WILL NEED
- *drinking straw*
- *plastic putty or tacky modelling clay*
- *stop-watch*

1 FEEL WITH your fingertips on the inside of your wrist, below your thumb, until you detect pulsations. Do not use the tip of your thumb, as that has its own pulse, which you may feel instead.

2 PLACE A blob of plastic putty at the place where you can feel the pulsations most strongly. Carefully push one end of the drinking straw into this blob so that it sticks upright from your wrist.

3 LET YOUR ARM lie flat on a table. The straw should twitch slightly to and fro, as the surge of blood produced by each heart-beat passes through your wrist into your hand, making the radial artery bulge. Measure your pulse rate by counting the number of times the straw rocks in one minute. The average resting pulse rate of humans varies with age. It is about 130 to 140 at birth, 110 to 120 at one year of age, 90 to 100 by three years, 80 to 90 by ten years, and 60 to 80 in adults.

■ Animal heart rates

In general, big mammals have hearts that beat more slowly than smaller ones. Humans are relatively large mammals, and therefore we have correspondingly slow heart-beats. This difference is partly due to the size of the heart. The huge heart of an elephant could not beat at the same rate as the mouse heart because the heart muscle is too bulky and heavy.

Mouse
This tiny mammal's pulse rate is over 500 beats per minute.

Elephant
This huge mammal has a resting pulse rate of 20 to 30 beats per minute.

■ Pulse points

The throbbing pressure-bulges of the pulse travel through all of the body's arteries. The wrists are not the only places where you can feel them, but they are usually the most convenient. The radial artery lies just below the skin and directly above the wrist bones, so the bones make a firm base on which to press the artery. There are several other sites where the pulse can usually be felt clearly, especially after you have been exercising. An especially important site is the carotid artery in the neck, which carries blood to the head and brain.

Around the body
Try to find your pulse at each of these places. Do not press too hard on the body parts when feeling for it.

Carotid artery in the neck

Brachial artery in the crook of the elbow

Radial artery in the wrist

Femoral artery in the groin

Popliteal artery in the back of the knee

Anterior tibial artery on the front of the ankle

Blood

BLOOD IS ESSENTIAL to human life. As the body's major transport medium, it has numerous roles. Blood carries life-giving oxygen to all body parts and collects carbon dioxide for removal by the lungs (p.71). It also distributes vitamins, nutrients, and energy-rich sugars from digested food, and picks up wastes such as urea (p.109) for disposal by the kidneys. Blood is a highway for the white blood cells that fight germs. It also carries hormones, the chemical messengers that stimulate and co-ordinate body processes (p.106). It evens out the temperature in the different parts of the body by taking heat from busy parts, such as the heart and active muscles, to warm the less active, cooler parts and the extremities (p.113). Blood protects the body by clotting at the site of a wound to prevent any leakage of body fluids. It then hardens into a scab to help the injury heal.

■ DISCOVERY ■
Karl Landsteiner

For centuries people tried to transfuse (transfer) blood from humans – and animals – into people with blood diseases or who had lost blood through injury. Most of these patients died. The Austrian physician Karl Landsteiner (1868–1943) discovered why in 1900 – one person's red blood cells agglutinate (clump together) on contact with blood from certain other people. This agglutination blocks the blood vessels. Landsteiner worked out that there must be a number of types of blood, which we call blood groups. His work led to the discovery of the ABO system (below left) in 1909. Landsteiner and others went on to find several other ways in which a person's blood can differ from another person's, such as the Rhesus system. This system shows the presence or absence of another agglutinating factor – the Rhesus factor – which is passed on in your genes (p.181).

■ The ABO system

Not everyone's blood is the same. There are a number of different systems for classifying blood. Everybody's blood has a combination of elements from each of these systems. One of these systems is the ABO system. In this system, blood may belong to group A, B, AB, or O. The group you belong to depends on the presence or absence of chemicals called antigens on the surface of your blood cells and chemicals called antibodies in the watery part of your blood (opposite).

ABO compatibility
In a blood transfusion, donated blood must be of the correct group. These arrows show which groups can safely be donated to, or taken from, which others. Each group is compatible with itself. O blood can be donated to any patient. Patients with AB blood can take from any donor.

■ Threads of fibrin

When body tissues are damaged, they trigger off a series of reactions in the blood. First, chemicals are released by platelets in the blood. Then these chemicals convert a protein called fibrinogen into microscopic threads of fibrin. These form a sticky mesh that traps blood cells, and in this way the clot builds up (opposite).

About to clot
This red blood cell is becoming trapped in threads of fibrin, as a clot begins to form.

■ What is in blood?

More than half of blood is a pale yellow fluid called plasma. Plasma is over nine-tenths water and contains sugars, nutrients, acids, salts, minerals, and proteins. The rest of blood consists of three types of blood cell – red cells, white cells, and platelets – as shown by an electron microscope (p.24) below.

Centrifuge test-tube

Water (about 50 per cent)

Plasma

Plasma substances (about 5 per cent)

White blood cells and platelets (less than 1 per cent)

Blood cells

Red blood cells (almost 45 per cent)

White blood cell

Red blood cell

Red blood cells (erythrocytes)
Shaped like tiny doughnuts, they carry oxygen.

Blood through a light microscope
Here red blood cells, one white cell, and a few platelets are seen through a light microscope rather than an electron microscope.

Separated blood
A centrifuge spins things around very quickly – faster than the spin cycle on a washing machine. Blood centrifuged in a test-tube separates into layers. The densest (heaviest) portion – red blood cells – is at the bottom. There are 5 million red cells in a pinhead-size drop of blood. Next come the white cells and platelets. There are about 10,000 white cells and 250,000 platelets in the same-sized drop. The lightest, watery portion of blood, called plasma, is at the top of the tube.

Platelets (thrombocytes)
These cell fragments take part in blood clotting.

Platelet

White blood cell (leucocyte)
Most of the many types of white cell fight germs.

■ Clotting and healing

A sticky lump known as a blood clot forms at the site of tissue damage, such as a cut in the skin. Unless the wound is large and gaping, the clot prevents more blood and other body fluids from leaking out. When the skin is cut, platelets become sticky and clump together at the site. Also, sticky strings of the clotting protein fibrin (opposite) make a tangled net that traps blood cells. Within a few minutes the clot starts to take shape. Gradually it shrinks and hardens, forming a tough scab. This protects the tissues while the cells in them multiply to heal the damage.

Platelet | *Red blood cell*

Damage
A sharp pin pricks into the skin and punctures a small blood vessel just under the surface. Blood, under pressure inside the body, oozes from the cut.

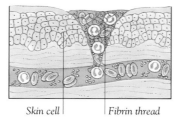

Skin cell | *Fibrin thread*

Young clot
Platelets clump together at the site. They release chemicals that turn the protein fibrinogen into fibrin threads, which trap more platelets and other blood cells.

Solid clot | *White blood cell*

Mature clot
The platelets trigger chemical reactions that make the clot harder and more solid. White blood cells attack invading germs. Skin cells below multiply to repair the cut.

Scab

Scab
The clot continues to dry and harden, and becomes a scab. By the time it loosens and falls off, the skin and blood-vessel wall will have healed any damage.

THE INTERNAL ENVIRONMENT

DELICATE MACHINES SUCH AS SUPERCOMPUTERS or medical scanners are kept in conditions that are constantly monitored. If there is a change in the temperature, humidity, or other conditions around these machines, their immensely complex circuits may fail. The same is true of the body. The workings of its fragile cells (pp.24–25) are easily disturbed by changes in temperature, fluid levels, or chemical concentrations. The body must constantly check and adjust its internal conditions.

Test the cooling effect of evaporation from the skin by blowing on a "sweat substitute" (p.112).

Conditions outside the body can vary enormously. Yet inside the body they remain remarkably constant. The temperature stays at about 37°C (98.6°F), fluid concentrations are kept at certain levels, and so are the amounts of sugars, minerals, and other substances in the blood. In the 18th and 19th centuries, physiology – the study of the way the body works – developed into a major science. But physiologists found it difficult to carry out experiments on cells. When they removed cells from the body and put them in water to work on them, the cells swelled up and died. But gradually scientists found ways of producing fluids with concentrations of chemicals similar to those in the body. In these fluids, they could keep cells alive outside the body.

Homeostasis

In the mid-19th century, the French physiologist Claude Bernard (p.110) introduced the idea of "the constancy of the internal environment". He saw that many body processes, such as shivering and sweating (which help adjust the body's temperature), were designed to maintain a steady environment inside the body, so that its cells could work efficiently.

The American physiologist Walter Canon (1871–1945)

refined Bernard's theories. He coined the term "homeostasis", from the Greek "to stay the same". Homeostatic mechanisms in the body keep its internal conditions stable.

The kidneys are involved in many homeostatic mechanisms, such as regulating levels of water and minerals in the blood, and removing waste substances – particularly urea, which is poisonous if it is allowed to build up. This removal is carried out by the urinary system, which comprises the two kidneys, the bladder, and their connecting tubes (p.108).

The kidneys

The early anatomists knew that the kidneys make urine, but they did not understand how they work. The invention of the microscope changed this. One of the early microscopists was an Italian philosopher-turned-doctor, Marcello Malpighi (1628–1694). He was the first to describe the tiny structures in the kidneys that are now called

A hormone-making adrenal gland (p.108) sits on top of each kidney. These glands release hormones directly into the blood.

A pioneer in microscopic study, Marcello Malpighi made important discoveries about the kidneys, lungs, spleen, and other organs. He also studied silkworms and how chicks develop in their eggs.

Malpighian corpuscles. One corpuscle together with a micro-tube forms a filtering unit called a nephron (p.108). Blood entering a nephron flows through a knot of capillaries, termed a glomerulus. Water, wastes, and some salts and chemicals are squeezed through the capillary walls into a system of micro-tubes. From there, water and useful salts and chemicals are taken back into the blood as required. The remaining wastes and excess water flow into collecting tubes in the kidney medulla, and then leave the kidneys as urine.

Hormones

How are the body's many homeostatic mechanisms controlled? A comparison may help. In the modern world, we can send and receive information

The tiny red blobs in this light
microscope picture of a kidney are called glomeruli. They are knots of capillary blood vessels in nephrons (p.108), which filter substances out of the blood.

in different ways. One way is by telephone. The messages are represented by electrical signals that travel along wires. They go from the sender, through a series of exchanges, to the receiver only. Another method is by radio. The radio waves are

If your brain detects that your blood
has become too concentrated, you feel thirsty and hormones are sent to instruct the kidneys to retain water.

produced by a transmitter and broadcast over a wide area. Anyone with a receiving set that is tuned in can pick up the waves.

Similarly, the body has two communications systems. Together they control and co-ordinate homeostasis. One is the nervous system (pp.118–119). The nerves are "wires", like telephone wires, through which

signals go from the sender to the receiver, usually with the brain as the "exchange".

The second system is the endocrine system (pp.106–107). It uses "waves" of body chemicals called hormones, like radio waves. These are produced by hormonal glands, which are "transmitters". There are several types of hormonal gland, such as the adrenal glands on top of the kidneys. Also, certain organs, such as the stomach, pancreas, kidneys, and ovaries and testes (p.23), make hormones as well as carrying out their other roles.

The hormones spread around the whole body, carried by the blood. But they affect only certain parts, the target organs, which, like radio receivers, are "tuned" to detect them.

Early anatomists had seen and described the hormonal glands, but they did not really know how they worked. They could see that these glands do not have tubes leading from them, unlike glands such as the salivary glands, which pour their products along a duct. For centuries, hormonal glands – which gained the alternative name "ductless glands" – were virtually ignored by scientists.

Physiological research gradually showed that chemicals from these glands were transmitted around the body. The true nature of the glands was then understood, and the science of endocrinology (p.106) was established.

Fight or flight

The nervous system controls the actions of the body that take place over a very short period of time – such as speaking or writing. In contrast, the endocrine system controls actions that take place over a long period of time. For example, the hormone thyroxine controls

the body's growth. But often the two systems work together.

The "fight or flight" response is a very good example of this. This is the choice of response that you must make if you find yourself threatened – you must face the situation (fight) or avoid it (flight). The hypothalamus in your brain (p.126) alerts several organs and glands through the autonomic nervous system (p.118). Among these are the

The nervous system
and the endocrine system work together to prepare your body for physical activity.

adrenal glands. These release the hormones adrenaline and noradrenaline, which spread through the blood and body tissues to their target organs. As a combined result of nerves and hormones, whether you fight or flee, your heart beats harder and faster, your lungs breathe more rapidly, blood is diverted from your skin and inner organs to your muscles, and your liver releases high-energy glucose to give your body energy. You are ready for action.

Because of its lack of the hormone
thyroxine, the axolotl never grows up. It breeds while it is still a "tadpole".

Hormones

YOUR BODY HAS two control systems. One is the nervous system (pp.118–119), which sends messages around the body in the form of nerve signals. The other is the endocrine system, which sends messages around the body in the form of chemicals called hormones. Hormones are made in special glands called hormonal glands. Each gland releases its hormone directly into the bloodstream. As the blood carries the hormone through the body, the hormone affects the working of specific body parts, called its target organs. The higher the level of a hormone in the blood, the greater its effect on its target organs. The amounts of hormones released are controlled by the nervous system and by other hormones, mostly produced by the pituitary gland.

■ DISCOVERY ■
Ernest Starling

The study of hormones is called endocrinology. This branch of physiology (the workings of the body) did not begin until the late 19th century. The name "hormone" comes from a Greek term, meaning "to set in motion". It was coined in 1905 by the English scientist Ernest Starling (1866–1927), a professor of physiology in London, England. In 1902, Starling and a colleague, William Bayliss, isolated (separated out) a hormone for the first time. The hormone was secretin, a digestive hormone made by the small intestine. Starling also studied the lymphatic system (p.23) and other body fluids, and the kidneys. A scientific law that predicts the amount of blood pumped out by the heart under various conditions is named after him.

■ Hormones and glucose

The body needs a relatively constant level of glucose sugar (p.181) in its blood to supply energy to its millions of cells. If the glucose level falls too low, cells run out of energy and die. If the glucose level rises too high, the extra glucose disturbs the working of the kidneys. Follow the arrows in this chart to see how the pancreas (p.85) can release either of two hormones – called insulin and glucagon – to maintain steady levels of glucose in the blood.

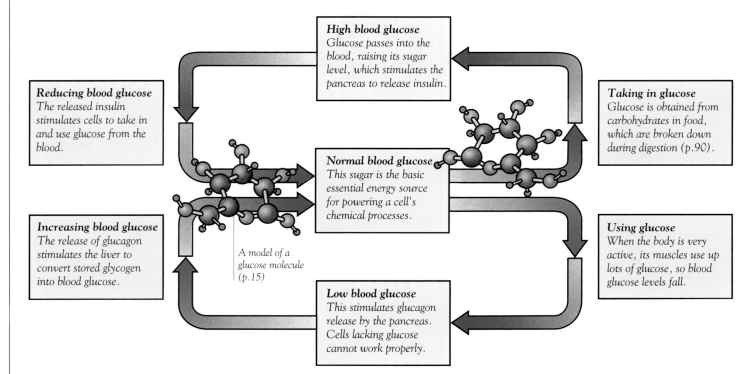

High blood glucose
Glucose passes into the blood, raising its sugar level, which stimulates the pancreas to release insulin.

Reducing blood glucose
The released insulin stimulates cells to take in and use glucose from the blood.

Taking in glucose
Glucose is obtained from carbohydrates in food, which are broken down during digestion (p.90).

Normal blood glucose
This sugar is the basic essential energy source for powering a cell's chemical processes.

Increasing blood glucose
The release of glucagon stimulates the liver to convert stored glycogen into blood glucose.

A model of a glucose molecule (p.15)

Using glucose
When the body is very active, its muscles use up lots of glucose, so blood glucose levels fall.

Low blood glucose
This stimulates glucagon release by the pancreas. Cells lacking glucose cannot work properly.

Dual functions

Several body organs make hormones, in addition to their other roles. One example is your pancreas (p.85). It makes insulin and glucagon (opposite). These pass directly into the blood that flows through the pancreas. The pancreas also produces enzymes, which flow along a tube called the pancreatic duct into the small intestine, to digest food.

Hormone-making in the pancreas
This microscope photograph shows an islet of Langerhans, one of a million hormone-producing knots of cells inside the pancreas.

Long-term control

The nervous system tends to control rapid, short-term body functions, such as muscle movements. The endocrine system is concerned more with the control of slower, long-term processes, such as digestion, fluid balance, the body's mineral levels, and growth and sexual development.

Child to adult
Male voices deepen in adolescence as more of the hormone testosterone is produced. This hormone affects the growth of the vocal cords.

Hormones through a day

We are usually less aware of the actions of the endocrine system than those of the nervous system. But each day dozens of hormones from various hormonal glands and other organs circulate in the blood, regulating and co-ordinating the activities of their target organs and tissues. The activity of the hormonal glands is mainly controlled by other hormones and by nerves. Most of the hormone-controlling hormones are produced by the pea-sized pituitary gland, just beneath the brain. The pituitary gland is the "chief gland" of the endocrine system. It is connected by a short stalk to the hypothalamus (p.126), which monitors levels of hormones and other substances in the blood. The hypothalamus instructs the pituitary gland to release the appropriate hormones into the body. Here are some examples of hormones released during various situations that you might find yourself in – some normal, some less so.

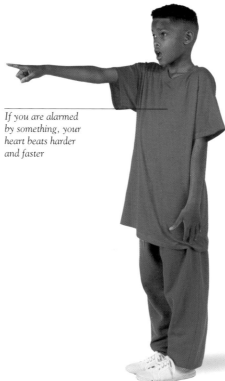

If you are alarmed by something, your heart beats harder and faster

Stress situations
If you are under stress, the adrenal glands, above the kidneys, make adrenaline. This hormone works with the nervous system to raise blood pressure, and heart and breathing rates (p.105).

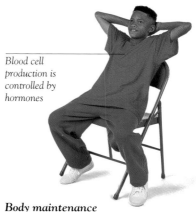

Blood cell production is controlled by hormones

Body maintenance
Even as the body rests, hormones are at work. The kidneys make the hormone erythropoietin, which stimulates the production of new red blood cells at the rate of two million each second.

Hormones make the stomach rumble as digestive juices are prepared

Digestion
As you eat a meal, your stomach stretches. This stretching triggers the release of hormones such as gastrin and secretin, which prepare the stomach, pancreas, and intestines for digestion.

Low fluid intake makes the blood more concentrated, which stimulates feelings of thirst

Fluid balance
Another adrenal hormone is aldosterone. When fluid intake is low, it stimulates the kidneys to conserve salts and water. After you have a drink, the level of aldosterone goes down.

Cleaning the blood

A CAR EMITS exhaust fumes. A heating furnace gives off smoke and soot. These are waste products. The body produces wastes, too. Most body wastes are end-products of chemical reactions that are carried out in cells (pp.24–25), as the cells build up new substances and break down old ones. Examples of wastes include urea, containing broken-down proteins, and creatinine, produced when muscles contract. These wastes are collected by the blood, the body's main transport fluid. They are filtered and removed from the blood as it flows through the two kidneys in the upper rear abdomen. The filtered wastes and excess water form a fluid, called urine, which is stored in a stretchy bag, the bladder, before being expelled from the body.

EXPERIMENT
Invisible wastes

The body's waste fluid, urine, is mainly water, with a yellowish tinge. It does not look as if it carries dozens of waste substances. It does – but they are in dissolved form. Show this principle using ordinary table salt and water. If the water was removed from urine in a similar way, it would leave a thimbleful of solid wastes daily.

Disappearing salt
Stir two tablespoons of salt into a jar of warm water. The salt grains dissolve and disappear. Pour some of this salt solution on to a plate.

Reappearing salt
Leave the plate in a warm place. Gradually the water evaporates. It leaves behind the salt, which has become visible again.

■ Urinary system

The kidneys, bladder, and connecting tubes make up the urinary system. The kidneys receive a huge blood flow – up to 2,000 litres (440 gallons) a day. Each kidney has a million tiny filtering units, called nephrons, which extract wastes from blood to form urine. The left kidney in this illustration has been cut away to show its interior.

Bladder lining
This microscope photograph shows the lining of the bladder. It is made of a type of tissue (p.185) called transitional epithelium, which is strong and stretchy, and resists the corrosive chemical attack of urine.

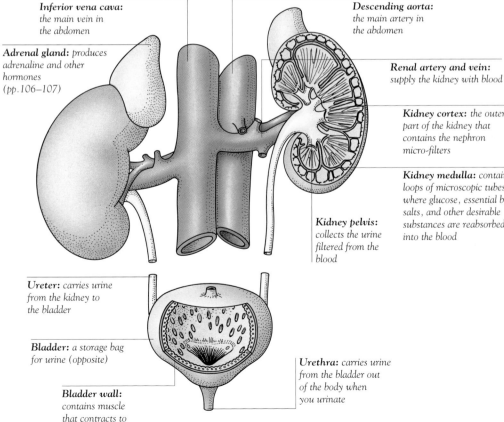

Inferior vena cava: *the main vein in the abdomen*

Adrenal gland: *produces adrenaline and other hormones (pp.106–107)*

Descending aorta: *the main artery in the abdomen*

Renal artery and vein: *supply the kidney with blood*

Kidney cortex: *the outer part of the kidney that contains the nephron micro-filters*

Kidney medulla: *contains loops of microscopic tubes where glucose, essential body salts, and other desirable substances are reabsorbed into the blood*

Kidney pelvis: *collects the urine filtered from the blood*

Ureter: *carries urine from the kidney to the bladder*

Bladder: *a storage bag for urine (opposite)*

Urethra: *carries urine from the bladder out of the body when you urinate*

Bladder wall: *contains muscle that contracts to expel urine*

■ The bladder

The kidneys of an adult produce on average 1 litre (nearly 2 pints) of urine each day. The exact amount is controlled by hormones (p.106). These adjust the filtering and water-absorbing rates of the kidneys. If you have plenty to drink, the kidneys produce a lot of dilute urine so that the excess water is disposed of. If you drink only a small amount, the kidneys do not expel much water in urine, so the urine is more concentrated. From the kidneys, the urine oozes down the ureters into the bladder. The tough, stretchy walls of the bladder can expand to hold up to 500 ml (almost 1 pint) of urine. However, the desire to urinate begins when the bladder is about half full.

Lining of empty bladder
Cells of the transitional epithelium lining the bladder are tall and rounded.

Lining of full bladder
Cells of the transitional epithelium are stretched thin and flat.

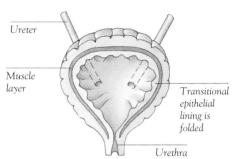

Ureter

Muscle layer

Transitional epithelial lining is folded

Urethra

Empty bladder
The multi-layered bladder wall thickens and folds up as urine flows away along the urethra. The empty bladder looks like a wrinkled prune.

Ureter

Transitional epithelial lining is stretched

Urethral sphincter

Full bladder
The muscle wall stretches thin as the bladder blows up like a balloon. The urine is held in by a muscular ring, the urethral sphincter.

■ Filtering and sorting

A series of various-sized pores (holes) in the nephron micro-filters retain selected chemicals – according to the size, shape, and other features of their molecules – and allow other chemicals through. In the same way, this model kidney has holes that filter out balls of certain sizes only. Red blood cells are big, and so do not pass into the filtering system at all. Urea passes through all filtering stages and ends up in urine. Glucose, salts, and other essential chemicals are first filtered out, in the cortex, but then taken back into the blood in the medulla.

Glucose, salts, and other chemicals (green, orange, and blue balls), and urea (yellow), taken out of blood here

Glucose, salts, and other chemicals taken back into blood here; urea is not taken back and carries on into urine

Red blood cells (red balls) stay in the blood

Balancing body fluids

NOW AND THEN, you may feel that you need a drink. But have you ever been truly thirsty? A lack of body fluid brings on a powerful, basic urge to take in water – because water is essential for life. All of the chemistry that takes place in your body occurs in a watery environment. Only when chemicals are dissolved in water are they able to move and react, combine and separate, diffuse and osmose. These reactions and processes take place constantly among the billions of cells in your body. Several body systems (pp.22–23) play a role in making sure that your fluid levels are balanced. These include the urinary and the endocrine systems. It is the job of the brain to detect when blood and other body liquids have become too concentrated, which means that water is running low.

Droplets of moisture from the skin

■ DISCOVERY ■
Claude Bernard

During the 18th and 19th centuries, chemistry developed into a major science for the first time. Researchers began to delve deep into the chemistry of the body. Some of the most important discoveries were made by the French physician Claude Bernard (1813–1878). Instead of simply observing nature, Bernard carried out many experiments, on animals and in test-tubes. He suggested that the body has mechanisms that maintain and stabilize its internal conditions – such as fluid balance, nutrient levels, and temperature. This idea led him to the concept of homeostasis, or "the constancy of the internal environment" (p.104). Bernard also made discoveries about the stomach, liver, intestines, pancreas, blood vessels, and curare – a muscle-relaxing drug extracted from a poisonous plant root. In 1865 he wrote the classic *Introduction to the Study of Experimental Medicine.*

EXPERIMENT
Always in a sweat

Adult help is advised for this experiment

Although you sweat most when you have been very active in hot conditions, the body loses small amounts of water all the time, as shown by this simple experiment.

YOU WILL NEED
● *clear plastic bag* ● *adhesive tape* ● *microscope* ● *slide* ● *red dye*

1 PUT YOUR hand in the bag, and tape it loosely to your wrist. Study the bag after 10 to 15 minutes. Can you see tiny, misty drops condensing on the inside of the bag? This is some of the moisture (sweat) that is constantly evaporating from the skin in small amounts. *Caution: Do not tape the bag to your wrist too tightly. Do not leave it on when the experiment is finished.*

2 REMOVE THE BAG. Smear the slide on your hand to collect moisture. Look through the microscope (p.178) to see crystals of sodium chloride (salt) in the sweat. Dye the crystals red to make details stand out.

■ Water in and out

Water evaporates from the skin and the lungs. It is also needed to carry dissolved wastes, such as urea (p.108), from the body. This lost water must be replaced by water in drinks and food – especially leafy vegetables and juicy fruits. This chart shows the average daily flow of water in and out of a child's body – although the amounts vary, according to factors such as the surrounding temperature.

In

Metabolic water
(made in the body by
chemical reactions)
150 ml (¼ pt)

Water in food
300 ml (½ pt)

Water in drink
750 ml (1¼ pt)

Total
1200 ml (2 pt)

Out

Water in sweat
100 ml (⅙ pt)

Water in faeces
100 ml (⅙ pt)

Water evaporating
from the skin
200 ml (⅓ pt)

Water evaporating
from the lungs and
breathing airways
200 ml (⅓ pt)

Water in urine
600 ml (1 pt)

Total
1200 ml (2 pt)

■ Survival without water?

Some desert animals never seem to drink. But they do need water. The main reason that they can drink so little is that they expel very little water. The urine that they produce is highly concentrated, and their droppings are dry. Also, desert animals avoid the hot, drying sun, by being active only at night. Much of the water that they obtain comes not from drink, but from food, such as moist leaves and seeds, and the juicy bodies of other creatures.

Drought in the desert
The gerbil rarely has to drink. It can survive on the water in seeds and other plant foods.

■ Why we feel thirsty

The desire to drink, like all conscious urges, comes from the brain. Water flows in and out of cells and around the body, mainly in the blood and also in the lymphatic system. When water levels fall, the concentrations of various substances in the blood rise. If this happens, the part of the brain called the hypothalamus (p.126) triggers the feeling we call thirst, so that we try to obtain more water. The hypothalamus also communicates by hormones (pp.106–107), which instruct the kidneys to retain some of the water that would otherwise be lost as urine. This makes the urine more concentrated, giving it a darker colour.

Getting thirsty
When your body becomes hot, it cools itself by sweating more. As a result of sweating the body loses water. This is why you feel thirsty after you have been active and sweating.

■ Water in the body

About two-thirds of your body weight is water. Two-thirds of this water is inside body cells (intracellular), where it acts as a solvent in which cell chemicals dissolve. It also maintains the shape and size of the cells. The other third of the body's water is outside cells (extracellular).

Non-water substances
These include proteins, fats, and minerals. They make up about one-third of your body weight

Intracellular water
Two-thirds of body water is inside cells. It can pass in and out of the cells by osmosis

Extracellular water
One-third of the water is in blood plasma and lymph, and in the spaces between cells

Body temperature

HAVE YOU BEEN in a small room that is crowded with people? Even if it is cold at first, the room soon begins to warm up. It may become uncomfortably hot. This is because human bodies give off heat, like very slow-burning fires. A fire turns the chemical energy of its fuel, such as coal or wood, into rapidly released heat. To obtain the energy that runs its thousands of chemical processes, the body "burns" its own type of fuel – food. It turns chemical energy in foods into slowly released heat. This warmth helps to keep your body at 37°C (98.6°F), the temperature at which its cells work most efficiently. A whole range of processes prevent your body from becoming too hot or too cold.

The body's "heat map"
A thermograph is a map of body heat. Here, cool parts are red, warm ones purple and green.

■ Warm-bloodedness

All mammals, from hares to humans, are warm-blooded, maintaining a high body temperature even in cold weather. To keep warm and active in the cold, mammals need lots of food to burn as fuel. The greater our body surface, the more heat we lose from it. Closely related animals that live in different climates may have body features with very different surface areas, to help them adapt to the climate.

■ Keeping cool

If the body gets too hot, part of the brain called the hypothalamus (p.126) registers this and triggers body-cooling processes such as sweating and flushing.

Sweat glands release sweat that oozes on to the skin and cools it by evaporation (left): this is called perspiration

Blood vessels near the body surface become wider, so that more blood flows through them, giving off more heat – which makes the skin flushed

Loose, light clothing lets air blow past and carry heat away from the body

---

EXPERIMENT
Cooling sweat

 Adult help is advised for this experiment

When a puddle evaporates (turns into vapour), it uses a tiny amount of the sun's heat. Similarly, when sweat evaporates from your skin it draws heat from your body. Show this with surgical spirit, a liquid that evaporates faster than water.

YOU WILL NEED
● *surgical spirit* ● *cotton wool*

1 POUR A little spirit on to the cotton wool, and dab the back of your hand.

2 BLOW ON your hand to speed the evaporation. Does the patch feel cool as the spirit draws warmth from the skin? (Wash your hands afterwards.)

Big ears in hot places
The jackrabbit's huge ears help to get rid of excess body warmth in the hot, dry scrub and grassland.

Small ears in cold places
In the icy Arctic, the snowshoe hare has small ears, so there is less area for heat loss.

▪ Keeping warm

In cold conditions, the cooling body processes (opposite) are reversed, to conserve heat. You can help these natural warmth-retaining reactions by putting on thicker clothes. A hat is particularly useful, since up to two-fifths of all heat coming from your body is lost from your head and face.

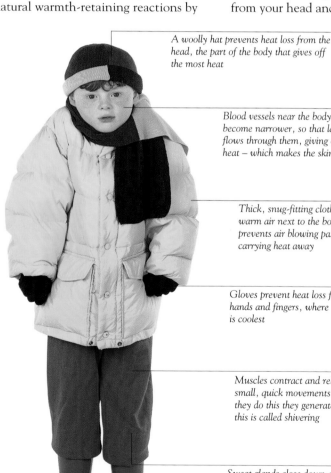

A woolly hat prevents heat loss from the head, the part of the body that gives off the most heat

Blood vessels near the body surface become narrower, so that less blood flows through them, giving off less heat – which makes the skin paler

Thick, snug-fitting clothing keeps warm air next to the body and prevents air blowing past and carrying heat away

Gloves prevent heat loss from the hands and fingers, where the body is coolest

Muscles contract and relax in small, quick movements, and as they do this they generate heat: this is called shivering

Sweat glands close down and release hardly any sweat

EXPERIMENT
Where's warmest?

Adult help is advised for this experiment

The temperature of the brain, heart, and other vital organs is 37°C (98.6°F). But blood cools as it flows to the extremities, like the fingers and toes. So one part of the body frequently has a different temperature from another. Measure the differences with a clinical thermometer. *Caution: If the thermometer cracks, do not touch it. Get help from an adult.*

YOU WILL NEED
● *clinical thermometer* ● *cotton wool*

1 SHAKE THE thermometer so the silver mercury goes into the bulb. Place the thermometer against your finger ends, and hold it in place with cotton wool for two minutes. Read off the temperature shown by the mercury thread.

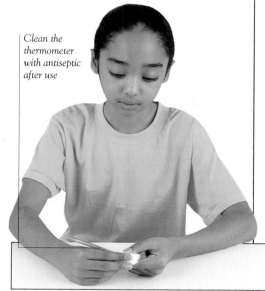

Clean the thermometer with antiseptic after use

2 SHAKE THE thermometer again. Take temperatures in the crook of your elbow, behind your knee, between your toes, and elsewhere on your body. Where is it warmest, and where coolest?

Thermometer use
Hold the bulb with cotton wool so that heat from the fingers holding the thermometer does not affect the results.

The CONTROL NETWORK

The ultimate bio-computer
*Looking like a grey blancmange, and the same weight
as a large grapefruit, the human brain (above) is the
control centre for all body functions. The smaller,
darker part on the lower left is the cerebellum (its
interior is shown in close-up, left). It co-ordinates
nerve signals for complex body movements.*

THE VAST, COMPLEX MAZE
of nerves that makes up the
human brain controls all
body processes – both
conscious and autonomic
(automatic). The brain
receives information from
the sense organs and other
body parts in the form of tiny
electrical nerve signals. And
it sends out information in
the same form. The outgoing
information controls muscle
movements and body
functions. The brain is
responsible for your
intelligence, creativity,
memories, perceptions,
reactions, and emotions.

THE BRAIN AND NERVES

SCIENTISTS HAVE LEARNED AN ENORMOUS AMOUNT about the workings of the human body. But many mysteries remain about the part that allows us to gather this knowledge, the powerful brain. The brain has a huge number of jobs. Its automatic functions include the control of heart-beat, digestion, and dozens of other body processes that happen every minute. Its conscious functions (those you are aware of) are as varied as catching a ball, recalling a memory, and creating a work of art.

The brain is the centre of all mental processes, from a fleeting memory of a face or smell, to a task that requires great thought and concentration – such as working out a complex puzzle. You are conscious (aware) of these processes. However, your brain does much more, without your realizing it. It controls your body functions such as the heart-beat, breathing, and digestion. It monitors the concentrations of substances such as glucose and carbon dioxide in blood, adjusts water and nutrient levels, and brings on feelings of hunger and thirst when supplies of food or fluids run low.

You may have forgotten how you learned simple actions such as pouring from a jug. "Re-live" the experience of learning by trying to pour a different substance from a different height (p.133).

Your brain also screens the gigantic amounts of information that are gathered continuously by your senses and filters out all but the most important features. If the brain did not do this, your attention would be overwhelmed.

Our knowledge of the brain is less complete than our knowledge of most other organs. This is partly due to the astonishingly complicated micro-structure of this organ. At the microscopic level the brain is incredibly

active. It weighs only one-fiftieth of the weight of the body, yet it is so chemically active that it uses up to one-fifth of the body's glucose-sugar energy supply.

Ancient views

In ancient times, many people thought the heart was the centre of all the emotions. The brain was not considered important. When the Ancient Egyptians preserved a body as a mummy, the heart and certain other organs were carefully put in their own containers. But the brain was pulled out in pieces through the nose and thrown away.

The Greek philosopher Alcmaeon of Croton (born c.500 BC) held that the brain, not the heart, was the seat of the senses and the centre of intellect. The great philosopher Plato (428–347 BC) agreed. But Plato's pupil Aristotle (384–322 BC) returned to the view of the heart as the home of thoughts and emotions.

Galen's ideas

Galen (p.13) of Ancient Rome believed that the spinal cord, protected by the vertebrae

*The dinosaur **Stegosaurus** had a tiny brain. But this was sufficient for its lifestyle of roaming wooded plains. The species survived for millions of years.*

The spinal cord (p.119) inside the vertebrae (backbones) is the body's main nerve. Its branches extend throughout the trunk (torso) and limbs.

(backbones), was an extension of the brain. He proposed that, through the spinal cord and its branching network of nerves, the brain was "plumbed in" to all parts of the body, especially to the muscles and the sense organs.

Galen suggested that a mysterious fluid substance, "animal spirit", formed in chambers known as ventricles inside the brain, and that it flowed along the nerves to muscles, making the muscles contract (p.57). This theory of brain and nerve function was incorrect, although it was not challenged for more than 1,500 years. It is true that the brain has ventricles, and that the ventricles contain a fluid, called cerebrospinal fluid. But the main role of this fluid is to carry nourishment to the nerve tissues and to collect their wastes.

■ Nerve cells

With the invention of the microscope in the early 1600s, the brain and nerves were found to be packed with huge numbers of nerve cells, also called neurons (p.119).

By chance, research into nerve cells led to the invention of the electrical battery by the Italian professor Alessandro Volta (1745–1827). Volta's work was inspired by an argument with another Italian scientist, Luigi Galvani (1737–1798) about the nature of electricity. Galvani believed that animals produced electricity, whereas Volta was convinced

Test your reactions by making a "react-o-ruler". When you react, nerve signals pass from the senses to the brain and then to the muscles (p.122).

The term "nerve centre" refers to the control centre of a complex communications system, such as this air traffic control room in an airport. There are also different nerve centres in the brain that receive messages from each of the senses.

that electricity came from contact between metals and other chemicals. In an experiment, Galvani made a frog's leg twitch by touching it with a metal knife. However, he misinterpreted the result. The leg had not twitched by "animal electricity" generated by the frog. It did so because the contact between the metal and the chemicals in the cells of the nerves and muscles had made a simple battery.

Volta did further experiments with metals and chemicals, and by 1800 he had produced the first intentional battery. Yet Galvani's theory was correct in a sense – the body does produce electricity in the form of signals to and from the brain along nerve cells, and as electrical "ripples" in heart muscle and other muscles.

■ Brain parts

The brain has three main structural parts (pp.126–127). These are the cerebellum, the cerebrum, and the brain stem.

The cerebellum mainly co-ordinates complex muscle movements, from pouring a drink to flying a helicopter.

The cerebrum is responsible for complex thoughts. In humans it is very highly developed. The cerebrum has two wrinkled halves, the cerebral hemispheres. Each of these is divided into five lobes, mostly named from the curved bones of the skull around them. The prefrontal lobes are positioned over the eyes, the frontal lobes below the top of the forehead, the parietal lobes on the top, the temporal lobes on the sides, and the occipital lobes at the lower rear.

The thin surface layer of the hemispheres is known as the cortex. It looks much the same all over, but different areas are specialized for different functions. A wide strip of cortex, running from ear to ear over the top of the brain, receives signals from the skin about touch, pressure, and pain. This strip is called the somato-sensory cortex and is the brain's "touch centre". Similarly there are nerve centres for sight, hearing, smell, and taste, and for body movements. These centres are not always related to any particular lobe or any combination of lobes.

Some parts of the cortex are called non-specific areas. Scientists have not yet worked out what their purpose is. For instance, the aspects of behaviour that we call "personality" seem to be based in the prefrontal and frontal lobes, but they do not seem to have any identifiable centre.

The third main structural part of the brain, the brain stem, is concerned mainly with the vital life processes that take place automatically in the body. The brain stem consists of several parts. The hypothalamus, which sits deep in the centre of the brain, is a centre for homeostasis (p.104). The heart-beat, breathing, and blood pressure are centred in the medulla, the lowest part of the brain stem, which merges into the spinal cord. The point where nerve fibres from the body come together to cross into the upper parts of the brain is the pons.

In proportion to their overall brain size, the sight centres of birds are much larger than those of humans.

The brain's information store is as great as that of a library. Scientist believe that in the brain information is organized into various types of memory (p.128).

The nervous system

LIKE THE circulatory system, the nervous system has branches all over the body. Its nerves divide many times. The thickest nerves look like pieces of cream-coloured rope, and the thinnest are narrower than a hair. Nerves are made of bundles of nerve cells (opposite). These cells are specially designed to carry tiny electrical messages. Some nerve cells are called sensory cells. They carry signals from the sense organs, such as the eyes and ears, to the brain, where they are analysed. Other nerve cells are called motor cells. They carry nerve signals from the brain and spinal cord to the muscles, telling them when to contract and when to relax. Many nerves contain both sensory and motor nerve cells.

■ DISCOVERY ■
René Descartes

The French scientist René Descartes (1596–1650) was a brilliant mathematician and a founder of philosophy. He believed that there was a connection between the body and the soul (the human spirit) and proposed that a small part of the brain, the pineal gland, linked the two. This idea was incorrect, but another idea Descartes had – that reflex actions (p.120) happen automatically and that they are controlled by nerves – was accurate. He understood that a reflex is caused by signals from a sensory nerve, which travel to the spinal cord and then to a motor nerve, often without entering the brain.

■ Voluntary actions

When you read, your eyes scan back and forth, and your brain interprets the image patterns that your eyes see

When you eat, your jaw muscles make your teeth chew, and your tongue moves the food around in your mouth

As you sit, you may not be aware of your body posture, but you constantly keep your balance and you regularly change position to rest muscles

■ Autonomic actions

As food reaches the back of your throat and you swallow, automatic muscle movements take over

When you digest, your stomach mashes the food you have eaten and muscles in your intestinal walls push it along

Muscles in the walls of the arteries make them wider or narrower to direct blood where it is needed

Part of the nervous system is voluntary. In other words, the movements and actions that these nerves are responsible for – such as reading, walking, chewing, or sitting upright in a chair – are under your conscious control. You are aware of them, and you can stop or start them at will. Most voluntary actions originate in the cortex (p.127). These actions are controlled by nerves that send signals to the body's skeletal muscles (p.59).

Part of the nervous system is autonomic, which means that it controls itself. Muscles in body parts such as the arteries, stomach, and intestines work without you thinking about them. You are usually unaware that they are working, and you cannot stop or start them at will. These muscles are under the control of parts of the brain stem (p.126). Autonomic actions are controlled by nerves that send signals to the body's smooth muscles (p.59).

■ Brain and main nerves

The main nerves of the body branch out and reach every nook and cranny. This system has two main sections. The brain and the spinal cord are together known as the central nervous system. The rest of the nerves, which spread out through the body, are called the peripheral nervous system. The peripheral nerves communicate with the brain via the spinal cord. There are also 12 pairs of nerves, called cranial nerves, that join the brain directly to important parts of the head. These include the cochlear nerves from the ears (p.152) and optic nerves from the eyes (p.139).

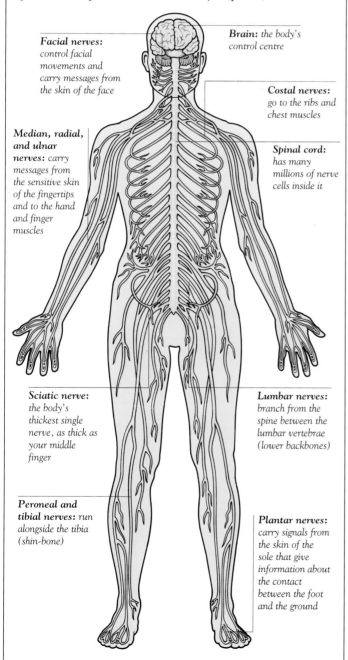

Facial nerves: *control facial movements and carry messages from the skin of the face*

Brain: *the body's control centre*

Costal nerves: *go to the ribs and chest muscles*

Median, radial, and ulnar nerves: *carry messages from the sensitive skin of the fingertips and to the hand and finger muscles*

Spinal cord: *has many millions of nerve cells inside it*

Sciatic nerve: *the body's thickest single nerve, as thick as your middle finger*

Lumbar nerves: *branch from the spine between the lumbar vertebrae (lower backbones)*

Peroneal and tibial nerves: *run alongside the tibia (shin-bone)*

Plantar nerves: *carry signals from the skin of the sole that give information about the contact between the foot and the ground*

■ Nerve cells

Intermediate nerve cell

Intermediate nerve cell body

Motor nerve cell body

Dendrite of intermediate nerve cell

Synapse

Dendrite of motor nerve cell

Dendrite of sensory nerve cell

Synapse

Sensory nerve cell body

Axon of motor nerve cell

Motor nerve cell

Sensory nerve cell

Myelin sheath insulates the axon

Sensory nerve cell axon

Motor end plate (junction between nerve and muscle)

Path of nerve signal

The nerve signal arrives at the muscle fibres

Touch sensor in skin generates the nerve signal

One nerve cell
This is a single nerve cell, seen through a light microscope. The dark-blue patch in the middle is the cell body. Three thin dendrites stretch out from either side of the cell body.

The nervous system consists of billions of linked nerve cells (neurons). Each nerve cell has a body (main part), finger-like dendrites, and a long, wire-like axon. These three elements can be arranged in various ways. Dendrite tips almost touch other dendrites at junctions called synapses. Dendrites pick up nerve signals and send them along the axon to the next nerve cells. In this illustration a nerve signal from a touch sensor in the skin travels along a sensory nerve cell to an intermediate nerve cell, then to a motor nerve cell, which passes it to a muscle.

Reflexes

HAVE YOU EVER been startled by a loud noise that made you jump before you could stop yourself? This is an example of a reflex – an automatic reaction that happens incredibly fast, before you even have time to think about it. A reflex occurs by itself, even if your attention is elsewhere. This is because a reflex is programmed and predictable – you do not have to use your brain to decide what action to take. In a reflex, nerve signals (p.118) are produced by a sense organ, such as the eye or ear, that detects the stimulus (something that provokes action). They go to the spinal cord or the brain, then to the muscles around the body that move in response. Most reflexes are quick responses to possible danger or harm to the body, such as jerking your finger away if it touches something hot.

■ On the alert

In the animal world there are many possible dangers, such as being attacked by a predator. An animal's senses are tuned to the slightest sound, scent, or movement. Even while feeding or resting, the senses monitor the surroundings. If anything startles the animal, its reflexes are called into action and it is ready to respond at once.

What's that noise?
Even tamed animals such as horses are wary. Hearing a strange sound behind, the horse automatically looks around.

EXPERIMENT

Blinking reflex

See how a sudden loud noise near the face causes the eyelids to close automatically to protect the eyes.

Loud claps
Clap your hands loudly 15 cm (6 in) in front of a friend's face. (No closer, to prevent accidents!) See how your friend blinks immediately. Can your friend override this reflex with practice?

■ A bundle of reflexes

Babies cannot control many of their movements, and they cannot feed or clean themselves. But they are far from helpless, as they do many things automatically. A baby is a "bundle of reflexes", several of which are important for basic survival. As you grow, you learn to control or override some of these reflexes. Other types of reflex fade away.

The Moro reflex happens if the baby suddenly falls back or is startled. The baby throws out his or her arms and legs, as if to catch hold of something

Bowel and bladder reflexes expel the contents of these organs automatically when they are full. A child eventually learns to control these actions

The rooting reflex helps feeding. If touched on the cheek, the baby turns to that side and moves his or her mouth to find the mother's breast or bottle

The stepping reflex happens only in the first few days. If the baby's feet touch a firm surface, he or she makes stepping movements

EXPERIMENT
The knee-jerk reflex

Testing the body's reflexes can give a physician useful information about how nerves and muscles work. One simple test is the knee-jerk reflex (below). When your knee is tapped, nerve signals travel from stretch sensors in the knee to the spinal cord and then back to the leg muscles. Meanwhile, other signals travel up the spinal cord to the touch centres of the brain (p.117). As a result, you become aware of your leg's response, but usually too late to stop it from happening.

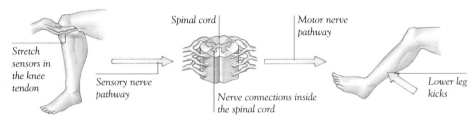

Stretch sensors in the knee tendon

Sensory nerve pathway

Spinal cord

Nerve connections inside the spinal cord

Motor nerve pathway

Lower leg kicks

Stimulus
A tap just below your kneecap stretches the tendon (p.185) there. Stretch sensors in the tendon send out nerve signals.

In and out
The signals pass along sensory nerves to your spinal cord. This sends signals back at once along motor nerves.

Response
The signals travel to the muscles in the front of your thigh. These contract and jerk the lower leg upward.

1 SIT IN A CHAIR. Cross your legs so the lower knee fits snugly into the hollow at the rear of the upper knee. Ask a friend to tap your upper knee firmly – on the soft part just below the kneecap – with the edge of his or her open hand.

2 WHAT HAPPENS? Does your lower leg twitch? You may need practice to find the right site. Can you use will power to stop your knee from jerking?

■ Protecting eyes and face

If an object comes toward your head, you may respond with a sequence of actions, almost without thinking. These actions protect your eyes and other parts of your face in the event of possible danger. The pupils of the eyes also have reflexes that respond to the varying brightness of light (p.141).

Eyes close
Your eyelids come together and facial muscles contract to tense and toughen your skin.

Head jerks
Your neck muscles twist the head back and to the side, so that your face is out of direct line.

Arms rise
Your shoulder and arm muscles lift your arms and hands in front of your face, as a shield.

Reactions

HUNDREDS OF TIMES a day we react to the world around us. When asked a difficult question, we may have plenty of time to think about the answer. At other times, fast reactions are vital, especially in dangerous situations such as driving. At 90 kph (55 mph) on the motorway, if an obstruction appears 50 m (165 ft) ahead, a driver has less than two seconds to see it, assess the situation, plan what to do, and take action. Each reaction in the body follows the same basic process. A sensory part, such as the eyes, ears, or skin, detects a stimulus. It flashes nerve signals along sensory nerves (pp.118–119) to your brain, at speeds of up to 100 m (330 ft) per second. Your brain becomes aware of the situation, makes a decision, and then sends signals out along motor nerves to your muscles, telling them how to respond.

■ Split-second timing

Many sports depend on quick reactions. When a top-ranked tennis player hits a mighty serve, the ball travels at more than 160 kph (100 mph). The opponent has less than a third of a second to note the speed and direction of the ball, move into position, watch for the bounce and ball-spin, and swing the racket for the return shot. The more someone practises such fast responses, the more quickly and smoothly the brain, nerves, and muscles can carry them out.

Life or death
Sports such as tennis are rarely a matter of life or death. But motor racing is. At 320 kph (200 mph), a racing car travels almost 100 m (330 ft) per second. The driver's safety depends on reactions measured in hundredths of a second.

sensory nerves (pp.118–119)

EXPERIMENT
Reaction time

In this experiment you find out the amount of time it takes to react to a stimulus. Here, the stimulus is feeling your right hand being squeezed. The reaction you must make is to squeeze the hand of a friend on your left. The time between these two actions is your reaction time. Six to ten of your friends must stand in a circle, hands linked. One is the starter. Another has the stop-watch and is the timer.

YOU WILL NEED
● *stop-watch*

EXPERIMENT
The "react-o-ruler"

Adult help is advised for this experiment

An individual's reaction time is often too fast to measure without complicated equipment. But you and your friends can compare your reaction speeds using this ruler with a coloured scale. The idea is to catch the ruler as soon as possible after it starts to fall between your fingers. Record the results. Do you get quicker at first, but then reach a time (colour) that you cannot improve?

YOU WILL NEED
● *scissors* ● *glue* ● *pencil* ● *ruler* ● *thick card 30 cm x 2.5 cm (12 in x 1 in)* ● *6 pairs of pieces of coloured paper 5 cm x 2.5 cm (2 in x 1 in)*

1 STICK SIX of the same-sized pieces of coloured paper along one side of the thick card. Repeat on the other side, keeping the same colour sequence. This is the "react-o-ruler".

2 GET A FRIEND to hold the react-o-ruler by the upper tip. Place your thumb and forefinger 2.5 cm (1 in) below the ruler, so that it will fall between them. With no warning, your friend lets go of the ruler. You try to catch it by closing your thumb and forefinger as fast as you can. Where are you holding it? The nearer the bottom of the ruler, the quicker your reaction.

Squeezing hands

The starter shouts "Go", and at exactly the same time squeezes the hand on his or her left. As soon as this friend feels the squeeze, he or she squeezes the next person's hand, and so on around the circle. When the starter feels his or her right hand being squeezed, he or she shouts "Stop". Meanwhile the timer starts the watch on "Go" and stops it on "Stop" to get the combined time for all the reactions. To find out the average reaction time of your friends, divide this combined time by the number of friends in the circle. Do your reaction times get faster if you go around the circle twice, or five times? (Do not forget to divide the final time by the total number of hand squeezes.) How much can you improve the times with practice?

Sensors in skin detect pressure

Sensory nerve pathway

Brain's somato-sensory cortex

Brain's motor cortex

Motor nerve pathway

Muscles make the fingers squeeze

Stimulus

When your right hand is squeezed by the person on your right, your skin sensors detect the increase in pressure. They send signals along sensory nerves, through your wrist, and up your arm and shoulder.

In and out

The sensory nerve signals pass into your spinal cord, then travel up to the somato-sensory cortex (p.127) of your brain. It is at this point that you realize that your hand has been squeezed, and you decide to respond.

Response

Signals pass from your brain's motor cortex (p.127), down through your spinal cord, and along motor nerves to the muscles in your hand. The muscles contract and squeeze the hand of the next person in the circle.

Starter

Timer

Reactions and decisions

IN A SIMPLE reaction situation, like the "Reaction time" experiment (p.122), only one response is required. But what if you have to decide between two or more responses? Your brain needs a split second to think about them and make a choice, before you act. The more complex the choices, the longer the decision time. As with most reaction situations, you get faster with practice.

YOU WILL NEED

● *for the chute: 3 lengths of plastic guttering (wider than a table-tennis ball), about 100, 60, and 40 cm (40, 24, and 16 in) long* ● *for the screen front: sheet of stiff card 50 cm x 40 cm (20 in x 16 in)* **(A)** ● *for the screen sides: 2 sheets of stiff card 50 cm x 20 cm (20 in x 8 in)* **(B)** ● *2 thin strips of card 55 cm (22 in) long* ● *for the screen base: stiff card about 50 cm x 30 cm (20 in x 12 in), shaped as* **C** ● *strips of felt* ● *tenon saw* ● *plastic beaker* ● *large bowl* ● *about 12 table-tennis balls painted at least 3 different colours* ● *plastic adhesive tape* ● *notepad* ● *pen* ● *double-sided adhesive tape* ● *scissors* ● *paint-brush* ● *non-toxic paints* ● *craft knife* ● *compasses* ● *metal ruler* ● *cutting mat*

EXPERIMENT
Making decisions

Adult help is advised for this experiment

The amount of time that it takes you to react depends on how rapidly your brain assesses a situation, and how many decisions you have to make. You and your friends can test your reaction times by seeing whether you can catch balls as they roll out of a chute. (The chute is lined with felt, so the balls do not make a warning sound as they roll.) This experiment tests how quickly you can react – firstly, when you have no decision to make because you can catch any ball, and secondly when you do have a decision to make, because you are allowed to catch only balls of a certain colour. How much quicker can you get with practice? Do you improve as quickly when trying the second part of the experiment as you do when trying the first?

1 LINE THE longest piece of guttering with felt, stuck on with double-sided tape. Place the shortest length of guttering on one end, to make a partial tube, and attach it with plastic tape.

Number the marked intervals on the thin card strips and position these strips so that the measure starts at the end of the tube

2 DRAW MARKS at intervals of 2 cm (1 in) along both of the thin card strips. Fix them to the outside edges of the exposed portion of the chute with double-sided tape.

3 CAREFULLY CUT a hole in the screen front, 30 cm (1 ft) from the bottom. Make it slightly larger than the guttering-tube. Tape together the sides, front, and base of the screen.

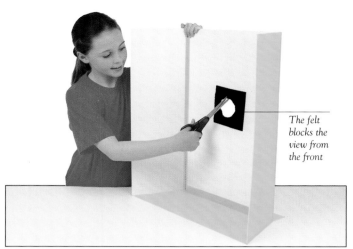

The felt blocks the view from the front

4 CAREFULLY CUT out a square of felt and tape this behind the screen hole. Trim a hole in the felt, slightly smaller than the guttering-tube. Snip slits into the felt to allow the tube to be pushed through.

Sliding cover

5 LAY THE THIRD piece of guttering on top of the chute, so that it sits between the measuring strips. This makes a cover that you can slide up and down the chute. Push the chute just through the hole in the screen.

The screen hides the feeder. The feeder should feed balls into the chute at random times, making as little movement as possible, so as not to give the catcher any warning

The lip on the screen base should stop the screen toppling. If not, put some books inside the screen to keep it stable

Holding the beaker
For this experiment it is best to place the whole assembly on a table-top. The lower end of the chute should hang slightly over the table edge. The catcher holds the beaker just to the side of the chute end. After each attempt at a catch, the catcher should move the beaker back out of the way of the chute end. Use the large bowl to hold balls that the catcher misses.

6 SLIDE THE chute cover to expose the maximum amount of open chute. Get one person to feed balls down the chute, and another person to try to catch each one in the beaker. Try several successive sets of 10 balls, scoring one for each ball. Does the catcher's score improve with each set? Move the chute cover down one mark on the scale and try again. Keep

sliding the cover down until the catcher misses all 10 balls – the limit of her or his reaction time. In the second part of the experiment, the feeder continues to feed all of the balls, but this time the catcher catches only balls of a certain colour. Is the reaction time the same as before? What happens if the catcher is allowed to catch balls of two out of three colours?

The brain

A COMPUTER ROOM full of printers, disk drives, and monitors would be still and silent without the central processor itself. Likewise, the body would be lifeless without the brain. The human brain has three main parts. The top part, making up nine-tenths of the brain's volume, is the wrinkled cerebrum. This is the thinking part of the brain. The back part of the brain is the cerebellum, a "mini brain" that deals mainly with balance, posture, and skilled movements. All of the other areas of the brain (including the pons, thalamus, medulla, and hypothalamus shown below) belong to a part of the brain called the brain stem. This joins with the spinal cord below it and the cerebrum above it.

■ DISCOVERY ■
Phineas Gage

For many years experts suspected that the front parts of the brain were involved in personality and the way we behave. In 1848 a discovery occurred by accident in the United States that supported these suspicions. Phineas Gage, the foreman of a road-building team, was injured when gunpowder went off accidentally. The explosion blew a metal rod up into his cheek, through the front part of his brain, and out of the top of his skull. Amazingly, Gage survived for 12 years, but his character changed. Once even-tempered, he became prone to rages. His case showed that the frontal lobes of the brain are involved in personality (p.117).

Hole in the head
This is the skull of Gage, beside a plaster cast of his head and face.

■ Inside the brain

This is a view through the middle of the brain, cut in half from front to back. Each of the two large wrinkled upper parts of the cerebrum is folded downward in the middle of the brain (as can be seen in the brain scan, right). Each of these parts is called a cerebral hemisphere. Some parts of the brain stem form emotions and feelings, some deal with memories (pp.128–129), and others carry out automatic processes, or produce basic motivations such as hunger. In the centre of the brain is a system of cavities, the ventricles. These are filled with cerebrospinal fluid, which cleans and nourishes brain tissues.

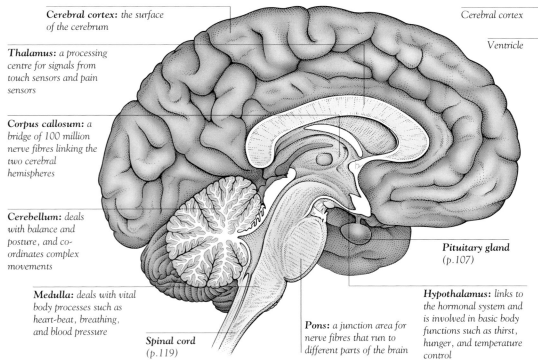

Cerebral cortex: *the surface of the cerebrum*

Thalamus: *a processing centre for signals from touch sensors and pain sensors*

Corpus callosum: *a bridge of 100 million nerve fibres linking the two cerebral hemispheres*

Cerebellum: *deals with balance and posture, and co-ordinates complex movements*

Medulla: *deals with vital body processes such as heart-beat, breathing, and blood pressure*

Spinal cord *(p.119)*

Pons: *a junction area for nerve fibres that run to different parts of the brain*

Hypothalamus: *links to the hormonal system and is involved in basic body functions such as thirst, hunger, and temperature control*

Pituitary gland *(p.107)*

Cerebral cortex

Ventricle

Right cerebral hemisphere

Left cerebral hemisphere

Brain slice
This is a computer-coloured photograph of a slice through a brain. The view is from the front. The wrinkled cerebral cortex at the surface of the cerebrum (right), where conscious thought takes place, is shown in yellow. Note how the cerebrum is folded downwards in the middle and divided into two cerebral hemispheres.

■ The cortex

Each cerebral hemisphere has a surface of "grey matter" about 3 mm (¹⁄₈ in) thick. This is the cerebral cortex. It is made of billions of nerve cells (p.119), whose axons run to the brain's centre and the spinal cord. The cortex is the site of nerve centres for the senses, and of consciousness (awareness), thought, and memory too. Each part of the cortex has a different set of jobs.

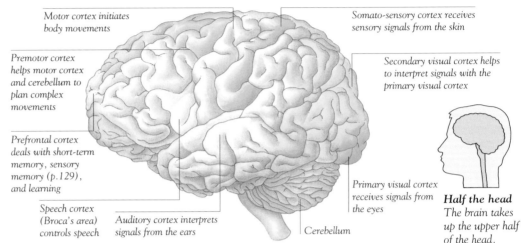

Motor cortex initiates body movements

Premotor cortex helps motor cortex and cerebellum to plan complex movements

Prefrontal cortex deals with short-term memory, sensory memory (p.129), and learning

Speech cortex (Broca's area) controls speech

Auditory cortex interprets signals from the ears

Somato-sensory cortex receives sensory signals from the skin

Secondary visual cortex helps to interpret signals with the primary visual cortex

Primary visual cortex receives signals from the eyes

Cerebellum

Half the head
The brain takes up the upper half of the head.

■ Brain size

When compared with the brains of other animals, the remarkable feature of the human brain is not its size – a sperm whale's brain is about six times larger. Instead it is the high proportion of brain size to body size, as well as the way the cerebral hemispheres are folded and wrinkled to give the cortex a large surface area – as big as the top of an office desk. This large surface area means that there is enough space for many highly complex and sophisticated nerve connections.

Cerebellum   Cerebrum

Frog
Most of the frog's small brain deals with basic body processes, co-ordination, smell, and sight.

Cat
A cat's brain has a substantial cerebellum, allowing the cat to carry out agile body movements and giving it very good balance.

Human
The cerebral hemispheres are so large that they wrap over and cover almost all of the rest of the brain.

EXPERIMENT
Making a mental picture

Adult help is advised for this experiment

The brain's imagination is amazingly versatile. For example, it can construct a mental picture from sound and touch.

YOU WILL NEED

● *shallow box with lid* ● *card* ● *scissors* ● *glue* ● *marble* ● *notepad* ● *pen*

1 TRIM THE card so that it fits into the box, making a triangular compartment, and glue it in place (left). Put the marble into the compartment, replace the lid, and shake the box to check that the marble stays in the triangle.

2 PASS THE closed box to a friend who knows nothing of the experiment. Let your friend tilt the box, listen to the rolling marble, and feel its impact against the inner surfaces. Can your friend work out the shape of the inner compartment? Ask your friend to draw on the pad the shape that he or she imagines. Now try other shapes of compartment.

Memory

CAN YOU REMEMBER what you had for lunch yesterday? Probably. Can you recall your lunch from 17 days ago? Probably not. The brain has an incredible and very selective ability to remember – and to forget. It is thought that there are several types of memory. Sensory memory (opposite) gives you a constant sense of where you are. Short-term memory (p.130) deals with information you have just received. And long-term memory is a memory for information, sometimes important, sometimes trivial, that you select out over days, weeks, or years.

■ Long memories

We remember some events for many years. These are often significant times such as examinations or birthdays. Memories of them can last for 70 years or more. These memories can be triggered by a chance stimulus of something stored in the memory, or they may be brought back deliberately. Recalling memories now and again helps to refresh them.

A day to remember
Many people recall their first day at school, but not their second, third, or subsequent days – unless something significant happened.

■ Memories in the brain

For centuries, scientists could not agree how memory worked in the brain. Recent research has begun to show where different parts of the memory processes take place. However, it does seem that the brain has no single site in which it stores memories. They are spread through several areas, especially around the cortex (p.127). Some of these areas are described here. It may be that different aspects of a particular memory – such as the sights, sounds, smells, and words associated with one event – are stored in different sites.

Prefrontal cortex:
the part of the cortex that deals with short-term memory and sensory memory (opposite)

Cortex: involved in sensory, short-term, and long-term memory

Amygdala: links deep-seated emotions from the brain stem (p.126) with conscious memories from the cortex

Hippocampus: part of the brain stem; it transfers information from short-term memory to long-term memory and back again

What are memories made of?
This diagram shows some of the brain parts involved in memory processes. It is thought that memories exist as patterns of connections between the nerve cells (neurons) of the brain. The connections occur at synapses (p.119). To store a memory, nerve signals flow along a specific set of routes through certain synapses. This particular memory returns each time nerve signals re-activate and pass again along this set of routes.

EXPERIMENT
Remembering without trying

You often recall things even if you do not consciously try to remember them. In this experiment you can test a friend's memory for faces. The brain seems to have a special facility for remembering human faces, which is very important for identifying people and communicating with them.

YOU WILL NEED
● *20 photographs of faces (or 20 pictures of faces from magazines): the pictures should be of similar size, and all either in colour or black-and-white*

Recognizing faces
Ask a friend to help you, but do not give him or her any details of the experiment. Select ten of the faces and show them to your friend, one by one, for about half a second each. After a short while, show all 20 faces in any order. Ask your friend to identify the ten already seen. Even though he or she did not try to memorize the faces, the results should be quite accurate.

■ Making sense of things

We can remember something much more easily if it makes some kind of sense – that is, if we can see some significance or a recognizable pattern in it. Seeing information as a pattern helps us to remember it from the vast amounts of other information flooding into the brain every second. We cannot remember everything, so we tend to ignore or forget things that have no meaning or that are not important in our lives.

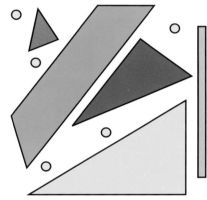

Can you remember this picture?
Study the picture above for 20 seconds, look away, and try to draw it. Can you make a good copy? When the brain sees something, it looks for a pattern or meaning. But this is a meaningless jumble of differently coloured shapes. It is difficult to remember.

What about this?
You could probably remember and redraw this picture more successfully. It consists of the same shapes as the top drawing. But their arrangement has meaning – a sailing boat.

EXPERIMENT
Using sensory memory

Have you ever walked along a street, near a lamp-post, when you were distracted and looked away? Did you then turn round and walk on – into the lamp-post? This is a rare failure of your sensory memory. This type of memory gives you an awareness of where you are in relation to objects and the space around you, so that you can move around without bumping into things. It lasts only a few seconds and depends mainly on vision. This experiment shows how sensory memory works and how it fades.

1 STAND FACING a friend, about 2 m (7 ft) away from him or her. Ask your friend to point at you. Now raise your arm and point so that your forefinger is aiming directly at your friend's forefinger.

2 CLOSE YOUR eyes, but try to keep a picture of your friend's position in your mind. Lower your arm. Your friend "freezes", with his or her eyes open and finger held in the same position.

Finger direction begins to wander

3 AFTER THREE seconds, with your eyes still closed, point at where you remember your friend's finger to be. Open your eyes. How accurate are you? Using your sensory memory, you stored a picture of your friend's posture and position in the prefrontal cortex (opposite). This part of the cortex is also called the "visual-spatial scratchpad". The sensory memory is short-lived, even when you try hard to retain it. To find out how long it lasts, try the same test, but keep your eyes closed for 5 seconds, then 10, then 30, and so on. After how long does the accuracy of your pointing fade significantly?

Short-term memory

HOW DO YOU MAKE a telephone call to an unfamiliar number? First you look up the number in the telephone book. Then you repeat the number to yourself as you dial, to help you remember it. You use your short-term memory for this type of task. As its name suggests, short-term memory has a very limited time span. If you look up the telephone number, then wait five minutes before dialling, you will probably forget it. But you can keep your short-term memory refreshed by repeating the number to yourself every few seconds. If someone interrupts you during this time, your short-term memory is usually taken over by the new information, and the number vanishes from your brain. The short-term memory has a limited capacity for information, as you can demonstrate with this memory-tester.

Assembly diagram
This diagram shows the main structural parts of the memory-testing machine and how they fit together.

Bulb window
Lid (A)
Switch hole
Lid hinge
End (D)
Divider (B)
Side (C)
Shallow cutout
Baseboard

Electrical note
The tester may also be built with a 6V or 12V battery, provided the bulb chosen is suitable.

Make a memory-tester

 Adult help is advised for this experiment

Make your own memory-testing machine to find out how many items – in this case coloured lights in a random sequence – you and your friends can hold in the short-term memory. Most people can remember seven or eight items in this way. Can you devise any ways of improving on this?

A
B
C
D

YOU WILL NEED
• *thick softwood baseboard 25 cm × 25 cm (10 in × 10 in)* • *hammer* • *18 U-shaped wire clamps with nails* • *for the lid (A): stiff card 25 cm × 24 cm (10 in × 9½ in)* • *for the dividers (B): 4 pieces of stiff card, each 25 cm × 5 cm (10 in × 2 in) with a shallow central cutout and slots 2.5 cm (1 in) long, 1 cm (½ in) from each end* • *for the sides (C): 2 pieces of stiff card, as for B but without the central cutouts* • *for the ends (D): 2 pieces of stiff card, as for C but with 4 extra slots, equally spaced between the 2 outermost slots* • *cutting mat* • *metal ruler* • *craft knife* • *scissors* • *pencil* • *compasses* • *notepad* • *8 squares of paper, sides 3.5 cm (1½ in), in 4 colours (2 of each)* • *4 normally open (on-while-pressed) switches* • *4 9V bulbs and bulb-holders* • *8 screws for the bulb-holders* • *4 pieces of cellophane or transparent plastic, 5 cm × 4 cm (2 in × 1¾ in), coloured to match the paper squares* • *screwdriver* • *9V battery* • *2 battery connecting wires with a battery attachment* • *2 wire connector blocks* • *4 lengths of coloured wire* • *glue* • *adhesive tape* • *pliers*

Circuit diagram
Each bulb is connected directly to its own switch by one wire. The other wires from each bulb and its switch go to the battery via the connector block.

Switch
Battery
Bulb-to-switch connecting wire
Battery connecting wire
Bulb
Connector block

1 ON THE UNDERSIDE of the lid, along one of its longer edges, mark out four 3.5 cm (1½ in) squares. Put one in the top left corner, 1.5 cm (¾ in) from each edge. Draw the next square after a gap of 1 cm (½ in), and repeat for the third and fourth squares. Carefully cut out the squares with the craft knife. The holes that you have made are bulb windows. In line with these windows, carefully cut small holes for the switches, 2.5 cm (1 in) from the opposite edge of the lid.

2 ON THE UNDERSIDE of the lid, tape the four pieces of coloured cellophane on to the bulb windows. Carefully cut small, round holes in each of the coloured paper squares. Glue the squares over the switch holes on both the top and bottom of the lid, to correspond to the positions of the pieces of coloured cellophane. The paper square on top of the lid shows the colour code for the switch. The paper square on the underside is a colour guide for when you connect the wires.

3 INSTALL THE switches. Depending on the way the type of switch is secured, you may need to unscrew a small collar from the stem, and push the switch through from below, before screwing the collar back on again. Or you may need to insert the switch from above, as shown. You can even attach the switch with tape. Whichever method is used, make sure the switch is attached securely enough to cope with the pressure when it is turned on by pressing it down.

4 SCREW THE bulb-holders to the base, so the bulbs will be under their windows. Run wires in L-shapes from the left, where one connector block will be placed, to one contact on each bulb-holder. It is helpful if the wire is the same colour as the window of the bulb it leads to. Do the same on the other side of the base, leaving the wire ends free to join the switches. Run another wire from the other contact on each bulb-holder to its corresponding switch. Secure all wires with clamps.

5 TAKE THE ENDS of the four wires from the bulb-holders, twist them together, and insert them into one side of one of the connector blocks. Screw the block into the baseboard. Do the same with the four wires that will be connected to switches, using the other connector block. Lie the battery on the lower left of the base. Attach each of the two connecting wires from the battery to a different connector block. Tape the battery in place. Now disconnect one of the battery wires to save power.

6 SLOT TOGETHER the dividers, sides, and ends as in the assembly diagram (opposite). Glue them together and into position on the base, so that the wires run under the shallow cutouts. Hinge the lid in position with tape, on the edge next to the switches. Connect the free ends of each pair of wires to the corresponding switch. Now reconnect the battery wire, lower the lid, and check that pressing each switch lights the corresponding bulb. The memory-tester is now ready to use.

7 WRITE DOWN RANDOM sequences of colours. Begin with two, such as red-blue, and finish with 12. Then, as a friend watches, tap out the first of these sequences, so that the lights flash in order. Can your friend repeat the order of lights? Which is the longest sequence your friend can remember correctly? Does your friend improve if you press the switches more slowly? What happens if he or she has to wait before repeating the sequence? Does it help your friend to divide long sequences mentally into several short groups of colours?

Learning

OUR CAPACITY FOR LEARNING depends mainly on the power of our memory. One type of learning involves physical skill, from simple movements such as pouring to complex ones such as writing. These skills are learned through a process of trial and error. We try certain muscle movements, assess the results, and store information on what we have done in the memory. Another type of learning involves ideas, inventions, and strategies rather than physical movements. This allows us to plan ahead – to think out, for example, the moves in a chess game. A third type of learning involves transferring facts and figures to the brain's memory, so that they can be recalled later.

■ Learning to laugh

From the age of only a few weeks, a baby learns to smile and then laugh. The baby learns that these actions produce reactions in those around and give them pleasure. At first, the baby's laughter is natural and unaffected. However, as the baby gets older, he or she learns that there are different ways to laugh, from a short chuckle to a loud guffaw, and that these different types of laughter convey different meanings. Learning to laugh is all part of learning to communicate our thoughts, emotions, and intentions to other people.

Waiting for a response
A baby may laugh and clap his or her hands to see how other people respond to such actions.

EXPERIMENT
Re-learning to write

Writing depends on a series of precise, controlled hand movements. Most of us learn to write with our preferred hand, which we have used since we were very young, for gripping objects and manipulating them. However, the brain can re-train itself and learn to use the other hand – with a certain amount of concentration and effort.

YOU WILL NEED
● *pen* ● *large sheet of paper*

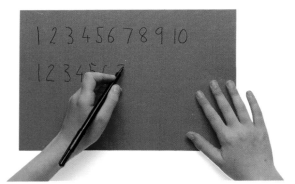

Writing with the wrong hand
With your usual writing hand, neatly write out the numbers 1 to 10, large and clear. Now hold the pen in your other hand. Write the same numbers again below. Are these numbers as neat and tidy as the first set? Keep practising with this hand, learning to control the pen. Compare your first attempt at writing with this hand to your last. Do the neatness and accuracy of your writing improve?

EXPERIMENT
Learning to draw

Drawing depends partly on physical control and co-ordination of hand movements. It also depends on the image of the subject that you hold in your mind, especially when you draw from memory. In turn, the accuracy of this image depends on your mental abilities, which usually become more accurate and sophisticated with age, as shown by this simple experiment.

YOU WILL NEED
● *paper* ● *pens* ● *head-to-toe photograph of a person*

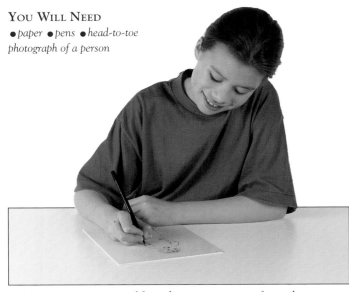

1 ASK FOR THE HELP of friends ranging in age from three or four years to adulthood. They do not have to be expert artists. Ask them to look at the photograph of a person for a minute, to close their eyes for 30 seconds, and then to draw the main features of the person in the photograph from memory.

Learning to play

As with other games, the basics of chess are relatively simple. Most people can quickly learn the moves for each piece. But learning to play chess well involves memorizing many hundreds of possible moves, as well as possible moves for each of these moves at the next turn, and so on.

So many combinations
In a chess game, moves must be thought out far in advance. This provides a complex challenge for the brain.

EXPERIMENT
Learning to pour

When you first learned to pour water from a jug, you probably spilled most of it. Now you can pour it smoothly. To see the body movements involved in pouring, "re-learn" this process by trying to pour from a greater height than usual, and by using sand, which flows in a different way from water. Wear protective goggles to prevent any sand from getting into your eyes. As you tip the jug, you must judge where to position it, when the sand will begin to slide out, and how it will fall sideways on its downward journey.

YOU WILL NEED
● large plastic jug ● plastic beaker ● fine sand
● protective goggles

Cascade of sand
Hold the jug of sand at head height. Try to pour the sand into a beaker on the table. You must learn to adjust your tipping speed and aim.

2 COMPARE the drawings to the original photograph. Which drawing is the most accurate? A sample set of drawings is shown here, based on the photograph above.

By a four-year-old
This shows a head, body, arms, and legs, but few details, even on the face. Young children may emphasize features that are important in their own lives. The person who drew this was learning to tie shoelaces!

By an eight-year-old
The body and limbs are now more in proportion. The arms and legs connect at the correct places, though one arm is rather long. The face and hair have more detail, and the shoes still figure prominently.

By a twelve-year-old
There is greater detail in this picture than in the previous two, and the lines of the drawing are finer. But some features of the photograph have been altered in the memory of this artist. Again, look at the shoes!

SENSING the SURROUNDINGS

Keeping eyes and ears open
When sound waves enter the ear, many thousands
of microscopic hairs deep inside the ear (coloured
yellow, left) are shaken by a vibrating membrane.
The movements of the hairs cause nerve signals to be
sent to the brain, which interprets them as sounds.
The eye (shown in the cutaway model, above) has
more than 130 million light-sensitive cells in its
wafer-thin inner layer, the retina.

YOUR SENSES ALLOW YOU TO
experience pleasure and
pain. They enable you to
appreciate art and music, or
the smell and taste of a
delicious meal. But they are
also vital for survival. You
can see and hear danger, and
feel if you are being harmed.
Sense organs transform
stimuli such as light rays,
sound waves, odours,
flavours, or physical contact
into a common form of
information – electrical
nerve signals. These signals
are instantly flashed to the
brain for interpretation and
identification.

THE BODY'S SENSES

Ask someone to name the body's senses. He or she will probably say sight, hearing, smell, taste, and touch, making a total of five. However, the body has other senses. We are not aware of most of them, since they are part of the automatic control mechanisms that keep internal body conditions stable (pp.104–105). Even the familiar five senses are not as simple as they seem. The sense of touch, for example, provides you with several distinct sensations such as pressure, heat, cold, and pain.

A cake tin and drinking straw show how sound waves are converted into ripples in the fluid of the inner ear (p.152).

An important feature of every animal's life is the ability to sense (detect) what is going on in the world around it. Even very simple creatures such as jellyfish and worms can sense light, moisture, vibration, and chemicals. This helps them to avoid possible danger, find food, and seek out suitable surroundings – all actions that are necessary for survival.

Each sense organ – such as the eye, tongue, or skin – converts the information about what it detects into the body's "language" of electrical nerve signals. These travel to the brain along sensory nerves (p.118). In the brain, the signals are sorted and processed, analysed and interpreted. The signals from each sense organ are dealt with in a specialized centre of the brain's cortex (p.127).

The sense organs are chiefly receiver-converters. This means that they receive a sensation and convert it into nerve signals, which go to the brain. Some initial sorting and processing take place, particularly in the eye, ear, and nose, but most interpretation happens later, in the brain. The incoming information is compared with other information already in the brain, in the memory. The brain tries to identify what the senses have

detected, and decides whether or not it is important.

The vast majority of information that the brain receives is not important, so it is discarded. You only become "aware" of information that does get through this sorting system.

Even when they are working efficiently, our senses detect only a small part of the information available to them. Some animals have senses that are far more acute than ours. For example, a dog can smell many more odours than a human, and at far weaker concentrations. An eagle can see the size and colour of a rabbit, when, for a human, the rabbit would look like a tiny speck.

■ Early beliefs

The idea that we have five senses is a traditional one. It goes back at least to the time of the great philosopher Aristotle of Ancient Greece (384–322 BC), who listed the five over 2,300 years ago. Some early beliefs about certain sense organs seem

The bloodhound's nose gives a sense of smell that is hundreds of times more sensitive to certain odours than a human nose.

The cells that see, rods and cones, are packed in the eye's retina (p.139). In this microscope photograph rods have been coloured purple and cones blue.

very strange today. These misconceptions arose partly from a lack of knowledge of the body, and partly from a lack of understanding of the nature of light rays, sound waves, odours, and flavours.

For example, some Ancient Egyptians believed that the body both listened and breathed through the ears. They thought that a substance called "life-breath" entered the right ear, and, when the time came, another substance, called "death-breath" entered the left ear.

Many Ancient Greeks and Romans thought that we could see because light beamed out of the eye on to the objects that we looked at. In fact, the reverse happens – light rays travel from the object on to light-sensitive cells in the eye.

■ Renaissance ideas

During the Renaissance there was steady progress in the knowledge that scientists gained about the sense organs.

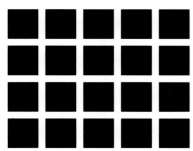

Look at these squares. Do you see spots between them? You may, even though there are none. Unusual images like this one can confuse the eye and brain (pp.150–151).

In 1562 the first thorough book on the ears was written, by the Italian anatomy professor Bartolomeo Eustachio (1520–1574). The tube linking the middle ear cavity (p.152) to the throat is called the Eustachian tube in his memory.

Some Renaissance scientists believed that light was detected by the eye's iris (the coloured front part) or the transparent lens just behind it. But the Frenchman René Descartes (p.118) showed that in fact the lens focuses an upside-down

Onion-shaped taste buds sense the flavours of food. They are visible in this microscope photograph of a section through the surface of a tongue.

image on to the sensitive retina lining the back of the eye.

Descartes also believed, this time incorrectly, that the optic nerves (p.139) were hollow tubes that carry a mysterious substance called "animal spirit" from the eyes to the brain. In fact each optic nerve, like other nerves, is a bundle of fibres.

Microscopes, invented in the early 1600s, revealed that the eye's retina is crowded with millions of light-sensitive cells of two main kinds – rods and cones (p.142). The Englishman Thomas Young (1773–1829) and the German Hermann von Helmholtz (p.139) believed that there were three types of cones – one type to detect red light, one for green, and one for blue.

However, new research shows that colour vision is more complex than Young and von Helmholtz suggested. The research shows that what we perceive as a certain colour depends also on the colours of surrounding objects.

Chemosenses

Biologists include the senses of smell and taste in a group called chemosenses, because these senses work in a very similar way to each other. Fish and other water creatures rely on chemosenses, because they detect chemicals in the water by smell and taste.

Thousands of microscopic receptors are scattered around the nose and tongue. In the nose they are found on a surface called the olfactory epithelium (p.158). On the tongue they are found on the taste-bud cells (p.160). Each receptor has a pit of a specific shape. Only molecules of a certain chemical are the right shape to fit neatly into the pit. When these molecules slot into the pit, they trigger nerve signals to the brain. This is the "lock-and-key" principle. With many types of receptor pit, shaped to receive a variety of chemicals, your nose and tongue can detect a wide range of substances.

Other senses

Scientists continue to investigate the astonishingly intricate workings of the sense organs.

These include not only the main five senses, but other sensors inside the body as well.

Stretch sensors in muscles, tendons, and joints tell the brain about the position and posture of the body. They are part of the proprioceptive sense (p.146). Pressure sensors in certain blood

Skin can help you "see". You can form a mental picture of an object by touch alone (p.167).

vessels, such as the carotid artery in the neck, inform the brain about blood pressure. And in the brain, chemosensors monitor concentrations of carbon dioxide, glucose, and other substances in the blood.

Each of these sensing systems is designed to adjust and maintain the environment inside the body automatically. So they leave the parts of the brain that deal with your conscious thoughts free to concentrate on other things.

Many machines can sense things that we cannot, such as ultraviolet light or magnetic fields. We often make other machines to mimic our own senses. For example, this moon-rover carries cameras and soil samplers to "see" and "feel" the moon's surface.

The eyes

YOUR TWO EYES provide an incredibly detailed, constantly updated, three-dimensional, colour view of the world. Light rays enter the eye through the cornea, a domed window at the front. They are detected by the retina, a layer of light-sensitive cells. The retina is not much larger than a postage stamp – and even thinner. From the pattern of light rays, the eye generates patterns of nerve signals and sends them to your brain. The parts of your brain specialized for dealing with sight, the visual centres (p.117), analyse all the information coming in from the eyes. It is your brain that tells you what kinds of shapes and forms, shades and colours, positions and movements you are looking at. The following pages explore the intricate structure and workings of your eyes and brain.

■ Moving the eyes

As you read these words, or glance around, your eyes flick back and forth. Their movements are produced by a team of six long, slim muscles behind each eyeball. The muscles work together to move the eyes in different directions.

Lateral rectus pulls the eye to look out

Medial rectus pulls the eye to look in

Looking out and in

Superior rectus pulls the eye to look up and in

Inferior rectus pulls the eye to look down and in

Looking up, down, and in

Superior oblique pulls the eye to look up and out

Inferior oblique pulls the eye to look down and out

Looking up, down, and out

■ Cleaning the eyes

Tear fluid is made continually in two small, lumpy glands, the lacrimal glands. They are just above the outer side of each eye. The tear fluid oozes from the eyelid each time you blink, and washes away dust and germs. The fluid drains into the lacrimal ducts (tear ducts), and then into the nose.

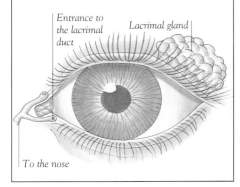

Entrance to the lacrimal duct

Lacrimal gland

To the nose

EXPERIMENT

Looking at your eye

Are your irises both exactly the same colour? Can you see the film of tear fluid over the front surface of the eye, the conjunctiva? Can you see into the pupil? Gently pull down your lower eyelid to see the tiny hole into the lacrimal duct.

YOU WILL NEED
● *small plastic-edged mirror*

Eyelash

Eyelid

Iris

Pupil

Sclera (white of the eye)

Position of the lacrimal duct

Using the mirror
Stand in good light and look at one eye closely in a mirror. Which parts of the eye can you see?

■ Inside the eye

This is a cutaway diagram of an eye, seen from above. The eyeball is about 2.5 cm (1 in) wide. Its outermost layer is the sclera, visible from the front as the white of the eye. Within this is the choroid, rich in blood vessels to nourish other eye parts. On the inside of the choroid is the retina. This has light-sensitive cells that detect light rays that have entered the eye through the cornea. The cornea, which partly focuses the rays (p.140), is so transparent that you can hardly see it when looking at your eye in a mirror. Next the light rays pass through a clear fluid, the aqueous humour, and then through the pupil, the central hole in the ring of muscle known as the iris. Then the rays pass through the lens, which focuses them further. They shine through the clear, jelly-like vitreous humour that forms the bulk of the eyeball, before reaching the retina.

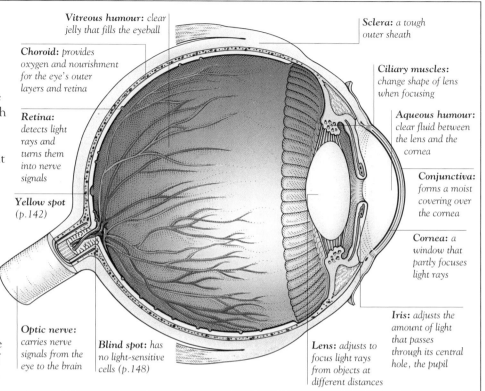

Vitreous humour: clear jelly that fills the eyeball

Choroid: provides oxygen and nourishment for the eye's outer layers and retina

Retina: detects light rays and turns them into nerve signals

Yellow spot (p.142)

Optic nerve: carries nerve signals from the eye to the brain

Blind spot: has no light-sensitive cells (p.148)

Sclera: a tough outer sheath

Ciliary muscles: change shape of lens when focusing

Aqueous humour: clear fluid between the lens and the cornea

Conjunctiva: forms a moist covering over the cornea

Cornea: a window that partly focuses light rays

Iris: adjusts the amount of light that passes through its central hole, the pupil

Lens: adjusts to focus light rays from objects at different distances

■ A view into the eye

An ophthalmoscope is a medical instrument for lighting up the inside of the eye and looking into it through the pupil. With it, your doctor can check that the inside of your eye is healthy. The ophthalmoscope also allows blood vessels in the eye to be seen clearly, giving valuable information about the general state of blood vessels in the body.

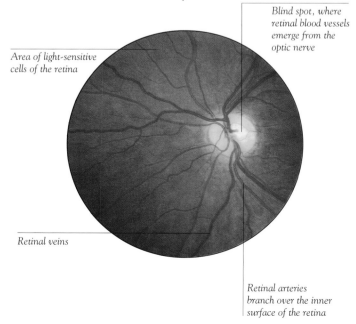

Area of light-sensitive cells of the retina

Blind spot, where retinal blood vessels emerge from the optic nerve

Retinal veins

Retinal arteries branch over the inner surface of the retina

■ DISCOVERY ■
Hermann von Helmholtz

A remarkable German scientist, Hermann von Helmholtz (1821–1894), combined work in anatomy and physiology with mathematics, electricity, and optics. In 1850 he measured the speed of tiny electrical nerve signals in living nerves. These, he discovered, travel at about 25 to 40 m (80 to 130 ft) per second, and some go even faster. The next year he developed an early version of an ophthalmoscope (left). Von Helmholtz also wrote *Handbook of Physiological Optics* (published in several volumes, 1856–1866). This book was a landmark in the study of how the eye works. In it he explained how cone cells in the retina contain pigments that are sensitive to one of three different colours of light – red, green, or blue. This is the reason that the eye can see in colour.

Seeing

WHEN YOU USE binoculars, you adjust them to see things nearby clearly, and then readjust them for faraway objects. This is called focusing, and it is done by moving the lenses in the binoculars. The lenses in your eyes also change when they focus on objects at different distances. But the eyes' lenses do not move; they change shape. Ciliary muscles around each lens make the lens fatter (to bend the light rays more) for nearby objects, or thinner (to bend the rays less) for distant objects. The eye also controls how much light enters it. Muscles in the iris shrink the pupil in bright light. This automatic reaction is called a reflex. If the eye did not do this, too much light would enter the lens and damage the delicate retina.

■ Turning the world upside-down

When a newborn baby sees the world for the first time, he or she has no idea of what is up or down, left or right. As the baby reaches out for objects, he or she realizes that when the image of the object falls on a certain part of the eye's retina, then the object is in a certain position. The eye's lens – like any other lens – inverts the image, so that on the retina it is upside-down. But the baby never knows anything different. From the very start of our lives we turn images the "right way up" in the brain as an automatic part of seeing.

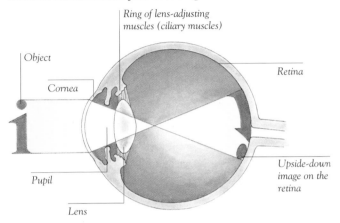

Ring of lens-adjusting muscles (ciliary muscles)

Object

Cornea

Retina

Pupil

Lens

Upside-down image on the retina

EXPERIMENT
Magnifying-lens eye

Adult help is advised *for this experiment*

Make an "eye" with a magnifying lens and tracing paper. Move the lens to and fro to focus on objects in the room.

YOU WILL NEED
● *thick card* ● *tracing paper* ● *magnifying lens*
● *craft knife* ● *pencil*
● *adhesive tape* ● *ruler*
● *scissors, for cutting tape*

1 USE THE pencil and ruler to draw a window frame around the edges of the sheet of card.

2 CAREFULLY cut out the "window". Tape tracing paper over it. This represents the eye's retina.

3 HOLD UP the frame between your face and the magnifying lens, which represents the eye lens. Look at a bright object, such as a window. Move the lens backwards and forwards until an image of the object appears on the screen. Is the image upside-down? Find another bright object that is nearer. Which way do you need to move the lens to bring this object into focus? Now try an object that is farther away.

As you look towards a window, an image of it appears on the screen

■ Seeing sharply

In some eyes the cornea and lens do not focus correctly. In short-sighted eyes, light from distant objects focuses in front of the retina, so images of these objects on the retina itself are blurred. In long-sighted eyes, light from nearby objects focuses behind the retina, so these objects seem blurred too. Long-sighted or short-sighted people can wear spectacles or contact lenses to correct the eye's focus.

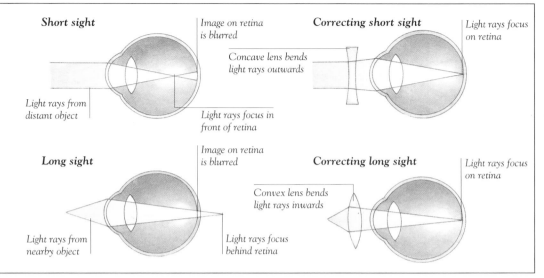

Short sight
Light rays from distant object
Image on retina is blurred
Light rays focus in front of retina

Correcting short sight
Concave lens bends light rays outwards
Light rays focus on retina

Long sight
Light rays from nearby object
Image on retina is blurred
Light rays focus behind retina

Correcting long sight
Convex lens bends light rays inwards
Light rays focus on retina

EXPERIMENT
Pupil reflex

Adult help is advised for this experiment

See your own eyes adjust their pupil size to allow in the right amount of light.

YOU WILL NEED
- cutting mat ● rectangular card sheet ● double-sided adhesive tape ● small plastic-edged mirror ● cardboard tube ● craft knife ● pencil ● scissors

1 HOLD THE tube near a short edge of the card sheet, and draw around it with the pencil.

2 WITH THE knife, carefully cut out the circle that you have drawn, so that the tube fits snugly into the hole.

3 TAPE THE mirror on to the card. Its near edge should be about 2 cm (1 in) from the tube hole.

4 PUSH THE tube into the hole, and hold it up to one eye, so that you can see your other eye in the mirror. With both eyes open, look at a bright window, then a dark corner. See how your pupil narrows in the light and widens in the dark. What happens if you put your hand over the end of the tube and look towards the window? Because your pupils always widen or narrow together, the pupil that is not covered widens at the same time as the covered one, even though it is looking towards the light.

The sensitivity of the eyes

THE AMAZINGLY DETAILED VIEW of the world sensed by each eye is detected by more than 130 million light-sensitive cells in the retina (p.139). When light falls on one of these cells, the cell sends a tiny electrical signal to the brain. There are two types of light-sensitive cell – rod cells and cone cells, so-called because of their shapes. The 125 million rods in each eye are extremely sensitive, even when it is almost dark. But, like black-and-white film, they detect only shades (amounts of light) and not colours. The 6 million cones detect an object's details and colours, but do not work well in dim light.

■ Retinal rods and cones

Rods and cones are arranged unevenly in the retina. When you look straight at an object, its image falls on an area called the yellow spot, at the back of the retina. This is packed with cones, which see shapes and colours well. At the front of the retina, there are more rods and fewer cones.

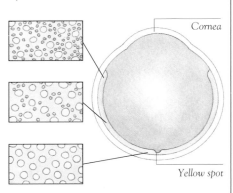

Front of retina
Mostly rod cells, so colour vision is poor.

Side of retina
A mixture of rod and cone cells.

Back of retina
Yellow spot is packed with close-set cones.

Cornea

Yellow spot

EXPERIMENT
Fading colours

As light dims in the evening, your vision "greys out" and colours seem to fade. This is because the cone cells, which let you see colour, do not work in faint light. Instead, you rely on the "black-and-white" rods. Study colour-fade with this simple test.

YOU WILL NEED
● *oranges* ● *other fruit, such as apples and bananas* ● *paint-brush* ● *non-toxic red paint*

1 PAINT ONE of the oranges red, and let it dry. Put it with the other fruit on a table. Dim the lighting in the room so that it is almost dark, allowing you to see the shapes of the fruits – but not their colours. Give your eyes time to adjust to the new light conditions, then dim the lights further if necessary.

2 ASK A friend who knows nothing of the experiment to enter the room. Wait until his or her eyes have adjusted to the dim light. Hold up the fruits in a random order and ask your friend to identify them and their colours. Now make the room brighter to reveal the colour of the painted orange!

EXPERIMENT
The "vision-meter"

Adult help is advised for this experiment

The concentration of rods at the sides of the retina and cones at the back means that your eye's sensitivity varies. It changes across its field of vision (the area you see) from side to centre. Make a "vision-meter" to gauge the point in your field of vision at which you can first see an object – here, a card strip. At what point can you tell the object's colour? When can you make out more details?

YOU WILL NEED
● *sheet of thick grey card 75 cm x 50 cm (30 in x 20 in)* ● *long ruler* ● *70 cm (28 in) strip of wood* ● *2 strips of grey card 20 cm x 2.5 cm (8 in x 1 in)* ● *short, thin strip of stiff grey card* ● *paper-clips* ● *strips of coloured card 25 cm x 4 cm (10 in x 1 1/2 in)* ● *short wooden rod* ● *glue* ● *pen* ● *protractor* ● *map pin* ● *thread* ● *craft knife*

Extend the two larger half-circles by 15° at each end

Attach thread to pin, to guide pen

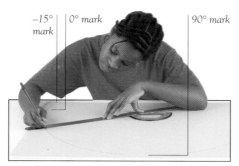

−15° mark *0° mark* *90° mark*

Do not cut all the way to edge of sheet

Leave card uncut here too

1 MARK A SQUARE with 12-cm (5-in) sides halfway along one of the sheet's long edges. Stick the pin halfway along the square's inner side. Draw three half-circles with radii 6 cm (2½ in), 34.5 cm (13¾ in), and 35 cm (14 in). Extend the two larger half-circles as above.

2 PLACE THE PROTRACTOR with its base parallel to the sheet's long edge and the centre of the base where the pin was. Use the ruler, pen, and protractor to mark every 5° around the 34.5-cm (13¾-in) half-circle and the extra 15° at each end. Label each of the marks.

3 ON A SUITABLE surface, carefully cut out a slot between the two larger half-circles, as well as the extra 15° at each end of the half-circles. But do not cut beyond the −15° marks, or for 10° each side of the centre line (a line from the pinhole to the 90° mark).

0° mark

4 CUT OUT the 12-cm (5-in) square and smallest half-circle to make a neck hole. Fold a short part of the thin grey strip and glue it to the sheet at the centre line, so that its main part sticks upright. This is the vision-meter's sight.

5 TURN OVER the whole sheet. Glue the wooden strip along the long edge opposite the neck hole as a stiffener. Now glue the wooden rod directly under the sight as a handle. The vision-meter is ready to use.

6 ASK A FRIEND to wear the vision-meter. Make sure that each 0° mark is level with his or her eyes, and that your friend looks directly along the centre line at the sight straight ahead.

7 FOLD ONE of the 20-cm (8-in) strips in two, and then fold the tips of each of the two ends outward. This is your test-card holder. Place it in the slit in the vision-meter, so that the folded tips stop it from falling through. Now start the experiment. Insert a coloured strip into the holder so it sticks upward. This is a test card. Secure it with a paper-clip. Your friend must keep staring straight ahead at the sight. Starting from the −15° mark, slide the test card 5° around the slot every few seconds. Note the angle at which the test card first comes into the edge of his or her vision. Can your friend tell you what colour the test card is, or do you need to move it further? Stick shapes on the test cards (like those opposite). At what angles can your friend identify these shapes too?

Folded tip of test-card holder *Coloured test card*

−15° mark

0° mark

0° mark

−15° mark

90° mark

Seeing 3-D images

WHY DO WE HAVE TWO EYES? One reason is that two eyes can judge distances more accurately than one. Each eye's visual field covers a slightly different area, and each eye sees an object from a slightly different angle. The brain receives these two different, overlapping views of an object, but it combines them, so we see only one image. The different angles and surfaces in this combined, 3-D (three-dimensional) image provide clues about how far away the object is. Seeing with two eyes is called binocular or stereoscopic vision.

EXPERIMENT
Two views

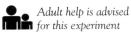 *Adult help is advised for this experiment*

Photographers make "3-D pictures" by printing two slightly different views of the same scene (right), which overlap, but which are in different colours. You can use glasses with coloured filters so that each eye sees only one view. The brain combines the two views into a 3-D scene.

YOU WILL NEED
● *cutting mat* ● *metal ruler* ● *card 15 cm x 8 cm (6 in x 3 in)* ● *blue and red transparent cellophane from packaging, sweet wrappers, or similar* ● *craft knife* ● *pencil* ● *glue*

1 DRAW THE SHAPE of some spectacles on the card, and carefully cut them out. Cut out two "lenses" from the cellophane, slightly larger than the lens holes in the spectacles. Use blue for the right eye and red for the left. Glue in place on the card.

2 LOOK THROUGH your 3-D spectacles at the cityscape (right). The blue filter lets only blue light through, so the right eye sees only the blue view. The red filter lets only red light through, so the left eye sees only the red view. Do you see the scene in 3-D?

EXPERIMENT
Holey hand

Normally, the images from your two eyes are very similar. The brain combines them into one view. In this experiment, the images are quite different. One of your eyes looks at your hand. The other eye looks through a tube and sees a small circular part of the scene in front of you. But the brain still combines the two images as usual. So it looks as if you have a see-through hole in your hand.

YOU WILL NEED
● *tube about 30 cm (1 ft) long and 3 cm (1½ in) in diameter*

Two views into one
Keep both eyes open. Hold the tube up to one eye. Place your other hand at the side of the end of the tube, with the palm facing you. Slowly bring your palm toward you along the side of the tube. You should see a hole appear in the middle of your hand.

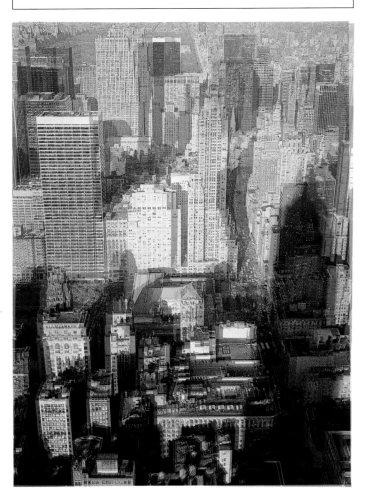

■ Combining views

Look at an object, such as a die, about 30 cm (1 ft) away. Cover one eye, then the other, as you study it. Each view is different, because each eye looks at the object from a different position. See how the angles of the object's edges and the shapes of its surfaces alter slightly between the two views. Each eye sends different messages to the visual cortex (p.127), which has two sides. The two sets of messages combine in the brain to give binocular vision.

Visual pathways in the brain

Turn this page sideways so that you are looking in the same direction as the person in the diagram. The pictures A, B, and C show the view that you would expect to see with the left eye, the right eye, and both eyes respectively.

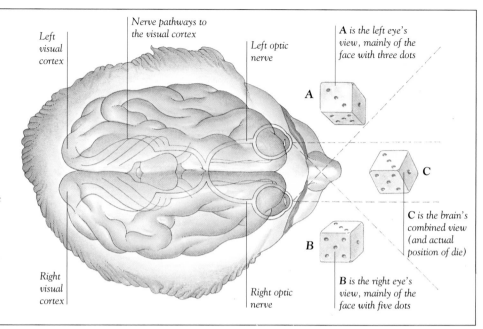

Nerve pathways to the visual cortex

Left visual cortex

Left optic nerve

A *is the left eye's view, mainly of the face with three dots*

A

C

C *is the brain's combined view (and actual position of die)*

B

B *is the right eye's view, mainly of the face with five dots*

Right visual cortex

Right optic nerve

EXPERIMENT
Judging distance

Adult help is advised for this experiment

In this experiment you aim to hit a target with balls of modelling clay. Your binocular vision helps you judge distances accurately, while the same test is difficult with one eye covered.

As soon as you think that the clay ball will land on the bullseye, tell your friend to drop it

1 DRAW AND CUT OUT five circles of paper. Make the first 5 cm (2 in) in diameter, the next circle 5 cm (2 in) larger, and so on. Make alternate circles different colours. Glue them together to make a target.

2 PLACE THE TARGET on a table. Stand about 1.2 m (4 ft) away, and cover one eye. A friend holds a ball over the table. Ask the friend to move the ball left or right, forward or backward, so that the ball drops on to the target. Is it easier to hit the bullseye using one eye or two?

Eyes and co-ordination

CLOSE YOUR EYES. Without looking, you can sense the positions of your head, neck, torso (trunk), and limbs. This is because millions of microscopic stretch sensors, called proprioceptors, in the muscles and joints are continually sending nerve signals to your brain. These signals tell the brain which muscles are relaxed or contracted, and which joints are bent or straight. But sometimes this inner awareness of body position (proprioception) is not accurate enough. To get a good sense of the positions of your hands and arms, for example, you regularly look at them. This is especially important when you are making precise movements or carrying out rapid, co-ordinated actions such as catching a ball (opposite). It is called "hand-eye co-ordination", though in fact the brain is the vital link between hand and eye.

YOU WILL NEED
● *cardboard shoebox* ● *several sheets of paper* ● *craft knife* ● *felt-tipped pen* ● *modelling clay* ● *plastic-edged mirror to fit inside the shoebox* ● *metal ruler*

Adjusting the mirror
Before you start to draw, look through the top hole to check that you can see the stars reflected in the mirror. If not, adjust the angle of the mirror by moving the clay blobs.

Mirror drawing

 Adult help is advised for this experiment

You use your eyes to monitor the marks you make when you draw or write (opposite) and to check small adjustments. But in this experiment your eyes are tricked as you draw a star shape, because your hand movements are reversed in a mirror. See how confusing and frustrating this can be.

1 USING THE felt-tipped pen, draw two neat stars, one slightly inside the other. Do this on several sheets of paper. (The paper should fit inside the shoebox.)

2 VERY CAREFULLY cut four rectangular panels from the shoebox, using the craft knife and ruler. Make sure that you use a suitable cutting surface. Remove the panels shown on the left: most of one of the ends of the box; three-quarters of each side nearest the cut-out end; and one-quarter of the top, farthest from the cut-out end. This is your drawing chamber. Slide the mirror through the top hole and lean it at an angle against that end of the box. Use blobs of modelling clay to prevent the mirror from sliding down into the box.

3 PLACE ONE of the star shapes in the drawing chamber. Hold your pen inside the chamber. Now try to draw a new star between the existing two sets of lines, watching your hand in the mirror only. Looking in the mirror, your eye gives your brain information about the hand's position – but it is the reverse of the information sent by your proprioceptors. So you may mean to move your hand one way, yet it goes the other! Does your drawing improve with practice?

EXPERIMENT
Keep your eye on the ball

Watch a friend throw a tennis ball up and catch it. He or she watches the ball on the way up and down. The hands are positioned exactly in the line of the ball's falling path. If your friend looks away while the ball is in the air, a secure catch is much more difficult.

Holding out hands
The eyes watch the ball, while the brain monitors the positions of the arms and hands by the inner proprioceptive sense, and adjusts the arm and hand muscles. At the last moment, the eyes see both ball and hands together. Now try to throw and catch a ball with your eyes closed. Is it possible?

EXPERIMENT
Writing without seeing

As you write, your eyes continually scan the sizes, shapes, and positions of the letters. You make adjustments as you go along. If you close your eyes, you no longer have this visual feedback, so your writing may become messy.

YOU WILL NEED
● pen ● large sheet of paper

Writing blind
On the paper, neatly write something familiar, such as numbers from 0 to 10. Then write the numbers again, but with your eyes closed. Are the letters as evenly sized, shaped, and spaced as the first version? Muscles and joints can give some feedback about hand movements and positions, but the eyes provide precise detail.

EXPERIMENT
Which finger is which?

Your eyes watch your hands to confirm their positions as monitored by your proprioceptors (stretch sensors, opposite). But if your hands are in an unfamiliar position, the information from proprioception and your eyes may not match – often with confusing results.

1 HOLD YOUR ARMS out and crossed so that the palms meet. Interlock your fingers.

2 BEND YOUR ELBOWS to move your hands down and in toward your body.

3 KEEP BENDING your elbows and wrists so that your hands come up past your chest.

4 HOLD YOUR fingers in this position. Ask a friend to point to one finger, without touching it. Try to move that finger quickly. Did you move the correct finger? Is it easier if your friend touches it?

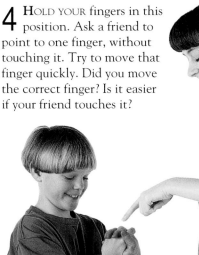

The limits of the eyes

PROFESSIONAL PHOTOGRAPHERS change their cameras and lenses for different tasks, such as achieving a wide field of vision or photographing in dim light. No single lens is suitable for all shots. In the same way our eyes have limitations – many of which are due to their design and structure. For example, objects that are moving very quickly appear blurred to us. Also, there are areas in our field of vision (the area we see) that are blank. If the brain could not "fill in" these areas, we would see patches of shadow.

EXPERIMENT
Seeing what isn't there

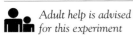 *Adult help is advised for this experiment*

This experiment reveals the hole that the blind spot causes in vision. It also shows how the brain fills in the blank area using information from the colours, shapes, and patterns around it.

YOU WILL NEED
● *sheet of card about 20 cm* **x** *20 cm (8 in* **x** *8 in)* ● *ruler*
● *felt-tipped pen* ● *compasses*
● *protractor*

1 WITH THE compasses, draw two concentric circles of diameters 15 cm (6 in) and 2 cm (¾ in) on the card.

2 PLACE THE centre of the protractor on the centre of the circles. Draw marks at 15° intervals all around. Do the same with the protractor upside down, so you have 24 marks in a full 360° circle.

3 DRAW A line from each 15° mark to the compass hole to make a spoked-wheel pattern, leaving the central circle empty. Mark a spot near the end of the right horizontal spoke, as shown.

■ The blind spot

As you look around, you seem to have an uninterrupted view. But each eye has a blank area in its field of vision. This blank area is due to the blind spot – where the optic nerve and its blood vessels join the retina (p.139). There are no light-sensitive cells on that part of the retina, so images are not detected there. We do not normally notice the blind spot for several reasons. Firstly, an image that falls on the blind spot of one eye is usually seen by the other eye. Secondly, our eyes are continually darting around, so they rarely look at the same scene long enough for the brain to notice the gap. Thirdly, the brain learns to fill in missing parts of the image (left).

Sclera

Choroid

Retina

Blind spot (optic disc)

Optic nerve and blood vessels

Blind spot position *The illustration above is an enlargement of the rear of an eyeball (right).*

Stare straight at this spot with your left eye

4 COVER YOUR right eye with your hand, and hold the card at arm's length. Staring at the spot, move the card toward you. Soon the centre of the wheel falls on your blind spot. At this point the spokes seem to join in the middle. Your brain "fills in" the area that the eye does not see with an image that it expects to exist. In this case, it is a fully spoked wheel, and not the blank circle that really exists.

■ Complementary colours

The retina has three types of cone cell (p.142). Each type mainly detects only one colour of light – red, green, or blue. However, our perception of the colour of an object is affected by other factors, such as how long we look at it. Cones may stop working after they have been exposed to their colour for a long period of time. The other cones then take over, and, if we look away from the object, we often see a "ghost" colour that is different from the original. This is called a complementary colour. Which complementary colours do you see after you stare at the picture below?

Find the Japanese flag
In bright light, stare at this picture for 20 seconds, then look at a blank white surface. Can you see an after-image in complementary colours?

EXPERIMENT
Seeing your own retina

This experiment should not be attempted by children alone. Ask an adult to hold the candle for you

The retina has blood vessels that cast shadows on the light-sensitive cells beneath. However, we usually concentrate on images formed by light shining through the central area of the lens. This light always casts shadows in the same places on the retina, so the brain learns to fill in the gaps in vision made by them. But a light source that comes from the side and jumps about, such as a candle flame, can reveal these shadows.

Retinal shadows
In a dark room, an adult helper holds a candle 15 cm (6 in) from the side of your head (but no closer), level with your eyes. Look straight ahead. You may see shadows of retinal blood vessels. The brain is unused to the flickering light coming from the side, so it is unable to fill in the gaps made by these shadows.

EXPERIMENT
Seeing a blur

Adult help is advised for this experiment

The eye's rod and cone cells respond to light by sending nerve signals to the brain. The nerve signals are caused by a chemical reaction set off by the energy in light. Each rod or cone cell needs a recovery period to reform its chemicals before it can make another signal. This recovery takes no more than a few thousandths of a second. Even so, the scene that you see can change in a much shorter time. As you look at something, some cells are responding while others are recovering. So fast-changing images seem to blur together into a continuous sequence. Study this blurring effect with a spinning disc.

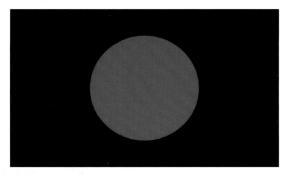

YOU WILL NEED
● *cutting mat* ● *compasses* ● *pencil*
● *white card* ● *string or thread*
● *ruler* ● *craft knife*
● *coloured felt-tipped pens*

1 USE THE compasses to draw a circle about 8 cm (3 in) in diameter on the card. Cut out the circle to make a disc. Draw a butterfly on one side and a flower, in a different colour, on the other.

2 MAKE TWO HOLES, at opposite edges of the disc. Feed equal lengths of string through each hole, and tie the ends of each length to form a loop. Hold the loops in your hands, and whirl the disc to twist the strings. Now pull on both strings. As they untwist, the disc spins so fast that the two sides blur into one image. See how the butterfly seems to sit on the flower.

Tricking the eyes and brain

FROM BIRTH, WE LEARN to look and make sense of what we see. The brain devises various ways and methods of interpreting and making sense of the images detected by the eyes. When the eyes see an unusual or novel series of images, the brain may not be able to interpret them in the usual way. The results can be very confusing, as shown by the "visual tricks" on these pages.

Expanding disc

 Adult help is advised for this experiment

If a spiral on a card disc is spinning one way, your brain gets the impression that the disc is expanding. If the spiral turns the other way, it seems to contract. In a short time, your brain gets used to this movement. If you quickly look at something else, then it too may seem to expand or contract for a moment.

YOU WILL NEED
●hammer ●cutting mat ●ruler ●sharpened pencil ●thick marker pen ●craft knife ●compasses ●nail ●cotton thread ●wooden board ●thick card square with sides of 15 cm (6 in)

1 DRAW A CIRCLE on the card using the compasses, and cut out a disc. Hammer the nail carefully through the centre of the disc a short way into the board. Tie a loop in one end of the thread to fit the pen barrel, and tie the other end to the nail. Put the pen barrel into the loop.

3 REMOVE THE nail and push the sharpened pencil through the centre of the card, so that about 2.5 cm (1 in) sticks out below. With your fingers, twist the pencil steadily on its point to spin the disc. Does the disc seem to expand or shrink? Twist the disc the other way. Is the effect reversed? Watch the card as it "expands" for 20 seconds, then quickly look at a stationary object nearby. Does the object seem to expand or shrink?

2 TWIST THE pen so that the cotton winds neatly around the barrel, pulling the pen towards the nail, but without marking the disc. Then make a spiral with the pen, by drawing in a circular motion as the string unwinds. Keep the string taut as it unravels.

Moving circles

 Adult help is advised for this experiment

When you look at close-set circles, their lines become confused and your brain may imagine spinning motions that do not exist.

YOU WILL NEED
●card ●scissors ●felt-tipped pen ●compasses ●pencil ●ruler

1 WITH COMPASSES and pen, draw 12 concentric dark circles on a card square at intervals of 5 mm (⅛ in), beginning with one 2.5 cm (1 in) in diameter. Repeat on another square.

2 ON A SMOOTH surface, move one of the squares in small circles. Your brain cannot follow the fast-changing positions of the lines, and the circles appear to rotate. Hold the squares next to each other and move one. Is there any effect on the other?

EXPERIMENT
Colours from black and white

Adult help is advised for this experiment

When microscopes were first invented, lens-makers had some problems. For example, a glass lens bends some colours in the light spectrum more than others. This produces coloured fringes around objects seen through the lens. A solution is to combine two or more lenses to correct the difference. The eye's own lens can produce similar effects, and sometimes we see colours that don't really exist.

YOU WILL NEED
● *cutting mat* ● *ruler* ● *glue* ● *white card disc 15 cm (6 in) in diameter* ● *protractor* ● *craft knife* ● *compasses* ● *black card semi-circle to match the white card disc* ● *sharpened pencil* ● *thick, black felt-tipped pen* ● *eraser*

1 DRAW A LINE through the centre of the white card disc. With protractor and pencil, divide half of the disc into four 45° segments. Dab some glue on to the black semi-circle, and stick it to the other half of the white disc.

2 DRAW THREE arcs, 5 mm (³/₁₆ in) apart, in one segment. Begin 1.5 cm (½ in) from the centre. Draw three more in the next segment – the same distance apart. Begin 5 mm (³/₁₆ in) further out.

4 PUSH THE pencil through the disc, so that about 2.5 cm (1 in) sticks out below. Spin the pencil. What do you see? The black arcs are all different lengths, so each one spends slightly more or less time in your vision than its neighbour. With each revolution the arcs are replaced by the black semi-circle. The combined effect is that coloured edges appear as the arcs pass by the eye's lens, although the disc is only black and white. What happens if you spin the pencil at different speeds?

3 REPEAT TO make four sets of three arcs in pencil. Carefully draw over each one of the pencil arcs with the felt-tipped pen, as shown. Now erase the pencil marks from the disc.

EXPERIMENT
Thiéry's figure

Adult help is advised for this experiment

To understand an object's shape we use clues such as surface shadows. If there are no shadows, a structure can seem ambiguous – that is, you can interpret it in different ways. One such structure is called a Thiéry's figure. You can make one yourself.

YOU WILL NEED
● *card* ● *scissors* ● *adhesive tape* ● *protractor*

120° angle

60° angle

1 CUT OUT a cross with four arms, as above. The cross is made of five diamonds, each with 60° and 120° angles, and sides of 5 cm (2 in) each.

Centre surface

Arms folded forward

Arms folded backward

2 FOLD TWO arms forward, and tape together. Fold the other two arms backward, and tape these too. (Stick tape to one side of the figure only.)

3 POSITION THE figure, untaped side forward, in dim light that comes from several directions. Does the centre surface seem to slope toward or away from you? Can you turn the figure inside out in your mind?

The ears and hearing

Have you ever been in a truly silent place? Even in the quietest countryside, there are still sounds, such as wind, singing birds, and buzzing insects. Sound travels as invisible waves through the air. Your ears are specially designed to detect sound waves, turn them into nerve signals, and send these nerve signals to the brain, which analyses them and identifies the sound.

The ear flaps (pinnae) on the sides of your head are the most obvious, but least intricate, parts of your hearing system. Each ear flap funnels sounds along a small tube, the ear canal, to the hidden parts of the ear inside your head. These delicate inner parts – the eardrum, tiny ear bones called ossicles, and the cochlea – are contained in an area about the size of your thumb's tip, just behind each eye. Some animal ears are more sensitive than ours to certain sounds. For example, we cannot hear the deep, low-pitched rumbles that an elephant detects, or the high-pitched squeaks that dogs and bats can hear.

EXPERIMENT
Make a model ear

 Adult help is advised for this experiment

Sound waves consist of vibrations of the gas molecules in the air. You cannot see them, because the gas molecules are too small. But you can "see" sound waves by converting the invisible vibrations of molecules in the air into visible vibrations, in the form of ripples in a fluid. This is exactly what happens in the ear (below). In this model ear the large, flexible, cling film surface acts as the eardrum. When you make sound waves, it vibrates and makes the straw rock to and fro very fast. The straw works like the ossicles (ear bones). Attached to a table-tennis ball, it makes ripples in the water in the bowl, which represents the fluid in the cochlea. Try sounds of different pitch (highness or lowness), like a high squeak or a low growl. Do the the ripples change in size or number?

■ Inside the ear

Sound waves pass along the ear canal to the eardrum, a piece of thin skin about the size of your little finger's nail. The waves make the eardrum vibrate. The vibrations pass along a chain of three tiny bones, the ear ossicles, which bridge a small air space called the middle ear cavity. The ossicles then transfer the vibrations into the fluid that fills the coiled, snail-shaped cochlea. As the vibrations ripple through fluid in the three chambers inside the cochlea, they shake a delicate membrane that runs along its whole length. Attached to the membrane are microscopic hairs, embedded in hair cells. When the membrane shakes, it pulls the hairs and causes the hair cells to make nerve signals, which pass to the hearing centres of the brain (p.117). The part of the cochlea containing the hairs and hair cells is called the organ of Corti.

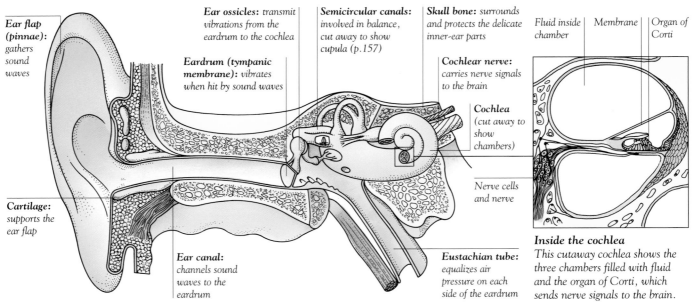

Ear flap (pinnae): gathers sound waves

Cartilage: supports the ear flap

Ear canal: channels sound waves to the eardrum

Ear ossicles: transmit vibrations from the eardrum to the cochlea

Eardrum (tympanic membrane): vibrates when hit by sound waves

Semicircular canals: involved in balance, cut away to show cupula (p.157)

Skull bone: surrounds and protects the delicate inner-ear parts

Cochlear nerve: carries nerve signals to the brain

Cochlea (cut away to show chambers)

Nerve cells and nerve

Eustachian tube: equalizes air pressure on each side of the eardrum

Fluid inside chamber | Membrane | Organ of Corti

Inside the cochlea
This cutaway cochlea shows the three chambers filled with fluid and the organ of Corti, which sends nerve signals to the brain.

1 DRAW A RECTANGLE with two slits on the thick card. Then draw around half of the cake tin, as shown. Carefully cut out the shape you have drawn. Now do this again.

2 CUT OUT TWO rectangles of card, each with two slits at either end of the top edges. Join all of the card pieces at the slits. This is the stand that the "ear" rests on.

YOU WILL NEED

● *pen* ● *elastic band* ● *craft knife* ● *double-sided adhesive tape* ● *glue*
● *table-tennis ball* ● *bendable drinking straw* ● *metal ruler* ● *cutting mat*
● *thin card* ● *cling film* ● *glass bowl* ● *water* ● *detachable cake tin sides*
● *thick card* ● *card with a grid of squares drawn on it*

Flap

3 PUT A LARGE piece of cling film over one end of the tin. Hold it in place with the elastic band, and make sure that it is stretched tight.

4 CUT A LARGE triangle of thin card, with a flap along half of the long edge. Fold the triangle in two. Dab glue on the flap.

Split straw end

Card triangle

Click your fingers, clap, shout, and make other noises to make the cling film vibrate like an eardrum and create ripples in the water

5 GLUE ONE END of the straw to the inside of the triangle. Split the other end of the straw. Use double-sided adhesive tape to attach this split end to the ball, and also to attach the triangle to the cling film. Make sure the end of the straw is at the centre of the circle.

6 PLACE THE TIN on its stand, so the ball just dips into water in the bowl. Put the grid card below the bowl to make it easier to see ripples in the water. Now make lots of different sounds behind the drum, and watch the water's surface. Do different sounds make different ripples?

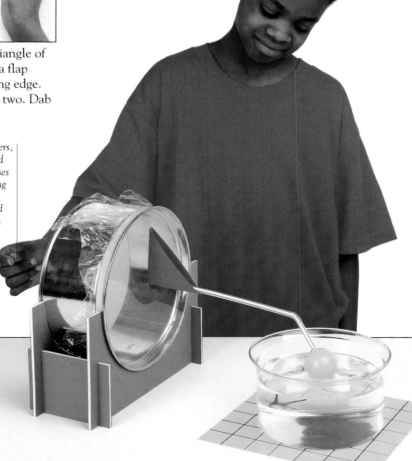

Judging sounds

EVEN UNDER WATER you can hear certain sounds – noises from above and sounds from within the water. This is because sounds travel not only through air but also as vibrations through liquids and solids. In fact this happens in the bones and fluid inside your own ears (p.152). When you speak, sound vibrations from your larynx (p.71) travel to your ears both through the air and through bones and body fluids in your neck and head. This alters the quality of the sound, which is why your voice seems different when you hear it on a tape recording compared with when you speak. Sound waves also take time to travel. The split-second difference between a sound reaching one ear and then the other helps you to judge where it comes from.

■ An unfamiliar voice

Make a recording of your own voice and listen to it carefully. You may find that your voice sounds unfamiliar, because you detect the recording's vibrations only through the air, not through your neck and head too, as when you hear your own speech.

EXPERIMENT
Hearing through solids

Adult help is advised for this experiment

The medium (substance) through which sounds pass can have startling effects on what they sound like to you. Sounds travel through the air at 343 metres per second (1,125 feet per second), but through water they travel over four times faster, and through steel almost 15 times faster! Although sounds travel quickly through liquids and solids, many liquids and solids do not convey the full range of a sound's high and low notes, compared to air. This is why sounds coming through water or solids sometimes seem muffled or strange. In this experiment you can investigate how sound waves carried by different materials are different from one another.

When your friend taps the spoon, sound waves travel up the string into your ears, with surprising results!

YOU WILL NEED
● *about 1 m (3 ft) of string (kite string works well)* ● *modelling clay*
● *two metal spoons*

1 TIE ONE spoon handle to the string, halfway along the string's length. Press a blob of clay on to the string on the spoon to secure it. Wind one end of the string around one of your forefingers, then the other end around the other forefinger. Make sure the two lengths of string are equal. Now lean forward, so that string and spoon hang freely.

2 PLACE YOUR FOREFINGERS lightly on the entrance to each ear. Ask a friend to tap one spoon gently with the other. What kind of sound do you hear? What happens when you use wool, wire, or elastic bands instead of string?

EXPERIMENT
Judging the direction of sound

When sound waves arrive at one side of your head, they reach one of your ears slightly before the other. Your ears and brain detect this time difference, so you know the sound's direction.

YOU WILL NEED
● *blindfold* ● *chair*

EXPERIMENT
Sound mix-up

If a sound comes from directly in front, above, or behind you, it is difficult to work out its direction. This is because the sound waves reach both of your ears at the same time.

Clicking fingers
Sit blindfolded. Ask a friend to click his or her fingers above, behind, or in front of you, but always in line with the centre of your body. Can you point to the sound source each time?

Pointing out the sound source
Get your friends to sit in a circle around someone who is blindfolded, so that he or she cannot see the sound source. In a random order, each person should click his or her fingers. The blindfolded person points to where he or she thinks the sound comes from. In which parts of the circle are the guesses most accurate?

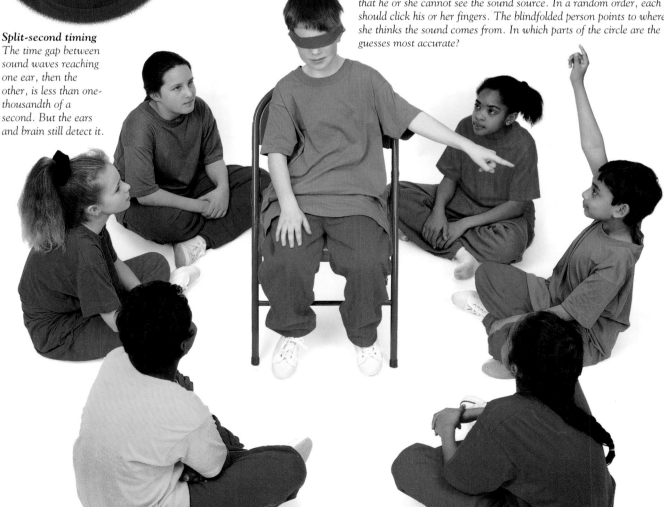

Split-second timing
The time gap between sound waves reaching one ear, then the other, is less than one-thousandth of a second. But the ears and brain still detect it.

Balance

IF ANIMALS SUCH AS DOGS OR CATS try to walk on their back legs, their unsteady movements show how difficult this is for them. Yet you walk on two legs almost without thinking. Your ability to balance is not a single sense, like eyesight. It is a continuous process, by which your brain receives information from sensory parts all over your body. These parts, described on other pages, include the semicircular canals and other parts of your inner ears, stretch detectors in your muscles and tendons, pressure sensors in your skin, and your eyes, which provide important visual information. Your brain builds up a picture of your body's position and posture in relation to the downward force of gravity. It constantly sends signals to your muscles to adjust the positions of your head, torso (trunk), and limbs.

■ Any way is up

High in space, the force of the Earth's gravity fades to almost nothing. Astronauts and anything in a spaceship that is not fixed down float about, weightless. There is no up or down. Conflicting signals coming from the inner ears, eyes, skin, muscles, joints, and other body parts confuse the body's balance process. Some astronauts feel dizzy and even nauseated for a time, a problem known as space sickness. This is similar to the motion sickness that you may feel in a car or boat.

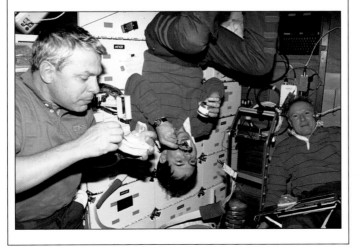

■ Keeping upright

Stand on one leg and tie your shoelace. Do you find it difficult? It will be at first, although you can probably do it with practice. Take note of how your body continually sways almost off balance. The different parts of the balance mechanism (below) send a constant stream of signals to your brain. Your brain assesses your body's position every split-second and tells your muscles to pull your weight back into a steady position. After standing on one leg for a time, the muscles in that calf and foot may begin to ache, because they each have to work harder than when you stand on two legs.

Ampullae (opposite) sense the position and motion of the head

Eyes report the position of the head in relation to walls, floors, and other visual clues

Stretch sensors in muscles, tendons, and joints send messages to the brain about the positions of the neck, torso, and limbs

Skin on the soles of the feet detects pressure as the body tilts from side to side and sways to the front or back

■ Motion detectors

Deep inside each ear (p.152) are three liquid-filled, C-shaped tubes called semicircular canals. As you move your head, the liquid lags behind the wall of each canal, in the same way that, when you turn a cup of water, the water moves more slowly than the side of the cup. The liquid bends a jelly-like blob, called the cupula, in the bulge known as the ampulla, at one end of the canal. This bending moves hairs embedded in the cupula. These are rooted in nerve cells, which send signals to the brain as the hairs move. All of the canals respond to most head movements, but each of them is also especially suited to one particular type of movement.

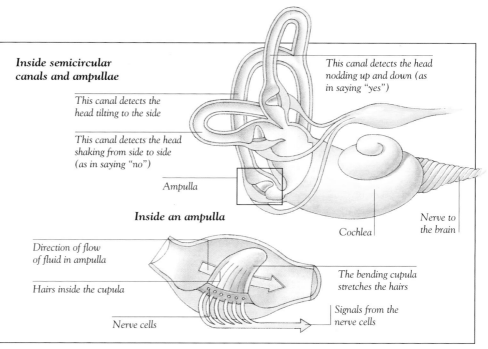

Inside semicircular canals and ampullae

This canal detects the head tilting to the side

This canal detects the head shaking from side to side (as in saying "no")

This canal detects the head nodding up and down (as in saying "yes")

Ampulla

Cochlea

Nerve to the brain

Inside an ampulla

Direction of flow of fluid in ampulla

Hairs inside the cupula

Nerve cells

The bending cupula stretches the hairs

Signals from the nerve cells

EXPERIMENT
Losing balance

Adult help is advised for this experiment

If you take away one part of the balance system, then another, and another, it becomes more and more difficult to carry out even simple tasks, such as standing up straight! In your bare feet, try the four steps shown here. Be sure an adult stands nearby, ready to catch you if you fall.

YOU WILL NEED
● *a safe place with no obstructions and a soft floor, such as a thick carpet, soft grass, or sand*
● *cushion* ● *blindfold*

1 STAND ON the cushion. This "blurs" information from the pressure sensors in the skin of the soles of your feet.

4 HOLD YOUR arms by your sides. Now you cannot swing your arms to correct yourself as you sway around. How easy is it to stand upright now?

2 STAND ON one foot. Now you have only half of the pressure information from the skin sensors in your feet.

3 ASK AN adult to blindfold you. Now you can no longer see objects and use them to judge if you are upright.

The nose and smell

YOUR NOSE IS THE MAIN AIRWAY for your respiratory system (pp.72–73). It is also an important sense organ. For example, it enables you to identify smells, such as smoke, that indicate danger. Inside your nose (p.183) is the olfactory epithelium – a postage-stamp-sized patch of nerve cells that have hairy projections. The projections are covered with receptors sensitive to odour molecules in the air. There are probably at least 10 million receptors in your nose – of at least 20 different types. Each type senses a different range of smell molecules. When the receptors detect an odour, they send nerve signals along the olfactory (smell) nerve to the smell centre in the brain (p.117). This analyses the signal pattern and identifies the smell.

Telling by smell

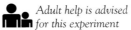 *Adult help is advised for this experiment*

Your sense of smell works closely with your sense of taste (p.160) to give you information about the foods and drinks you consume. You also identify foods by sight. When you look at something to eat, you often get a good idea of how it will taste. This experiment shows how difficult it can be to identify foods and other smelly substances by smell alone – without the help of taste or sight. Other smells, however, will be very familiar to you. Which smells are easy to identify?

Smell alone
Carefully cut the substances – the cut surfaces will give off fresh odours. Put them on saucers, and cover them with the glasses, so that the odours do not form a confusing mixture in the air. For each substance, remove the glass and hold the saucer while a blindfolded friend (who has not seen the substance) tries to tell by smell what it is. Are foods easier to identify than non-foods?

YOU WILL NEED
- cutting board ● blindfold
- kitchen knife ● 6 saucers
- everyday substances with odours, such as wax candle, lemon, chocolate, soap, apple, and potato
- 6 glasses

Lift the cover when smelling the substance

The glass keeps the odour concentrated and pure

EXPERIMENT
The smell threshold

There are smells in the air all around us. But most are too weak for the human nose to detect. There must be more than a certain number of odour molecules in a specific volume of air before you can sense an odour. This number is called the smell threshold concentration. You can test a friend to find out what the smell threshold is for vanilla essence and other familiar substances. At each stage of the experiment, air the room.

YOU WILL NEED
● *dropper* ● *substance with a characteristic odour, such as vanilla essence (you can try others, too, such as banana flavouring or strawberry essence)* ● *6 glasses* ● *card circles to cover the tops of the glasses* ● *large jug of water*

1 PUT 10 DROPS of vanilla essence into the jug of water. (The water in these photographs has been coloured so you can see the concentrations.)

2 FILL A GLASS with the solution. This is the strongest concentration. Cover the glass with a card circle. Half empty the jug, then fill it up again with water.

3 THE JUG NOW has half-strength vanilla. Pour this into another glass. Repeat Step 2 until you have six glasses, with lower and lower concentrations.

■ A trained nose

A person with a "trained ear" can pick out instruments in an orchestra. In the same way, learning to identify certain odours is called having a "trained nose". In fact, when you identify something by smell, it is not your nose you have trained, but your brain's ability to remember smells.

Blending smells
This perfume expert blends scents to make a new product. Winemakers, chefs, and many others need similar smelling skills.

4 ASK A FRIEND to smell the weakest solution. Can he or she identify it? The friend should try the next strongest, and so on, until the odour is identified – then take a breath of fresh air. Next, ask the friend to smell the solutions from strongest to weakest. Is the threshold at which the odour disappears the same as the one at which it appeared when smelling from weak to strong?

Keep the glasses covered to retain the odours

The tongue and taste

YOUR SENSE OF TASTE is governed by several thousand microscopic, onion-shaped clusters of cells called taste buds, scattered mainly over the surface of your tongue. The taste buds detect four basic flavours, using flavour sensors on the surfaces of their cells, similar to the odour receptors in the nose (p.158). The four flavours are sweet, sour, salty, and bitter. The substances in food that carry flavours must be dissolved in saliva before they can seep down into the taste buds. This is why you can taste dry foods, such as crackers, only after chewing them. The taste buds send nerve signals to your brain's gustatory (taste) centre (p.117). This analyses the signal pattern, so you can identify the taste.

Taste alone

Peel and cut the foods into cubes of equal size, to remove identifying clues such as their shape or skin texture. Ask a friend to be the taster and to wear the blindfold and noseclip, so that he or she cannot see or smell the food. Using the toothpick, rub a food cube on the taster's tongue for five seconds. Can the taster identify the food? Ask the taster to rinse his or her mouth out with water. Then try the other foods. When you have finished testing with each food, repeat the process, but without the taster wearing the noseclip. Is it easier to identify the foods?

EXPERIMENT

Telling by taste

 Adult help is advised for this experiment

Much of what we think of as "taste" is a combination of the taste sense and other senses, such as temperature and texture sensations in the mouth, smell, and even sight (p.162). Find out which foods you can identify using your taste buds alone.

YOU WILL NEED

● *cutting mat* ● *toothpicks* ● *kitchen knife* ● *water*
● *noseclip* ● *blindfold* ● *saucers of foods such as apple, potato, lemon, onion, cheese, chocolate*

Tongue, papillae, and taste buds

Look at your tongue in a mirror. Most of its upper surface is roughened by projections of various shapes, called papillae. These help to grip food and move it as you chew. At the front of the tongue you can see two types of papillae. The larger ones are fungiform papillae and the tiny hair-like ones are filiform papillae. At the back of the tongue are 8 to 12 large, rounded papillae called vallate papillae. Most of our taste buds are sited in tiny pores between and on the papillae.

The tongue surface
The electron microscope shows frilly filiform papillae and larger fungiform papillae.

Close-up of papillae
Greater magnification reveals thin, cone-shaped filiform papillae among rounded fungiform ones.

Taste bud
An even closer view shows the opening to a taste bud, set into the surface of a papilla.

Super-mobile muscles

The underside of the tongue is rooted at the back to the bones and muscles of the throat. But the main body of the tongue is extremely mobile and flexible. It consists mainly of eight interwoven muscles within the tongue itself, and another eight muscles that join the tongue to the surrounding parts. These muscles can contract in various combinations to give the tongue a huge variety of shapes. Tongue flexibility is important for eating and essential for speech.

The "th" sound
Watch your tongue in the mirror and feel the different shapes it makes as you speak. For example, to make a "th" sound (above) it comes forward between the teeth.

EXPERIMENT
How one taste masks another

Some flavours are so strong that even when they are present in small amounts, they mask or block out other flavours. However, the other, weaker flavours do not disappear completely. This experiment shows how salt masks out an equally strong second flavour, sugar. But, as you taste solutions of sugar that become increasingly strong, you may be able to detect that another flavour is present.

YOU WILL NEED
- *saucer of table salt*
- *saucer of sugar*
- *4 glasses of fresh water*
- *2 teaspoons*

You may need to adjust the concentrations of the salt and sugar in this experiment, to suit the different taste thresholds of different friends

1 STIR HALF A TEASPOON of salt into each glass of water. Stir sugar into all four glasses, putting half a teaspoon in the first, one in the second, one and a half in the third, and two in the fourth.

2 ASK A FRIEND TO SIP the solutions, beginning with the weakest. In which one can he or she taste a second flavour behind the salt? In which one can he or she identify it as sugar?

Taste expectations

THE TASTE BUDS ON THE TONGUE and the taste centres of the brain (p.117) work together to tell you the flavours of the foods you eat. You also use sensors in the mouth and gums, similar to those involved in the sense of touch (p.164), to detect the hardness, temperature, and consistency of food as you chew. However, what you think you taste when you put food in your mouth also depends a lot on your own likes and dislikes. You are born with some of your taste preferences (opposite), but many other preferences can be accumulated over years of experience and memory. For instance, you may enjoy certain foods because you associate them with happy events from the past. The colour and texture of a food, and its strength of flavour, also influence whether you like its taste.

(p.117)

(p.164)

EXPERIMENT

Fading flavours

When you first taste a flavour, it may seem very strong. But after continually tasting the same flavour over a few minutes, it seems to become weaker and you notice it less. This is known as habituation, and it also occurs with other senses such as smell and touch. You can demonstrate habituation of taste with solutions of sugar of two different strengths.

Weak sugar solution

Strong sugar solution

YOU WILL NEED
● 2 glasses of water ● white or brown sugar ● teaspoon

Diminishing flavour
Stir half a teaspoon of sugar into one glass and three teaspoons into the other. (The water has been coloured here for clarity.) Sip the weaker solution, and note how strong the flavour seems. Now sip the stronger solution eight to ten times, then go back to sip the weaker one again. Does it taste as strong as it did the first time you tasted it?

▇ An appetizing sight?

Usually, we look at something before we taste it. This is important because we can check with our eyes that the food is edible and has not gone bad. The sight of food also has a strong effect on what we expect it to taste like. Children often do not want to eat certain foods because of the way they look – perhaps they look slimy, or are strange shapes or colours. This attitude may have evolved in prehistoric times, as a way of self-protection, when humans had to hunt and forage for food. It would have made them suspicious of unfamiliar foods, until they were sure these were safe to eat. However, in the modern world, most foods are specially grown and prepared. There is no excuse for not eating your vegetables!

Colour confusion
There is something very strange about this meal of chicken, baby sweet-corn, courgettes (zucchini), and rice! Each food is the wrong colour. The chicken is green, the baby sweet-corn is brown, the courgettes (zucchini) are red, and the rice is blue. In fact, the foods are coloured with safe, flavour-free food dyes and taste perfectly normal. But would you eat them? What food looks like has a strong influence on how you think it will taste.

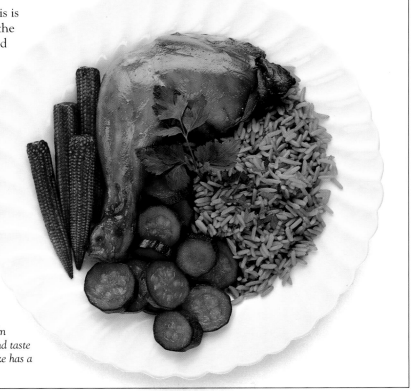

■ Likes and dislikes

What we eat depends on many factors, such as cultural tradition, food prices, and what we need for a balanced diet. But sometimes people – particularly young children – do not think about these factors. They eat what they want to. Generally, children prefer sweet flavours. Which of the foods below are your favourites? How about your friends? Do you think that you have chosen the most nutritional ones?

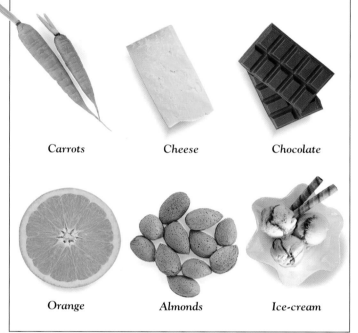

Carrots   Cheese   Chocolate

Orange   Almonds   Ice-cream

A lemon-flavoured potato

 Adult help is advised for this experiment

In the food we eat, there are many clues to tell us what the food is. But you can confuse the brain by combining the flavour of one food with the texture of another.

YOU WILL NEED
● small cube of potato
● lemon juice ● toothpick

Taste confusion
Soak the potato in lemon juice for ten minutes. Put it on a toothpick, and give it to a friend to eat. Make sure your friend's eyes are closed, so that he or she cannot see the food. Does your friend identify the food as potato or lemon? The brain receives conflicting information from different sensors, making it difficult to identify the food.

_____EXPERIMENT_____
Flavours and concentrations

Each of us has our own favourite flavours. But the strength or concentration of a flavour also has an effect on how much we like it. Some flavours are pleasant if they are weak, but become less so as they get stronger, while other flavours tend to taste better when they are stronger. You can study how the strength of a flavour affects how much you like it, by using the contrasting flavours of salt and sugar. When you do the experiment, make sure you do not take more than a small sip of each solution. (Do not drink all of the solution or you will feel sick.) Ask friends to try the experiment too. Do you find that most people have similar preferences? Do older and younger people have different preferences?

YOU WILL NEED
● *4 glasses of water* ● *sugar* ● *table salt* ● *teaspoons*

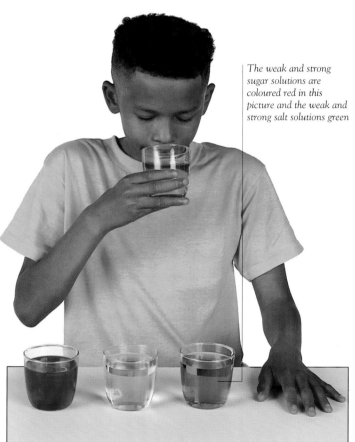

The weak and strong sugar solutions are coloured red in this picture and the weak and strong salt solutions green

Sweet and salty
Stir half a teaspoonful of sugar into one glass and three teaspoonfuls into another. Do the same with the salt, stirring half a teaspoonful into the third glass, and three teaspoonfuls into the fourth. Sip the weaker sugar solution first. Then try the stronger one. Rinse your mouth with fresh water, then taste the salt solutions in the same order. Which do you like most and which least? Most people prefer stronger sweet flavours and weaker salty ones.

Touch

YOUR SENSE OF TOUCH allows you to feel incredibly light sensations, such as a fly on your hand, as well as very heavy ones, such as a weight dropped on your foot. The sensation of touch comes from millions of microscopic touch sensors scattered all over the skin. In some places, such as the fingertips, the sensors are close together, so these parts are very sensitive. In other places, such as the back, the sensors are quite far apart. When the sensors are pressed, vibrated, or stimulated by heat or cold, they generate nerve signals that flash to the brain (p.117).

EXPERIMENT
Fading touch

If you are wearing socks, can you feel how high they are on your legs, without looking? Perhaps not. You did feel the socks when you first put them on, but the feeling soon fades. This fading is called habituation. It also happens with smell (pp.158–159) and taste (pp.160–163). Habituation dulls your senses to a continuing stimulus. You become aware of something only when it changes.

Forgotten feeling
With eyes closed, can you point exactly to the tops of your socks?

■ Types of touch sensor

The microscopic sensors in the skin are at the ends of nerves. The sensors are specially designed to convert physical sensations into tiny electrical nerve signals. Although we may think of touch as a single sense, there are a number of different types of touch sensor, each of which delivers a different pattern of nerve signals. The different sensors give us a wide variety of information about objects, such as their hardness, wetness, and surface texture.

Epidermis | *Dermis* | *Meissner's ending* | *Free nerve ending*

Pacini's ending | *Ruffini's ending* | *Merkel's ending*

Kinds of stimulation
Each type of touch sensor responds to several kinds of stimulation. But the sensors do have specialized jobs. The deeply set Pacini's endings react mainly to heavy pressure. Merkel's endings respond best to medium pressure. Meissner's endings respond well to light pressure and small, fast vibrations. Ruffini's endings sense changes in temperature and pressure. When free nerve endings are activated, you feel pain.

Slide guide | *Triangle marker* | *Slide-retaining strip*

Handle | *Slide*

Clip-holder

Bent end of paper-clip

Bent end of paper-clip

Base

Putting the touch gauge together
Use thick, stiff card to make the gauge. When you tape or glue the slide guides to the base, make sure that the slide can move backward and forward between them. Tape the two paper-clips to the edges of the base and clip-holder so that the straightened vertical ends are touching each other.

EXPERIMENT
A touch map

Adult help is advised for this experiment

To feel the surface texture of something, you probably use your fingertips, rather than the back of your hand or your forearm. The fingertips are extremely sensitive to light touch, due to closely packed microscopic skin sensors. Investigate the sensitivity to light touch of different parts of the body by making a touch gauge. Create a touch-sensitivity "map", by sketching a rough outline of a body and marking your results on it.

YOU WILL NEED

● *blindfold* ● *scissors* ● *2 paper-clips* ● *for the slide-retaining strips: 2 pieces of card 6 cm x 0.5 cm (2¹/₂ in x ¹/₄ in)* ● *for the handle: 2 pieces of card 4 cm x 1 cm (1¹/₂ in x ¹/₂ in), glued one on top of the other* ● *for the clip-holder: card square of sides 4 cm (1¹/₂ in)* ● *for the slide guides: 2 pieces of card 20 cm x 1 cm (8 in x ¹/₂ in)* ● *for the slide: card 24 cm x 4 cm (9¹/₂ in x 1¹/₂ in)* ● *for the base: card 20 cm x 6 cm (8 in x 2¹/₂ in)* ● *2 triangles of card about 1 cm (¹/₂ in) tall* ● *cutting mat* ● *metal cutting edge* ● *ruler* ● *craft knife* ● *adhesive tape* ● *double-sided tape, or glue* ● *notepad* ● *pen*

1 STICK THE TWO triangles to the slide guides, 1 cm (¹/₂ in) from the end, with double-sided tape or glue. Tape the guides to the base, with enough room to fit the slide between them.

3 PLACE THE SLIDE between its guides, with the scale facing upward, and the paper triangles pointing to zero on the scale you have drawn. Turn over the gauge. Straighten out half of each paper-clip, and bend it up at a right angle. Tape one bent paper-clip end to the edge of the clip-holder and the other to the base, so that the straight ends of the clips stick up vertically, touching each other.

2 DRAW A SCALE 15 cm (6 in) long – with divisions of 0.5 cm (¹/₄ in) – on the slide, starting 5 cm (2 in) from one end. Tape the clip-holder to the same end of the slide, on the reverse side.

4 TAPE THE slide-retaining strips across each end of the upper side of the gauge, so that they hold the slide to the base, but allow it to move. Then tape the handle to the slide at the opposite end of the scale to zero. Check that the slide moves freely in the guides, and that when zero on the scale aligns with the triangles, the points of the paper-clips are exactly together.

5 YOU CAN READ the gap between the paper-clip points on the scale of the touch gauge. Ask a friend to wear a blindfold. Begin with the maximum gap between the paper-clip points. Press both points lightly on the outside of the forearm, making sure they touch the skin at exactly the same time. Your friend then tells you whether he or she feels two points or one. If the answer is two, reduce the gap slightly, and try again. Repeat until your friend can feel one point only. When this happens, read the gauge and note the gap between the two points. This gives an indication of the distance between touch sensors at the site. Repeat the whole process for other skin sites, such as the upper arm, wrist, and finger. Which parts of the body are most sensitive, with the greatest concentration of touch sensors?

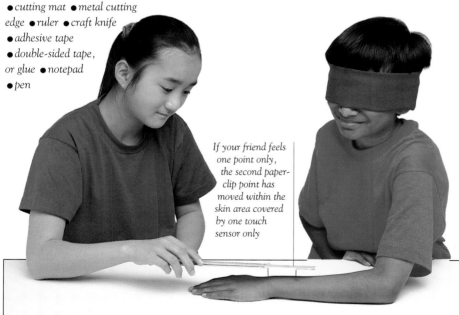

If your friend feels one point only, the second paper-clip point has moved within the skin area covered by one touch sensor only

The touch picture

YOUR SENSE OF TOUCH is a more complicated sense than it might seem. Think of the difference between feeling a warm cat and a cold lump of ice. The different microscopic sensors (p.164) in your skin respond to different stimulations, such as changes in temperature, light touch, or heavy pressure. They send complex patterns of nerve signals to your brain. Your brain assembles an overall "touch picture" from these nerve signal patterns. You describe different aspects of this touch picture with words such as "cold" and "warm", "soft" and "hard", "rough" and "smooth", "dry" and "moist". To learn more about the things that you touch, you use the information from other senses, particularly sight. Imagine how you would hesitate before touching an object that you knew nothing about. You would be sensible to do this – it might be burning hot!

Telling by touch

 Adult help is advised for this experiment

Focus on the sense of touch by blocking out other senses that usually accompany it. Use a noseclip and blindfold to block out smell and sight. Then feel various everyday things to find out whether you can identify them by touch alone.

YOU WILL NEED
● *cutting mat* ● *small kitchen knife* ● *noseclip* ● *blindfold* ● *saucers* ● *samples of everyday substances, such as candle wax, denim, coffee, soap, leather, and sugar*

Touch alone
Put the noseclip and blindfold on a friend. Hold up the samples of different substances one at a time for your friend to feel and identify. The shapes and surface coverings of some larger items would give extra clues, so cut these into small, similar-shaped chunks for the experiment. How many samples can your friend identify? Ask him or her to describe the sensations encountered, such as hardness, wetness, and slipperiness. Repeat the experiment with other friends. Which samples do they all find particularly easy or difficult to identify?

EXPERIMENT
Reading by touch

Adult help is advised for this experiment

Fingertips are very sensitive to touch. You can use them to "read" numbers or letters made of map pins stuck into cork tiles.

YOU WILL NEED
• *felt-tipped pen* • *plastic-headed map pins* • *blindfold* • *cork tiles*

1 USING MAP pins, you can make a system similar to the Braille system (below right) with its patterns of raised dots. Draw a large number or letter on each cork tile. Use simple shapes such as L, O, and 1, and also complex ones such as G, Q, and 4. Make all the figures the same size. Now push the pins into the numbers and letters to make their shapes. Do not push the pin points right through the cork tiles.

2 BLINDFOLD A FRIEND and hand him or her the cork squares, one at a time. Ask your friend to feel the pattern of pinheads, and see if he or she can read each letter or number. Which ones are easiest? Does your friend get quicker and more accurate with practice? What happens if you hand over the letter or number upside-down?

EXPERIMENT
Blurring the sense of touch

When you look through a window with frost on it, what you see is indistinct. Thick gloves create a similar effect for the sense of touch. Wearing gloves makes it more difficult to feel and identify objects. But there are clues that you can still use, even when blindfolded – such as weight, shape, and hardness.

YOU WILL NEED
• *padded or woollen gloves*
• *similar-shaped objects, such as a tomato, walnut, golf-ball, potato, and table-tennis ball*

Dulled sensations
Blindfold a friend. Ask him or her to put the gloves on. Pass over a series of objects to feel and identify. Are soft things easier to name than hard ones? Does it help to smell or bounce the objects?

■ The Braille system

Braille is a reading system for visually handicapped people. Patterns of raised dots in groups of up to six (as on a domino) are felt by the fingers. Each pattern represents a number, a letter, or a group of letters. The method is named after its French inventor, Louis Braille (1809–1852), who lost his sight when he was three years old.

Two-handed reading
Braille is read by the sensitive fingertip skin. Usually, one hand reads the dots while the other hand feels ahead for the next line.

The BODY'S LIFE-CYCLE

Egg to baby
The human ovum (egg cell) is one of the largest cells in the body – it is just about visible to the naked eye. If a male's sperm cell enters the female's ovum, the egg is fertilized (a sperm is shown at the very point of entry, left), and it develops in the mother's womb. Nine months later, this tiny egg will be a living, breathing, crying new baby (above).

DURING ITS LIFE, THE BODY progresses through well-defined stages. A baby grows from a tiny egg, develops in the mother's womb, and enters the outside world at birth. He or she grows through infancy, childhood, puberty, and adolescence, and matures through the adult years. Finally, the only certain thing about life is that it will end. But the reproductive process brings about new human beings. Parents pass on the blueprint of human life to their babies in the form of genes. And a new cycle of life begins.

NEW LIFE AND GROWTH

THE STAGES OF LIFE for a human body are the same as for any type of mammal. They include the coming together of an egg cell and a sperm cell to create a new individual, formation of the main organs while an embryo in the womb, birth as a baby, rapid growth in infancy, and becoming sexually mature and able to produce offspring. Humans also have important life stages based on culture and tradition, such as the school years, parenthood, and retirement.

The cell is the basic unit of life. All living things – plant or animal – are made from cells (pp.24–25). The cell is also the unit of growth. The body grows as its cells divide in two. Each of these new cells enlarges to the size of the original cell and then divides again. Even in a fully grown adult, cell division occurs at an amazingly fast rate. New cells are needed constantly by the body to replace cells that have died or have worn away. For example, two million new red cells are made for the blood every second. The cell is also the unit of reproduction. Each human body starts out as a single cell, a fertilized egg. These eggs are each smaller than the full stop at the end of this sentence.

A baby soon learns to smile at a friendly face, especially that of the mother. Mother and baby recognize each other by smell – from a day or two after birth.

Mother and father

Ancient people realized that after a woman and man had sexual intercourse, a baby could be conceived. But their ideas about how this happens were mistaken. For example, Aristotle (384–322 BC) of Ancient Greece believed that the mother provided only the physical body of the child, which grew from the blood in her womb (uterus). He thought that the role of the father was to provide the "soul" that made the baby alive.

During the Renaissance, Leonardo da Vinci (1452–1519) made accurate drawings of how the baby develops in the mother's womb. Unfortunately, his drawings were lost for several centuries, so later researchers did not benefit from them.

Cells from cells

From the 1600s onwards, the microscopists turned their lenses on to the reproductive process. They discovered egg cells (p.180) and sperm cells (p.185), and saw how a sperm joins with an egg at fertilization (p.172).

Some scientists believed that new cells were made when chemicals gathered together in a body fluid and attracted more chemicals to them, gradually building up a whole cell. However, this theory depended on the false assumption that living organisms can form from chemicals – in other words, from non-living material. This idea was known as spontaneous generation. The work of scientists such as the Frenchman Louis Pasteur (1822–1895) showed that

Milk from the mother's mammary glands is the complete food for baby mammals, such as these piglets. It contains proteins for building up the body, sugars for energy, fats for both, and germ-fighting antibodies.

Inside a man's testes there are coiled tubes (p.23), shown in cross-section by this microscope photograph. Millions of sperm cells develop here, then pass into the centres of the tubes before they are released.

cells do not simply "appear" from non-living matter.

German scientist Rudolf Virchow (1821–1902) studied the process of disease at the level of cells and tissues. He supported the idea, now proved correct, that new cells were made by the division of existing cells. He coined the famous phrase: "Every cell from a cell".

Genetics

In 1865 an Austrian monk, Gregor Mendel (1822–1884), published his work on the breeding of garden peas. In his writings he explained the basic laws of heredity – how certain traits (features) are inherited by offspring from parents.

Many people believed at the time that the traits of each parent "blend" in their offspring. But Mendel found that, over the generations, certain traits of pea plants do not blend – they either appear or not. He realized instead that features seem to be inherited as units, which we now call genes (p.176). Sometimes they do not show in one generation, but reappear in the next. Mendel also realized that some traits are dominant, "overpowering" other traits. However his theories produced little interest until the 1900s, when Mendel's laws became the basis for the new science of genetics.

We now know that genes are in pairs, and that one member of the pair can be dominant over the other. In a simplified example, each person has a pair of genes that control eye-colour, one from each parent. If both genes are for brown eyes, the eyes are brown. If both are for blue eyes, the eyes are blue. But if a person has one gene for brown eyes and one for blue, the eyes are not blue-brown. The brown gene is dominant, so the eyes are brown. The ideas of genes and dominance are central to modern genetic research.

By the early 1900s, the process of cell division had been studied in great detail. We now know that there are in fact two types.

This set of quadruplets is unusual *because humans generally have only one baby at a time. These babies will have different characteristics, but they will retain a family likeness.*

■ Mitosis

For growth and maintenance of the body, the cells divide by mitosis (p.182). The pairs of genes in each cell, which are in the form of the chemical DNA (p.180), are packaged into structures called chromosomes inside the nucleus. In mitosis, the chromosomes duplicate themselves when the cell is ready to divide, making a second set of gene pairs. The two sets then separate, each moving to one end of the cell. The cell membrane (p.28) grows through the middle of the cell, splitting it in two. So two complete new cells, each with an identical full set of genes, are formed from one parent cell.

Do you grow in spurts? *Find out by regularly measuring how tall you are (p.175).*

■ Meiosis

The other type of cell division is meiosis (p.182). This process has major differences from mitosis. Meiosis produces egg and sperm cells only. There are not two offspring cells; there are four. And each offspring cell contains single genes, not pairs.

Egg cells are made in the woman's sex glands, called ovaries (p.23). Each month, one egg matures, as part of a cycle controlled by hormones (p.106). The mature egg is released from a small bag in the ovary called an ovarian follicle (Graafian follicle) and travels along a tube, the oviduct, toward the womb. If sperm have entered the oviduct as a result of sexual intercourse, fertilization may occur.

Sperm cells are made in the man's sex glands, called testes. These hang in a small sac of skin, the scrotum, below the abdomen. Millions of sperm are made every day. If they are not released they die, break up, and are re-absorbed into the body.

As a result of meiosis, each egg and sperm has a single set of genes. When they join together at fertilization, their sets combine. So each cell in the developing baby has the usual set of gene pairs. We inherit one gene of each pair from our mother and the other from our father. Inherited genes are the reason why we resemble our biological parents.

By choosing pairs of beans from *two jars you can find out the chances of inheriting certain body features, such as a particular eye or hair colour (p.177).*

■ Human growth

During the first two months in the womb, all of the baby's major parts and organs are formed (pp.172–173). After nine months the baby is born. In the processes of birth and early infancy, humans are typical of mammals. For example, the baby feeds on milk made in the mammary glands (after which the mammal group is named) in the mother's breasts. However, the human child soon shows the intelligence that sets us apart from other mammals – by talking, reading, and so on. The next major stage is puberty, which takes place during the teens, when the sexual organs become mature and start to function. After this stage, it is possible to become a parent, and begin the cycle of life once again.

Louis Pasteur worked in this laboratory. *Scientists such as Pasteur helped to show that life comes from previous life, and that spontaneous generation of new living things from non-living matter does not occur.*

Reproduction

THE PARTS OF THE BODY concerned with producing babies are together called the reproductive system (p.23). In a mammal such as a cat or horse, a male animal and female animal come together and mate (have sexual intercourse). A sperm cell from the testes of the male fertilizes an egg cell from the ovaries of the female – that is, they join together. After fertilization, the egg grows and develops into a new baby animal in an organ called a womb (uterus), which only female mammals possess. After a period called pregnancy, the baby leaves the womb through the birth canal and is born. Reproduction in humans follows this typical mammal pattern. The human pregnancy period is, on average, 38 weeks from fertilization to birth.

■ DISCOVERY ■
Antony van Leeuwenhoek

Antony van Leeuwenhoek (1632–1723), the "draper of Delft", was a Dutch textile merchant. He used magnifying lenses, which he made himself, to count the threads in pieces of cloth. His lenses were tiny – many were no bigger than a pea. Van Leeuwenhoek was not an expert on the human body. But he used his lenses to study all kinds of microscopic objects, and the range and accuracy of his observations were astounding. He was one of the first people to see microbes (microscopic organisms) such as bacteria. He studied the movement and size of red blood cells. And he was the first scientist to see and draw sperm cells (below).

■ Tiny bodies

In the 17th century, some scientists believed that the eggs (ova) of female animals, including humans, contained tiny versions of the parents, waiting to grow into babies. These scientists were called "ovists". After the discovery of male sperm cells, which were originally called spermatic animalcules, other scientists – known as "animalculists" – argued that the tiny beings were not in the eggs, but in the heads of the sperm. Later it was realized that in fact egg and sperm contribute equally to the conception of a baby (right).

Inside the sperm
Early microscopists made fanciful drawings of imaginary tiny bodies curled up inside the heads of sperm cells.

■ Fertilization

Sperm cells pass into a woman's body during sexual intercourse. They swim through her womb and into the oviducts (also called Fallopian tubes), which connect the ovaries to the womb. If a mature egg cell is released by one ovary at about this time, the sperm cells are attracted to it. One of the sperm cells penetrates the membrane, called the zona pellucida, that is wrapped around the egg cell. Then the genetic material of egg cell and sperm cell combine (p.171). This event is called fertilization.

Sperm cells
These tadpole-shaped cells, shown here through a light microscope, are very small (p.26). They swim by lashing their long tails.

Egg cell
The zona pellucida around an egg cell looks like a halo under a light microscope. After fertilization, the membrane thickens to keep out other sperm.

Ball of cells
The fertilized egg cell divides into two cells, then into four, and so on. This electron microscope view shows the ball-like 16-cell stage.

■ A baby's development

As the fertilized egg continues to divide, each of the cells in the ball becomes slightly smaller. Living on its stored reserves of yolk, the ball floats along the oviduct to the womb. About a week after fertilization, it burrows into the thick, blood-rich womb lining and begins to feed on nourishment provided by the lining. The cells multiply, becoming hundreds in number, then thousands.

As they multiply, the cells begin to differentiate – in other words they change into different types, such as nerve cells, muscle cells, and so on. Slowly the baby's body takes shape.

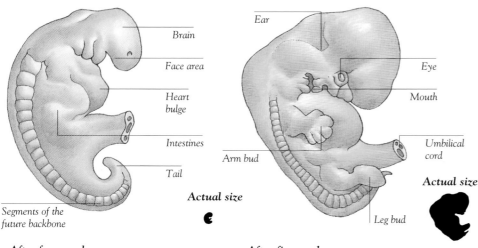

Brain

Face area

Heart bulge

Intestines

Tail

Segments of the future backbone

Actual size

Ear

Eye

Mouth

Arm bud

Umbilical cord

Leg bud

Actual size

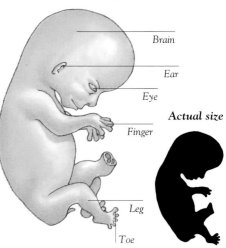

Brain

Ear

Eye

Finger

Actual size

Leg

Toe

Actual size

After four weeks
The future backbone forms a ridge. The baby has a tiny tail, and at this stage it is difficult to distinguish from other baby mammals.

After five weeks
The eye is recognizable, but the ear is slit-like. Limbs grow out of the trunk, and the tail shrinks away. At this stage the baby is called an embryo.

After eight weeks
From this age, the developing baby is called a foetus. It is only thumb-sized, yet all its main parts are formed, even fingers and toes.

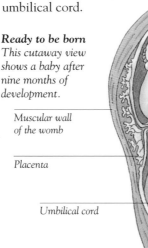
■ Nourishing the baby

Inside the womb, the baby floats in a pool of amniotic fluid. It cannot breathe air or eat food. Oxygen and nutrients pass to the baby from the mother's blood through the placenta, a disc-shaped organ in the womb wall. Blood flows between the baby and placenta along a flexible tube, the umbilical cord.

Bulging abdomen
The enlarging womb makes the mother's abdomen bulge.

Ready to be born
This cutaway view shows a baby after nine months of development.

Muscular wall of the womb

Placenta

Umbilical cord

Amniotic fluid

Amnion membrane (protective bag around the baby)

Cervix (neck of womb)

Birth canal

Growth and ageing

HAVE YOU WATCHED a young child learning to walk? He or she often topples over. This is partly because the brain, nerves, and muscles have not yet learned how to balance the body. It is also because the young child is "top-heavy". A baby has a very large head in relation to the body, compared with an adult. In the womb (p.173), the brain and head develop very early. By the time a child is about three years old, the brain and head are more than four-fifths fully grown, yet the body's bones and muscles are only about one-fifth of their adult size. In early childhood the body lengthens rapidly. From about nine or ten years, the arms, and then the legs, grow fastest – much more quickly than the torso. There is a rapid growth spurt just before and during puberty (p.171). The average person is physically fully developed by the age of 20 to 25. After 40 to 50 years, the changes of ageing become noticeable. The muscles become smaller, there is loss of height, and the skin develops lines and wrinkles.

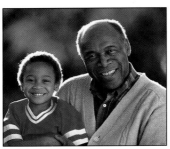

Different but the same
Often, many similarities can be seen in members of a family, even though the people may be at different stages of the ageing process.

EXPERIMENT
Growth rate

 Adult help is advised for this experiment

See how tall you are, and how fast you grow, by marking your height with a pen on a measuring pole (made from a length of wood or plastic). Do this at regular times – say, every four months. Your growth rate is the amount you have grown each year. Does it vary as you get older? Measure the growth rates for your family and friends too. Do people grow faster at certain ages? In particular, try to measure the growth rates of a baby, someone in their early teens, and an older person.

YOU WILL NEED
● pole 2 m (6½ ft) long ●pen ●paint-brush
● plastic pipe to slip over the pole ●strong glue
● paints ●ruler ●saw ●vice ●large set square

■ Changing proportions

In this series of photographs, the height of each person – from the new baby to the young adult of 20 years – has been adjusted so that he just fits into the panel. This makes all of the bodies exactly the same height. The photographs allow you to compare the body proportions and to see how they change with age. For example, the baby has a very large head, almost one-quarter of its total height. By adulthood, however, the head is only about one-eighth of the total height. Compare the legs and arms, too. The baby's legs make up roughly one-third of its total height. In a full-grown person they are almost half of the total height. Added to these general changes are many individual variations (pp.16–17). A person may have a relatively long body, or long legs, throughout his or her life.

2 months: 55 cm (1 ft 10 in)   *2 years: 86 cm (2 ft 10 in)*   *4 years: 110 cm (3 ft 8 in)*

1 ASK AN adult to saw the pipe, held in place by the vice, to the same length as the set square's shortest edge. Glue the pipe to this edge.

2 PAINT THE pole in stripes 30 cm (1 ft) wide, and allow the paint to dry. Slide the pipe on to the pole. Now measure your height. Stand upright next to the pole. Get a friend to slide the pipe down so that the set square rests on your head. The friend marks the pole below the pipe with a line and the date. To check your height, add up the number of whole stripes and measure the extra part of the last stripe with the ruler.

Changing faces

These details from self-portraits by the Dutch artist Rembrandt (1606–1669) show how he aged over a period of 40 years. Although facial features gradually change during life, we can still recognize the same person after many years from the face's overall shape, proportions, and expressions.

Age 23 (1629)

Age 31 (1637)

Age 44 (1650)

Age 63 (1669)

7 years: 120 cm
(4 ft)

12 years: 145 cm
(4 ft 10 in)

20 years: 175 cm
(5 ft 10 in)

Genes and inheritance

A COMPLICATED STRUCTURE such as a jetliner or a skyscraper must be built from a set of plans. The body also has "plans", called genes. These contain, in chemical code, all the instructions needed to build and run a body. There are about 100,000 different genes in each body cell. Each gene is a short section of a long molecule called DNA (p.179). DNA is packaged in chromosomes, arranged in pairs in the cell nucleus. However, sperm and egg cells contain not pairs of chromosomes, but single sets. This is due to meiosis (p.182). When a sperm fertilizes an egg, these single sets pair up in a new cell – which multiplies and develops into a baby.

■ Genes and chromosomes

Each body cell has 46 sets of gene-containing DNA molecules. The DNA molecules are coiled into 23 pairs of X-shaped structures called chromosomes in each cell nucleus.

Full set of chromosomes
There are 23 chromosome pairs. One chromosome of each pair comes from the mother, the other chromosome from the father.

Chromosomes in close-up
Each chromosome contains a thin DNA molecule, about 5 cm (2 in) long, coiled very tightly and protected by proteins called histones.

■ Family features

Every human body is unique, from its overall shape to its fingerprints. But most people resemble their biological parents, who are in turn like their parents, and so on. This is because offspring acquire parts of the genetic "body plan" from each parent. This is called inheritance. An example of a feature passed from one generation to the next is the "Habsburg jaw". Many of the Habsburgs, a European royal family, had a distinctive lower jaw and chin, as seen in these details from famous paintings.

Philip II, King of Spain
Philip II (1527–1598), here painted by Antonio Moro, shows the deep chinline that was characteristic of his family line.

Philip IV, King of Spain
Philip IV (1605–1665), the grandson of Philip II, here painted by Diego Velazquez, inherited the family jawline and slightly protruding lower lip.

The Infanta Margarita
Daughter of Philip IV, the Infanta Margarita (1651–1673), also painted by Velazquez, had very similar facial features to her great-grandfather Philip II.

■ DISCOVERY ■
Francis Crick and James Watson

In the 1940s individual genes were discovered to be sections of a chemical called DNA (deoxyribonucleic acid). In 1953 the Englishman Francis Crick (born 1916, left) and the American James Watson (born 1928, right) worked out the structure of a DNA molecule. It is like two corkscrew-shaped staircases, intertwined as a double-helix (p.179). Each "staircase" is twisted incredibly tightly. There are one million twists in a 3-mm (⅛-in) length of DNA. When a cell divides, the "staircases" separate, and each makes a mirror-image of itself. In this way genes are passed on as cells divide to form new body cells, or to produce sperm and egg cells.

EXPERIMENT
Chances of inheritance

Many of your body features are inherited in a complicated way, following instructions from many interacting genes. However, some features are inherited more simply, involving only one or a few genes. They include eye and hair colour, and the ability to roll the tongue into a U-shape. This experiment shows how genes from each parent can combine so that their offspring are bound to inherit some genes, but also how the offspring can inherit some genes by chance. In the experiment, genes are represented by beans and parents by containers. Any pair of beans in the parent container represents a gene pair. If the offspring has conflicting genes, such as one gene for blue eyes and one for brown – or one black bean and one red here – the body follows instructions in the dominant gene (p.171).

YOU WILL NEED
●notepad ●pen ●2 large containers ●at least 400 small objects of two different colours, such as dried red kidney beans and black beans

Keep your eyes closed to make sure that the choices are random

1 PUT BLACK beans in both containers. Take a bean from each to represent the offspring's gene pair. Repeat several times. Note the result.

2 PUT RED beans into one container and black ones into the other. Pick several pairs of beans, as in Step 1. Note the result.

3 COUNT EQUAL numbers of red and black beans into each container – say, 100 red and 100 black per container – and mix them well. With eyes closed, take one bean from each container and pair them. Repeat at least 50 times. What are the proportions of black-black, red-red, and black-red pairs?

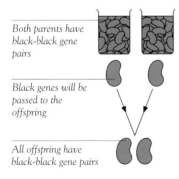

Both parents have black-black gene pairs

Black genes will be passed to the offspring

All offspring have black-black gene pairs

All the same
Genes are in pairs in the body (p.171). In this example, each parent has identical pairs of genes, and both parents are the same. The result is easily predicted. As genes are selected from each pair, from each parent, all the offspring have the same genes as each other and as the parents.

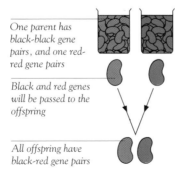

One parent has black-black gene pairs, and one red-red gene pairs

Black and red genes will be passed to the offspring

All offspring have black-red gene pairs

Same again
This time, one parent has identical pairs of genes. So does the other – but the two parents are different from each other. Even so, the results soon become obvious. All the offspring have the same combination of genes, which is black-red. This offspring becomes a parent in Step 3.

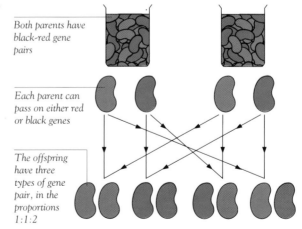

Both parents have black-red gene pairs

Each parent can pass on either red or black genes

The offspring have three types of gene pair, in the proportions 1:1:2

New combinations
In Step 3, both parents are the same – they each have dissimilar pairs of genes, one red and one black. Since the combinations follow the mathematical laws of chance, they produce predictable proportions of each different combination. In the body, for those pairs that are mixed (black-red), the dominant gene will dictate how the body develops.

Using a microscope

THE INVENTION OF THE LIGHT microscope revealed a previously unseen world. Light microscopes are essential scientific tools today in many places, from medical laboratories to school classrooms. A microscope is also useful for several of the experiments in this book. The one shown here can magnify objects by up to 200 times. To look through a microscope to see tissues, cells, and other tiny objects at first hand, helps you understand your body's structures and the functions of its parts. The basics of microscopy are not difficult to master. Some important guidelines for working with a microscope are described on this page.

■ The microscope

Focus knob: turned slowly to focus the specimen

Eyepiece: moves up and down as you adjust the focus. It contains lenses called the eyepiece lenses (in some versions these can be changed for different magnifications)

Objective lenses: on a swivelling turret, with each giving a different magnification, usually from about 50 to 200 times

Specimen stage: place the glass slide carrying the specimen here, and secure it with the two clips

Mirror: reflects the light source (left)

1. Lighting
This type of microscope needs a light source, such as a desk lamp or a powerful torch. The mirror reflects the light up through the specimen – as shown by the arrows (left), then through the objective lenses and eyepiece lenses into your eye. Adjust the mirror while looking through the microscope, until you find the most suitable angle for lighting the specimen.

2. Specimen preparation
The specimen should be very thin and not too large. Cut a slice of it, with adult help. It is often useful to add drops of water to the specimen and cover it with a small transparent cover slip. This stops the specimen from drying out. Rub a drop of water-based ink into the water with a cotton wool bud, while you lift the cover slip with a toothpick (as left), to stain important features.

3. Focusing
Put the slide on the stage, with the specimen under the lens. Look through the eyepiece and turn the focus knob to bring the specimen into focus (sharp view). Higher magnifications give more detail, but they have drawbacks. They need brighter light, the relevant part of the specimen is harder to find, and only a thin layer of the specimen is in focus at one time.

4. Studying
Always check that the objective lens does not move too low as you focus, or it may smash into the specimen and slide. Look away from the microscope every few minutes, to rest your eyes and your neck muscles.

Practice materials
Practise how to use your light microscope by looking at items that you can obtain easily and that are simple to handle, such as this human hair (p.40). Compare your hair to wool, cotton, and artificial fibres. Here you can see that the hair is not smooth, but has tiny scales.

GLOSSARY

The following seven pages explain many of the general terms used in this book. The explanations refer to the human body, although many of the terms also have wider uses – for talking about other animals and in general science. The terms apply mainly to the body as a whole. They do not include, for example, the scientific names of bones or muscles. If you want to find these, turn to the index (pp.186–191). Use the index, too, if you want to find out about a particular body organ, such as the heart, or a body system, such as the digestive system.

ABDOMEN The lower part of the main body (trunk or torso), below the thorax (chest cavity).

ABSORPTION Taking in or soaking up a substance. The intestinal lining absorbs the nutrients from digested food, which are in turn absorbed into the blood and passed to body tissues.

AMINO ACIDS The building blocks of proteins, which are the body's main structural substances, and also form enzymes. Different proteins are made from different sequences of amino acids. *See Proteins.*

AMYLASE An enzyme that breaks down the starches in food into their simpler sub-units during digestion. *See Enzyme.*

ANATOMIST A person who studies anatomy – the structure and physical make-up of the body (as opposed to physiology – the body's functions and chemistry).

ANTAGONISTIC MUSCLES Muscles that pull in opposite directions, with one member of the pair pulling the bone one way, and the other pulling it back.

ARTERY A large, thick-walled blood vessel that carries blood away from the heart. It divides to form capillaries.

ATOM A very tiny particle that cannot easily be split into anything smaller. Everything is made up of atoms. Elements consist of one type of atom only, but most things you see consist of many types of atoms, combined into molecules. *See Element, Molecule.*

BALANCE A mechanism by which the brain receives constant information from many sensory parts around the body, such as the ears, eyes, skin, muscles, and joints. Using this information, the brain adjusts the muscles to keep the body in a stable posture and stop it from falling over.

BILE A body fluid made by the liver and stored in the gall bladder. Bile is released into the small intestine, where it emulsifies the fats in food, so that they can be digested more efficiently. *See Emulsify.*

BLOOD A liquid that is the body's main transport substance. It carries oxygen, nutrients, energy-rich substances, salts, minerals, hormones, vitamins, and various cells, and distributes them to the tissues around the body. It also collects wastes for disposal by organs, such as carbon dioxide for disposal by the lungs, and urea for disposal by the kidneys. An oxygen-carrying pigment called haemoglobin makes blood red.

BLOOD VESSEL A tube that carries blood through the body. The main types of blood vessel are arteries, capillaries, and veins. Each of these is described elsewhere in the glossary.

BONE A strong body part, made chiefly of the protein collagen and various minerals. There are 206 bones in an adult skeleton. Bones are fairly rigid but also slightly flexible. *See Collagen.*

CAPILLARIES Microscopic blood vessels with walls only one cell thick. Oxygen and nutrients pass from the blood in the capillaries to the cells in body tissues. Wastes produced by the cells pass the other way, from tissues into the blood.

CARBOHYDRATES A group of chemicals containing carbon, hydrogen, and oxygen. They include sugars and starches, and are the body's main energy sources.

CARDIO- To do with the heart. The thick muscle that makes up the heart wall is called cardiac muscle. A machine that shows the pattern of electrical signals that pass through the heart is called an electrocardiograph.

CARTILAGE A tough, rubbery substance. It lines the ends of bones where they meet in a joint. It also forms structural parts in the nose and the larynx (voice-box).

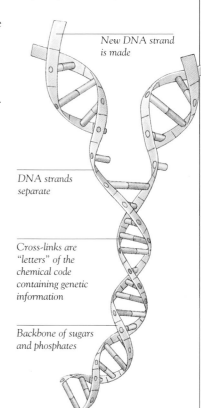

New DNA strand is made

DNA strands separate

Cross-links are "letters" of the chemical code containing genetic information

Backbone of sugars and phosphates

DNA
DNA has a double-helix shape – that is, like two intertwined corkscrews. As DNA duplicates itself, each helix separates and makes a mirror-image of itself.

CELLS The microscopic units, sometimes called building blocks, that make up all living things, including the human body. The body has more than 100 million million cells. A typical cell consists of a cell membrane surrounding a fluid substance called cytoplasm. Each cell contains tiny structures called organelles, such as the nucleus. *See Membrane, Nucleus, Organelle.*

CENTRAL NERVOUS SYSTEM The part of the nervous system that consists of the brain and spinal cord. *See Peripheral nervous system.*

CERVICAL To do with the neck or a neck-like structure. The cervical vertebrae are the backbones in the neck region. The cervix is the neck of the womb (uterus).

CHEMICAL REACTION A process in which chemical substances come together, split up, and recombine to produce a new set of chemical substances. Hundreds of chemical reactions happen every second in each cell of the body.

CHROMOSOMES X-shaped structures, containing the substance DNA, found inside cells. The DNA carries genes, which have all the information for the structure and growth of the body. *See DNA, Genes.*

COLLAGEN A tough, fibrous protein found in the dermis layer of the skin, and in cartilage and bone.

CONDENSATION When gas or vapour changes into a liquid. Usually the molecules or atoms in the gas are very far apart, so the gas is invisible. But in the liquid they are closer together, so the liquid is visible.

CONNECTIVE TISSUE A body tissue that is specialized to connect, support, or fill in between other tissues. Connective tissue is one of the four basic kinds of tissue in the body. It makes up most of bone, cartilage, fat, the lower layer of the skin, and blood. *See Tissue.*

CORPUSCLE A "small body". This term was used widely by the early microscopists to describe the new objects they saw. Several tiny body parts are still sometimes called corpuscles, such as red blood cells and some of the touch sensors in the skin.

CORTEX The outer layer or part of an organ. The cortex of the kidney contains microscopic filtering units called nephrons. The cortex of the brain is a thin grey layer, consisting of billions of nerve cell bodies and nerve connections, where sensations, thoughts, and movements originate.

DENT- To do with teeth. Dentine is the tough, shock-absorbing layer under the enamel covering of a tooth.

DIFFUSION The spreading out of a substance. The atoms or molecules of the substance move from where they are more concentrated to where they are less concentrated, so that eventually they are spread out evenly.

DIGESTION The process of breaking down substances into smaller, simpler substances. In the body the digestive system breaks down the large molecules in food into small ones that can be absorbed into the blood.

DIGESTIVE TRACT The long tube that goes through the body from the mouth to the anus. Its main parts are the mouth, pharynx (throat), oesophagus, stomach, small intestine, and large intestine.

DNA The abbreviation for deoxyribonucleic acid. This important substance is found in chromosomes inside the nucleus of a cell. It carries all the information, in the form of chemical codes, needed to build a human body and to keep it alive. The information is in units called genes. When any new cells are made (except egg and sperm cells), DNA duplicates itself, so the new cells contain exactly the same genetic information as the originals. *See Chromosomes, Genes.*

EAR The organ of hearing (the auditory sense). The flap on the side of the head is supported by flexible cartilage. Behind is a chamber called the middle ear cavity, set into the skull bones. This contains the tiny ear ossicles, which transfer vibrations from the eardrum. Deeper in the skull are the cochlea, in which the vibrations are converted into nerve signals, and the fluid-filled chambers and canals that contribute to the mechanism of balance. *See Balance.*

EGG CELL A female sex cell, made in the ovaries of a woman. Fertilized by a sperm cell from a man, it will develop into a new human being. *See Fertilization.*

ELASTIN A stretchy, rubbery protein found in the dermis layer of the skin and in other connective tissues.

Hair
A hair grows from a follicle – a cavity formed by the epidermis folding down into the dermis below.

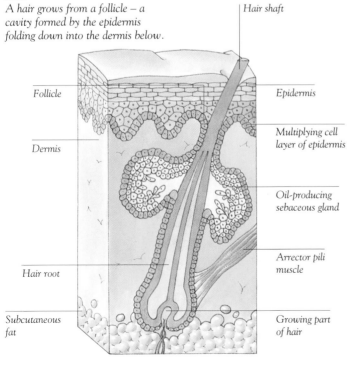

Follicle

Dermis

Hair root

Subcutaneous fat

Hair shaft

Epidermis

Multiplying cell layer of epidermis

Oil-producing sebaceous gland

Arrector pili muscle

Growing part of hair

Joint
A joint is lubricated by an oil called synovial fluid, which is produced by the synovial capsule, a bag-like membrane around the joint.

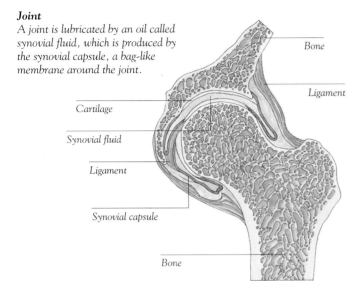

Cartilage

Synovial fluid

Ligament

Synovial capsule

Bone

Bone

Ligament

ELEMENT A simple substance that is made up of only one kind of atom, such as carbon, iron, or sodium. *See Atom.*

EMBRYO A baby in the early stages of development in the womb, between about two and eight weeks after fertilization. *See Foetus.*

EMULSIFY To break up a substance such as a fat into droplets, so that chemicals such as enzymes have more surface area to attack.

ENDOPLASMIC RETICULUM An organelle inside a cell. It is the site for making or storing proteins and cell products. Its membrane usually takes the form of a large bag, folded many times. *See Organelle.*

ENERGY The ability to do work, such as moving things or heating them. The body gets its energy from food.

ENZYME A special type of protein that controls a chemical reaction in the body. There are hundreds of

types of enzyme to regulate different aspects of the body's chemistry. *See Proteins.*

EPITHELIAL TISSUE Tissue that forms protective coverings or linings for body parts. Epithelial tissue is one of the four basic kinds of tissue in the body. It lines the digestive tract, airways, blood vessels, and other hollow tubes and parts. The skin cells in the epidermis are also epithelial cells. *See Tissue.*

EVAPORATION When a liquid changes into a gas or vapour. Usually, the atoms or molecules in the liquid are very close together, so the liquid is visible, but in the gas they are very far apart, so the gas is invisible.

EYE The organ of sight (the visual sense). The eyeball is a jelly-filled sphere with a lens at the front that focuses light on to the retina, the sensitive layer at the back. *See Retina.*

FATS Types of lipid, one of the body's main groups of chemicals. Fats provide both

energy and structural ingredients for cell membranes and many other cell parts. The subcutaneous fat layer just under the skin contains cells that are full of fat. *See Lipids.*

FERTILIZATION When an egg cell from a woman joins with a sperm cell from a man to form a single cell. This cell is a fertilized egg that will develop into a baby.

FIBRE A component of food, made mostly of plant material such as cellulose. Fibre cannot be digested to obtain energy or nutrients, but it helps to make digestion work efficiently and keep the intestines healthy.

FOETUS A baby during the middle and later stages of development in the womb, between about eight weeks after fertilization and birth. *See Embryo.*

FOLLICLE A small bag, sac, or cavity. In the skin, a hair follicle is a tiny cavity from which a hair grows. In the ovary, an ovarian follicle (Graafian follicle) is the fluid-filled container for the mature egg cell.

GENES Units of inheritance, passed from parents to their offspring. Genes are the plans for each feature of the body, such as bone shape, intestinal structure, and skin colour. Genes are sections of the chemical DNA, packaged into structures called chromosomes, arranged in pairs inside the nucleus of a body cell. Only a selection of the genes in any particular type of cell is active. *See Chromosomes, DNA.*

GENETICS The study of genes: what they are made of, how they work, and how they are inherited. *See Genes.*

GLUCOSE A type of sugar with small, simple molecules. It is obtained from digested food, either directly or through conversion from other types of food nutrients, such as carbohydrates. Glucose is the body's major source of energy and is often called "blood sugar".

GOLGI BODY A tiny organelle, inside a cell, specialized to store cell products and wrap them in membranes, so that they can leave the cell. *See Organelle.*

HABITUATION When the brain learns to ignore repeated signals from a sensor that do not seem to be important. *See Sensor.*

HAIR A long, stiff, rod-like structure that grows from a pit in the skin called a hair follicle. Hairs are made mainly of dead cells filled with the tough protein keratin. Hairs protect and insulate the body. Sensitive nerves wrapped around the bases of hairs detect when they are being moved.

HEPATO- To do with the liver – the part of the digestive system that processes and stores nutrients. Hepatocytes are the main types of cell in the liver.

HORMONES The body's "chemical messengers". Made in hormonal glands, they are chemicals that circulate in the blood and stimulate certain body parts – their target organs – into action.

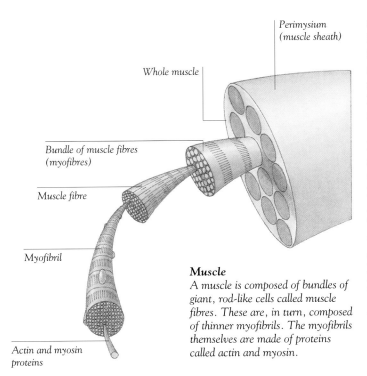

Perimysium
(muscle sheath)

Whole muscle

Bundle of muscle fibres
(myofibres)

Muscle fibre

Myofibril

Actin and myosin
proteins

Muscle
A muscle is composed of bundles of giant, rod-like cells called muscle fibres. These are, in turn, composed of thinner myofibrils. The myofibrils themselves are made of proteins called actin and myosin.

JOINT The part of the body where two bones meet. In some joints the bones are fixed firmly and cannot move, as in the skull. In other joints the bones move smoothly over a limited range. The bones in these types of joint are covered by cartilage and held together by ligaments.

KERATIN The tough, hard protein that makes up the body's outer layer of skin, hairs, and also nails.

LEVER A simple machine with a rigid bar that pivots (swings) about a point called the fulcrum. A lever makes it easier to move a heavy load. The body's bones work as levers.

LIGAMENTS Tough, elastic, strap-like parts that attach bones together at a joint, so that they do not come apart.

LIPASE An enzyme that breaks down the lipids (fats and oils) in food into their simpler sub-units during digestion. *See Enzyme.*

LIPIDS One of the body's main groups of chemicals. Lipids provide both energy and the structural ingredients for cell membranes and many other cell parts. They are made primarily from carbon, hydrogen, and oxygen. Lipids, which include fats and oils, do not mix with water.

LOBE A distinct, rounded segment, section, or part of a structure such as an organ. The liver has two lobes. The cerebrum of the brain has five lobes on each side.

LUMBAR To do with the lower back. The lumbar vertebrae are the backbones in the lower part of the back.

LYMPH A pale fluid that is like blood, but with certain parts, such as the red cells, removed. It carries nutrients

and germ-fighting cells. Lymph is formed from the fluid that collects between cells. It passes through a network of tubes called the lymphatic system and empties into the blood circulation.

LYMPH NODE A kidney-shaped organ connected to the lymphatic system. The largest lymph nodes are up to 3 cm (just over 1 in) long. They store germ-fighting white blood cells and help clean and filter lymph fluid. Lymph nodes enlarge and harden during some types of illness, when they are called "swollen glands".

MARROW The jelly-like substance inside certain bones. It makes new cells for the blood.

MEIOSIS A type of cell division by which a cell splits into four offspring cells. This type of cell division occurs only to make sperm and egg cells for reproduction. During meiosis, as in mitosis, a duplicate set of the parent cell's gene pairs is produced. However, unlike mitosis, this new set and the original set of gene pairs then both split in two, with the result that each of the four offspring cells has only a set of single genes, not gene pairs. When an egg joins a sperm at fertilization, a complete set of gene pairs is formed. *See Genes.*

MEMBRANE A flexible barrier around or within an object. A cell has a cell membrane enclosing it, and membranes inside it too. On a larger scale, most body organs are also covered or lined by membranes, which are themselves composed of

layers of cells. For example, there is a membrane around the lungs called the pleura and one around the heart called the pericardium.

MICROSCOPE A device that magnifies objects (makes them look bigger). A light microscope uses light rays and can magnify by about 1,000 times. An electron microscope uses beams of sub-atomic particles called electrons and magnifies by a million times or more.

MICROSCOPIST A person whose work involves using microscopes.

MICROTUBULES Scaffolding-like systems of rod-shaped molecules, such as proteins, inside cells. Microtubules give a cell shape and strength, and move parts such as organelles around within the cell.

MINERAL A simple chemical, usually an element, that the body needs to stay alive and healthy. Examples are calcium for strong bones and teeth and iron for healthy blood. *See Element.*

MITOCHONDRION A tiny organelle, specialized to break down substances from food to provide its cell with energy. *See Organelle.*

MITOSIS A type of cell division by which one original cell splits into two offspring cells. It is the normal method of cell multiplication in the body, for growth and to replace cells that die or are lost by wear and tear. During mitosis a duplicate set of the parent cell's gene pairs is produced, so that both of the offspring cells have identical gene pairs. Compare with meiosis. *See Genes.*

MOLECULE A chemical made from two or more atoms joined together. Some molecules consist of only one type of atom; some have several types. A molecule of oxygen has two atoms of oxygen. A protein molecule has thousands of atoms of various substances, such as carbon, nitrogen, and oxygen. *See Atom.*

MOTOR NERVE A nerve that carries nerve signals from the brain and spinal cord to the body's muscles.

MUSCLE A body part specialized to contract (get shorter). Muscle tissue is one of the four basic kinds of tissue in the body. It makes up all muscles, from major skeletal muscles to heart muscle and the tiny hair-erecting muscles in the skin. *See Tissue.*

MYO- To do with muscles. A myofibre is a thread-like fibre inside a muscle, and a myofibril is a thinner thread inside the myofibre.

NERVE A long, thin body part that is specialized to carry messages around the body in the form of tiny electrical signals. Nerve tissue is one of the four basic kinds of tissue in the body. It forms the brain, nerves, and parts of the sense organs. *See Motor nerve, Sensory nerve, Tissue.*

NERVE SIGNAL A tiny electrical signal that travels along a nerve. Nerve signals move along the membranes of nerve cells (neurons). The strength of a typical nerve signal is between 50 and 100 millivolts, that is about one fiftieth of the strength of a torch battery. The signal lasts for about 5 milliseconds ($\frac{1}{200}$ of a second).

NEURO- To do with nerves. A neuron is another name for a single nerve cell.

NOSE The organ of smell (the olfactory sense). The protruding part on the face has two nostrils (air holes), a flexible framework of cartilage, and hairs to filter the passing air. Behind is a hole, or chamber, called the nasal cavity, set into the skull bones. This contains the

olfactory epithelium, a patch of tiny projections that are linked to nerve cells. Nerve signals are sorted by the olfactory bulb and interpreted by the brain as smells. The nose is the major entrance and exit for air going to and from the lungs.

NUCLEOLUS A tiny structure inside the nucleus of a cell. The nucleolus transfers genetic instructions from the chromosomes in the nucleus out into the rest of the cell. *See Chromosomes, Nucleus.*

NUCLEUS A special type of cell organelle, that acts as the cell's "control centre". The nucleus contains the cell's genetic information in the form of DNA chemicals packaged into chromosomes. *See DNA, Organelle.*

NUTRIENTS Substances in food that the body can break down during digestion, absorb, and rebuild into its own cells and tissues.

OILS Types of lipid, one of the body's main groups of chemicals. Oils are greasy and do not mix with water. *See Lipids.*

ORGAN A major structural part of the body that carries out an important role. The heart is an organ that pumps blood. The kidneys are organs that filter wastes from the blood. Most organs are made of collections of tissues. *See System, Tissue.*

ORGANELLE A tiny structure inside a cell that carries out an important role. The nucleus is an organelle that contains genetic information. The mitochondria are

organelles that break down substances to provide the cell with energy.

ORGANIC To do with substances containing the element carbon. Carbon atoms are the main atoms of molecules, such as proteins and DNA, that are found in living things. The word "organic" also means substances that are, or were, part of an organism (living thing). *See Element.*

OSMOSIS The movement of a solvent, such as water, through a semi-permeable membrane, through which other substances may not be able to pass. *See Semi-permeable membrane, Solvent.*

OSTEO- To do with bones. Osteocytes are cells that make the hard material that forms bones.

PELVIC To do with the pelvis, which is the lowest part of the abdomen. The pelvic organs are those in the lower abdomen, such as the bladder and rectum.

PERIPHERAL NERVOUS SYSTEM The part of the nervous system that consists of the nerves that snake and twist through the body, connecting the brain and spinal cord to the many parts and organs. *See Central nervous system.*

PERISTALSIS When contents are pushed along a tube by waves of contraction of the muscles in the walls of the tube. Many substances pass through body tubes in this way, such as food through the oesophagus and intestines, and urine along the ureter from kidney to bladder.

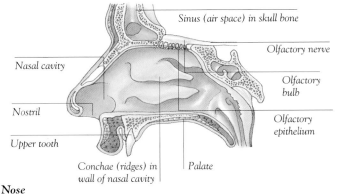

Sinus (air space) in skull bone

Olfactory nerve

Nasal cavity

Olfactory bulb

Nostril

Olfactory epithelium

Upper tooth

Conchae (ridges) in wall of nasal cavity

Palate

Nose
Behind the outer nose is an air chamber, the nasal cavity, which has the olfactory epithelium in its roof.

PHYSICIAN Generally, a medical doctor. The term is sometimes used in contrast to a surgeon, who performs operations.

PHYSIOLOGIST A person who studies physiology – the way the body works and its functions (as opposed to its anatomy, or structure).

PIGMENT A coloured substance. Artificial pigments are used in stains, dyes, and paints. The body has its own pigments, such as dark brown melanin, which gives colour to skin and hair.

PROPRIOCEPTORS Sensors that respond to body movements and changes in body position and posture.

Stretch sensors in muscles, tendons, and ligaments are all types of proprioceptor. *See Sensor.*

PROTEASE An enzyme that breaks down the proteins in food into their simpler sub-units during digestion. *See Enzyme.*

PROTEINS The body's main construction substances. They are the structural ingredients of skin, muscles, bones (with minerals), and many other parts. Proteins also form enzymes, which control chemical reactions. Proteins are made from building blocks called amino acids.

PUBERTY The period during which the sexual organs

become mature and functional. The male's testes start to make sperm, and the female's ovaries begin to produce mature eggs. Puberty is usually accompanied by a spurt in body growth, and various body changes, such as breast development in females, and the appearance of facial hair and a deeper voice in males.

PULMONARY To do with the lungs. For example, the pulmonary arteries carry blood to the lungs. The pulmonary circulation is the part of the blood circulation to and from the lungs.

RENAL To do with the kidney. The renal arteries carry blood to the kidneys for filtering and waste removal.

RESPIRATION The process of breathing: inhaling fresh air into the lungs to absorb oxygen, and then exhaling stale air. The term "cellular respiration" refers to the sets of chemical reactions inside a cell in which energy-rich substances, such as glucose, are broken down to yield their energy in a form that the cell can use. In cellular respiration the body uses oxygen and produces carbon dioxide as a waste.

RETINA The light-sensitive layer that lines the inside of the rear of the eyeball. Arranged around the surface of the retina are about 130 million special cells, called rods and cones. These change the energy of light rays into tiny electrical nerve signals. These signals are sent along other nerve cells to the optic nerve, which delivers them to the brain.

SCANNER A machine that scans the body, building up an image of its inner parts, line by line. Some scanners beam lines of weak X-rays through the body. Others transmit high-pitched sound, called ultrasound, through the body, or detect how certain body parts react in a strong magnetic field. A computer processes the results and displays them on a visual display unit (TV screen).

SEMI-PERMEABLE MEMBRANE A membrane that allows a solvent – in the body, water – to pass through, but prevents other substances from doing so. This selective letting-through process is called osmosis. *See Membrane, Osmosis, Solvent.*

SENSOR A structure that changes some kinds of stimuli into nerve signals. Some sensors are whole organs, such as the ear, which converts sound waves into nerve signals. Some sensors are microscopic bunches of cells, or even single cells, such as the stretch sensors in muscles and tendons, which produce nerve signals when stretched or distorted.

SENSORY NERVE A nerve that carries nerve signals from a sense organ, or another type of sensor, to the brain or spinal cord.

SKELETON The supporting framework of the body. In a developing baby it is composed mainly of cartilage. This changes to bone as the baby grows into an adult.

SKIN The organ of touch and the body's outer covering. The skin's millions of

Retina
The retina is only a few cells thick. Its light-detecting rod and cone cells are linked to the optic nerve by other nerve cells such as the ganglion nerve cell and bipolar nerve cell.

Surface of retina | Light rays

To the optic nerve

Path of nerve signals

Ganglion nerve cell

Synapse

Bipolar nerve cell

Rod cell

Cone cell

Choroid (blood-rich nourishing layer)

Sclera (tough outer sheath of eyeball)

microscopic sensors detect different aspects of touch, such as light touch, heavy pressure, heat or cold, vibrations, and the damage we feel as pain. The skin also protects the body from conditions outside and keeps its fluids in.

SOLUTE A substance, usually a solid, that is dissolved in a solvent. *See Solution.*

SOLUTION The result of a substance (called the solute and usually solid) dissolving in another substance (called the solvent and usually liquid). A common example is sugar (a solute) dissolved in water (a solvent). The atoms or molecules of the solute are freed from each other and can float around, so that the solute often seems to disappear in the solvent. An example of a solution in the body is urine, in which urea and other waste products are dissolved in water.

SOLVENT A substance, usually a liquid, in which other substances are dissolved. *See Solution.*

SPECIES A group of living things whose members can breed with each other, but who cannot breed with any other group. All human beings belong to one species, *Homo sapiens.*

SPERM CELLS Sex cells made in the testes. If an egg cell from a woman is fertilized by a sperm cell, it can then develop into a new human being. *See Fertilization.*

SURFACE AREA The amount of surface that an object has. The bigger the surface area of

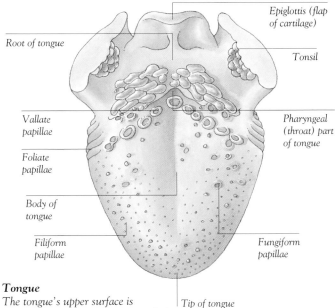

Tongue
The tongue's upper surface is covered by a variety of bumps, called papillae. The tonsils are masses of germ-fighting lymph tissue.

an organ, the more of a substance it can absorb (take in) through this surface. This applies to the insides of the lungs, for absorbing oxygen, and to the insides of the small intestine, for taking in nutrients from food.

SYNAPSE The tiny gap between two nerve cells (neurons). The two cells do not touch each other. Electrical signals travelling along the nerves change their form at this gap and cross it in the form of chemicals called neurotransmitters. *See Nerve signal.*

SYSTEM A group of organs or other parts that carries out one major role. For example, the heart, blood vessels, and blood form the circulatory system, which delivers oxygen and nutrients to all body parts and collects their wastes.

SYSTEMIC The part of the circulatory system that takes

blood to all of the body except the lungs.

TENDON The strong, rope-like part of a muscle, where it narrows toward its end and is attached to a bone. Tendons are often called sinews.

THORACIC To do with the thorax (chest). The thoracic vertebrae are the backbones in the chest region.

THORAX The chest – that is, the upper part of the main body (trunk or torso), above the abdomen.

TISSUE A collection of similar cells, all of which perform one main role or function. Strictly, the body has only four basic types of tissue: nerve, epithelial, connective, and muscle; but there are many variations on these types. Each of these kinds of tissue is described elsewhere in the glossary. *See Organ, System.*

TONGUE The organ of taste (the gustatory sense). Flavour molecules are detected by thousands of microscopic, onion-shaped cell clusters called taste buds. These are scattered on and among the larger bumps and lumps on the tongue, called papillae. Under its surface, the tongue is a mass of flexible, interwoven muscles.

VALVE A device to control the flow of a substance. A common example is a water tap. In the body, valves in the heart and main veins are one-way valves. They ensure that the blood flows the right way around the circulatory system.

VEIN A large, slack-walled blood vessel that carries blood back to the heart.

VESICLE A small, fluid-filled, bubble-like structure. In a cell there are numerous vesicles. They are made from membranes, and contain various items, such as fat molecules, or germs that have been engulfed by the cell.

VITAMINS Substances that are needed for the smooth running of the body's chemical reactions. Vitamins are not structural or energy-containing, but they "oil the wheels" of the body's chemical machinery.

X-RAYS Invisible waves that can pass through most of the body, except for hard parts such as bone. A radiograph is an "X-ray photograph" produced when X-rays that have passed through body tissue are exposed on a photographic plate, leaving bone-shaped shadows where no rays have got through.

Index

A

ABO system 102
absorption 81, 84, 90
Achilles tendon 58–9
acid, digestive system 81, 85, 91
actin 57
Adam's apple 89
adductor magnus muscle 65
adolescence 169
adrenal glands 23, 104–5, 107, 108
adrenaline 105, 107, 108
ageing 174–5
agglutination 102
airways 69, 70–1
Alcmaeon of Croton 116
aldosterone 107
alveoli 69, 71, 72–3
amino acids 81, 90
ribosomes 27
amniotic fluid 173
ampullae 156–7
amygdala 128
amylase 90
ankle bones 47
antagonistic pairs of muscles 56, 62
anterior tibial artery 101
antibodies 102, 170
antigens 102
anus 84–5
aorta 95, 96–7, 98, 108
appendix 85
aqueous humour 139
Aristotle 12
heart 116
breathing 70
reproduction 170
senses 136
arm bones 47
arrector pili muscle 34, 40
arteries
circulatory system 22, 94–5, 96
heart 98
pulmonary 72
pulse 100

structure 97
atoms 14–15
atria 98–9
auditory cortex 127
autonomic nervous system 115, 118, 126
endocrine system 105
senses 136
axons 26, 119, 127

B

babies 13, 23, 170
development 169, 172–3, 176
head size 174
learning 132
reflexes 120
skeleton 46
vision 140
backbones 46, 116
embryo 173
bacteria 33
anaerobic 70
tooth decay 86–7
Baglivi, Giorgio 45
balance 118, 156–7
brain 126–7
muscles 60
barium meal 91
Bayliss, William 106
Beaumont, William 91
Bernard, Claude 104, 110
biceps brachii muscle 59
biceps femoris muscle 59
biceps muscles 22, 57, 65
antagonistic pairs 60–1, 62–3
mechanical advantage 50
bile 85, 91
Hippocrates 94
binocular vision 144–5
birth 169, 170, 172
birth canal 172

bladder 23, 104, 108–9
blind spot 139, 148
blinking 120
blood 93, 102–3, 116
circulation 22
exercise 76
glucose 83, 106
heart 98–9, 100
lungs 69
muscles 57
nutrients 81
pulse 100
respiratory system 23, 69, 70–1, 72
urinary system 23
blood cells 25, 103
marrow 43, 45
blood groups 102
blood pressure 107, 117, 126
sensors 137
blood vessels 93, 97
alveoli 72
bones 44, 48
circulation 22, 94, 96
dermis 34
heart 98
retina 139, 149
tooth 87
body fluids 110–11
body proportions 16–17, 174–5
bolus 84, 88
bone cells 25, 48
bone matrix 45
bones 22, 43, 44–5
ear 152
calcium 81
growth 46–7, 174
joints 50
mineral storage 70
muscles 55, 58, 66
structure 48–9
Boyle, Robert 71
brachial artery 101
Braille, Louis 167
brain 13, 126–7
baby 173, 174
balance control 156
heart control 98
muscle control 55, 57, 58, 60, 64

nervous system 115, 116–17, 118–19
reactions 122–3
reflexes 120–1
sensory centres 136
skull 22, 43, 46
smell 158–9
sound 152, 155
taste 160, 162
touch 164, 166
vision 137, 138, 144–5, 150–1
water levels 111
brain stem 117, 118, 126, 128
breastbone 22, 44, 46
breasts 171
breathing 46, 70–1, 74–5
brain control 116–17, 126
rate 76, 107
water loss 111
Broca's area 127
bronchi 23, 69, 71, 72
bronchioles 69, 71, 72

C

calcaneous bone 47
calcium
bones 45, 48, 81
diffusion 27
calf-bone 46
calluses 36
cancellous bone 44
canine teeth 86
Canon, Walter 104
capillaries 95, 97
alveoli 71, 72
circulation 94, 96, 100
nephron 104–5
carbohydrates 14–15, 82
digestion 84, 90, 106
foods 80, 83
carbon dioxide
blood transport 102
diffusion 27
monitoring 116, 137
pulmonary vessels 95

respiration 70–1, 72, 74
yawning 75
carbon 15
cardiac muscle 57, 58–9, 98, 100
carotid arteries 97, 101, 137
carpal bones 52
carpal ligaments 59
cartilage
ear 152
joints 45, 51
trachea 72
young bones 46–7
cell division 170–1, 172–3
cell membrane 28–9, 80–1, 171
cells 12–13, 14–15, 24–5
bone 44–5
chromosomes 176
egg 26, 169, 172
environment 104
epidermal 33
epithelial 25, 26
fuel 81
hair 40
light-sensitive 135, 137, 138–9, 142
melanocytes 36
muscle 57, 59
skin 31, 32–3, 34–5
water 111
cellular respiration 57, 70–1, 72
cellulose 81
cementum 87
central nervous system 119
cerebellum 115, 117, 126–7
cerebral cortex 126–7
cerebral hemispheres 117, 126–7
cerebrospinal fluid 117, 126
cerebrum 117, 126–7
cervical vertebrae 46
cervix, womb 173
Cesalpino, Andrea 95
chemosenses 137
chewing 88–9, 118
childhood 169

chondrocytes 45
choroid 139, 148
chromosomes 171,
176
ciliary muscles
139, 140
circulatory system 22,
93, 94–5, 96–7
clavicle 46
clotting 49, 102–3
cochlea 152, 157
cochlear nerves 119,
152
collagen 80
bones 45, 48
dermis 34, 37
collar-bones 45, 46
colon 85, 91
colour vision 137,
139, 149
Columbus, Realdo
95
compact bone 44
condyle 53
cone cells 136–7,
139, 142, 149
conjunctiva 138–9
connective tissue 45
consciousness 116
co-ordination
146–7
copper 15
cornea 138–9, 140–1,
142
coronary arteries 95
corpus callosum 126
corrugator supercilii
muscle 61
cortex
cerebral 118–19,
126–7
kidney 108–9
memory 128–9
sensory centres
136
coughing 75
cranial nerves 119
cranium 43, 46
creatinine 108
creativity 115
Crick, Francis 13,
176
crown, tooth 87
cupula 157
cytoplasm 25, 27

D

Darwin, Charles 12
da Vinci, Leonardo 16
muscles 56
circulation 95
reproduction 170
skin 32
decay, tooth 86–7
deciduous teeth 86
decisions 124–5
de Graaf, Regnier 173
deltoid muscle 59, 61
dendrite 119
dentine 87
depressor anguli oris
muscle 61
depressor labii muscle
61
dermis 32–3, 34, 36,
164
Descartes, René 118,
137
diaphragm 72–3, 75
diet 16, 80, 163
diffusion 25, 26–7
capillaries 96–7
epidermis 34
digestion 80–1, 90–1
control 106–7, 116,
118
digestive juices 84–5
digestive system 14,
23, 79, 80, 84–5
digestive tract 80, 84,
91
digital blood vessels
97
DNA 12, 171, 176
dominance, genetics
171, 177
dorsal venous arch 97
ductless glands 105
duodenum 85

E

eardrum 152
ear canal 152
ear flap 152
ears 23, 135, 152–3,
154–5

embryo 173
hearing 136–7,
152–3
muscles 56
nervous system
118–19
semicircular canals
152, 157
sound waves 154–5
eating 80–1
ECG 98
egg cells 13, 26,
chromosomes 176
reproduction 23,
169, 170–1, 172–3
elastin 34, 36–7
electrical nerve
signals 26, 115, 118
light–sensitive cells
142
muscle control 58
sense organs 135,
136
speed 139
electrocardiogram 98
embryo 13, 170, 173
emotions 115, 116,
126, 128
enamel 86–7
endocrine system 23,
105, 106–7, 110
endoplasmic
reticulum 27
energy 80–1, 82–3
mitochondrion 26–7
muscles 57, 65
respiration 70
enzymes 80–1, 85,
90–1, 107
epidermis 32–3, 34,
36, 164
melanin 36
epididymis 23
epiglottis 88–9
epithelial cells 25, 26
epithelium 108–9
Erasistratus 56–7
erythrocytes 103
Eustachian tube 137,
152
Eustachio,
Bartolomeo 137
evolution 12, 47
excretory system 23
exercise 16, 76, 99

extensor digitorum
muscle 60
extensor digitorum
longus muscle 59
external oblique
muscle 59
eyeball 139, 148
eye-colour
inheritance 171, 177
eyes 135, 138–9
and balance 156
co-ordination 146–7
embryo 173
facial features 18–19
focusing 140–1
limits 148–9
nervous system
118–19
sense organs 23,
136–7
sensitivity 142–3
stereoscopic vision
144–5
visual tricks 150–1

F

Fabricius,
Hieronymus 95
faces 18–19
facial expressions 61
facial muscles 56,
61, 121
facial nerves 119
faeces 23, 25, 81, 85
water loss 111
Fallopian tubes 172
fast-twitch muscles
65
fats 15, 82
digestion 84, 90–1
energy store 81
foods 80, 83
marrow 45
subcutaneous 34, 36
fatty acids 80–1
female reproductive
system 23
femoral artery 97, 101
femur 44, 48
height 16
knee 52–3
skeleton 22, 46

fertilization 13, 169,
170–1, 172–3, 176
fibre, dietary 81, 83
fibres, muscle cell 26,
57, 58
fibrin 102–3
fibrinogen 102
fibroblasts 49
fibula 46
fight or flight
response 94, 105
finger flexing muscles
60, 64, 66
fingernails 32, 40
fingerprints 32, 38–9,
176
flavours 160–1, 162–3
flexor digitorum
muscle 60
flushing 112
focusing 137, 140–1
foetus 173
follicle
Graafian 171, 173
hair 34, 40
foot bones 47
forearm bone 46, 52,
63
Fosbury, Dick 21
free nerve endings 34,
164
frontalis muscle 59,
61
frontal lobes 126
fulcrum, levers 51

G

Gage, Phineas 126
Galen 13
brains 116
circulation 94–5
digestive system 80
lungs 70
muscles 56
Galilei, Galileo 44
gall bladder 84–5, 173
Galvani, Luigi 117
gases, digestion 90
gastric blood vessels
97
gastrocnemius muscle
59

genes 27
  fertilization 169,
    171, 176–7
  melanin 36
  shaping the body 13
twins 19
genetics 12, 170–1
germs 32
  digestion 81, 90
  white blood cells
    102–3
glomeruli 104–5
glucagon 106–7
glucose 15, 106–7
  brain monitoring
    105, 116
  chemosensors 137
  diffusion 27
  food 80
  energy 83, 105, 116
  muscles 57
  nephron 109
  respiration 70
gluteus maximus
  muscle 56, 59
glycogen 106
Golgi bodies 27, 28
Golgi, Camillo 28
Graafian follicle 171,
  173
grey matter 127
gristle 46
growth 170–1, 174–5
  food 79, 82
  hormones 23, 105,
    107
gums 87, 162
gustatory centre 160

H

habituation 162, 164
Habsburg jaw 176
haemoglobin 81, 93,
  94–5
hair 22, 40–1
  colour 177
  follicle 34, 40
  skin 31, 32–3, 34–5
hand 60, 66–7
  bones 47
Harvey, William 95,
  96

Havers, Clopton 48
Haversian systems 44,
  48–9
healing
  blood clotting 102–3
  bones 49
hearing 135, 136–7,
  152–3, 154–5
  centres 117, 152
heart 98–9
  cardiac muscle
    56–7, 59
  circulatory system
    22, 94–5, 96
  efficiency 21
  embryo 173
heart–beat 94, 99,
  100–1
  brain control
    116–17, 126
  ECG 98
  energy 83
  hormone control
    105, 107
  muscles 56
  rate 76, 95, 100
heat sense 136
height 16, 174
Henry, Edward 39
hepatic portal vein 80
hepatocytes 14–15
heredity 170
hiccups 75
hip-bone 46
hippocampus 128
Hippocrates 13, 94
histology 28
histones 176
homeostasis 104–5,
  110, 117
Hooke, Robert 24, 26,
  71
hormonal glands 23,
  106
hormones 23, 105,
  106–7
  blood transport 102
  heart 94, 98
  hypothalamus 126
  kidneys 109, 111
  ovaries 171
humerus 46, 52
humours, Hippocrates
  94
hunger 116, 126

hydrochloric acid 81,
  90
hypothalamus 117,
  126
  blood monitoring
    105, 107, 111
  endocrine system 23
  temperature control
    112

I

ileum 85
iliac blood vessels 97
incisors 86
infancy 169, 170
inferior vena cava 97,
  108
inheritance 176–7
insulin 106–7
integumentary system
  22
intelligence 115, 116,
  171
intercostal muscles
  72–3
intestinal cell 26
intestines 23, 79,
  80–1, 84
  digestion 91
  embryo 173
  muscles 56–7, 59
involuntary muscle
  57, 58–9
iris 137, 138–9, 140
iron 15
  haemoglobin 81, 95
islet of Langerhans
  107

J

jawbone 46
  teeth 86–7
jejunum 85
joints 50–1, 52–3
  hand 66–7
  jaw 88
  skeleton 43, 44–5
  stretch sensors 156
jugular veins 97

K

keratin 32
  nails 40
  protein 80
  skin 34, 37
kidneys 106
  blood transport 102
  homeostasis 104–5
  hormones 111
  renal vessels 97
  urinary system 23,
    108–9
kneecap 46
knee-jerk reflex 121
knee joint 52–3

L

lacrimal glands 138
lamellae, bone 48
Landsteiner, Karl 102
large intestine 23,
  80–1, 85
larynx 71, 72, 89, 154
latissimus dorsi
  muscle 59
laughter, learning 132
Lavoisier, Antoine
  70–1
learning 116, 132–3
  baby 170
  child 174
lenses 137, 139, 151
  focusing 140–1
leucocyte 103
levator labii muscle
  61
levers 45, 50–1
  jaw, chewing 88
life-cycles 169, 171
ligaments 59, 66–7
light rays 135, 136,
  138
  focusing 139, 140–1
light-sensitive cells
  135, 137, 138–9,
  142
lipase 91
lipids 15, 28
  digestion 90
  food 80

liver 14
  digestive system 23,
    79, 80, 84–5
  hormonal control
    105, 106
  storage 70
lobes, brain 117
long-sight 141
long-term memory
  128
lumbar nerves 119
lumbar vertebrae 46
lungs 69, 70–1, 76–7
  breathing 74–5
  circulation 94–95,
    96
  efficiency 21
  respiratory system
    23, 72–3
lymph 23, 81
lymphatic system 23,
  111
lysosomes 27

M

magnesium, bones 45
maintenance, body,
  79, 80, 82
male reproductive
  system 23
Malpighian
  corpuscles 104
Malpighi, Marcello
  13, 24, 70, 95, 104
mammals 12, 20, 47
  development 170–1
  reproduction 172
  warm blood 112
mammary glands
  170–1
mandible 46
marrow 43, 44–5
masseter muscle 61
mating 172
matrix, bone 49
mechanical
  advantage 45, 50
median nerves 119
medulla
  brain 117, 126
  kidney 108–9
meiosis 171, 176

Meissner's ending 33, 34, 164
melanin 33, 36
melanocytes 36
membrane
  cell 25, 26–7, 28–9
  organelle 27
memory 115, 116–17, 126–7, 128–9
  learning 132
  senses 136
  taste 162
Mendel, Gregor 170–1
mentalis muscle 61
Merkel's ending 164
metabolic water 111
metacarpal bones 52, 47
metatarsal bones 47
microscope
  electron 27
  invention 13, 24, 26
  use 178
microtubules 25
microvilli 84–5
middle ear 152
milk 12, 170–1
milk teeth 86
mineral crystals, bone 48
minerals 14–15
  blood 103, 104
  bones, 43, 44–5, 70
  diffusion 27
  foods 81, 83
  hormonal control 107
  reabsorption 81, 85
mitochondrion 15, 26–7
mitosis 171
molar teeth 86–7, 88
molecules 13, 14–15
  chemosensors 137
  diffusion 27
  DNA 176
  glucose 106
  haemoglobin 93, 94
  nutrients 90
  water 25
Moro reflex 120
motion sickness 156
motor cells 118
motor cortex 127

reactions 123
motor end plate 58, 119
motor nerves 57, 119, 121, 122–3
mouth 18–19
  digestive system 23, 80, 84
  epithelial cells 26
  muscles 61
  respiratory system 70, 72
  teeth 86
  touch sensors 162
mucus 75, 81, 94
mummies, Egyptian 37
muscles 55, 58–9, 60–1, 65
  balance 156
  cells 26
  exercise 16, 36, 76
  eyeball 138
  fibres 26, 57, 119
  glucose 83
  growth 174
  hand 66–7
  heart 95
  nerve control 116–17, 118–19
  pairs 57, 62–3
  proteins 80
  reflexes 120–1
  respiratory system 23, 69, 72, 75, 77
  skeletal system 50, 53
  stamina 21
  strength 21, 64–5
  stretch receptors 137, 156
  tongue 161
muscular system 22, 56–7
myelin sheaths 81, 119
myofibrils 57
myology 56
myosin 57

N

nails 22, 31, 32, 40

neck-bones 46
nephrons 104–5, 108–9
nerve cells 25, 26
  cerebral cortex 127
  memories 128
  myelin sheaths 81
  nervous system 117, 118–19
  olfactory epithelium 158
nerve centres 117, 127
nerve fibres 28
  brain 126
  optic nerve 137
nerves 116–17
  bones 44
  brain 115
  dermis 34
  Haversian system 48
  muscles 55, 57, 58, 64
  nervous system 23, 118
  skin sensors 33
  tooth 87
nerve signals
  eye 138
  heart 94
  semicircular canals 157
  sense organs 135
  sodium 81
  sounds 152
  tongue 160
  touch 164
nervous system 23, 105, 106–7, 118–19
neurons 117, 119
  memories 128
noradrenaline 105
nose
  epithelial cells 26
  respiratory system 23, 69, 72
  smell 136–7, 158–9
  sneezing 75
nucleolus 27
nucleus
  cell 24, 26–7
  chromosomes 171, 176
nutrients 15, 82
  bones 44

capillaries 96
cells 13, 26, 81
circulation 93, 94
diet 80, 83
digestion 80, 90
epidermis 34
exercise 76
membrane 25
mitochondrion 27
transport 102

O

oblique muscles, eye 138
oesophagus
  digestive system 23, 80, 84–5
  peristalsis 89
  swallowing 88
oils 15, 82
  digestion 90–1
  food 80
olfactory epithelium 137, 158
olfactory nerve 158
ophthalmoscope 139
optic nerves 119, 137, 139, 144
  blind spot 148
orbicularis oculi muscle 59, 61
orbicularis oris muscle 61
organelles 14–15, 24, 26–7
organ of Corti 152
organs 12, 14
osmosis 25, 26, 28–9, 110
ossicles 152
osteoblasts 49
osteocytes 25, 45, 48
osteology 44
osteons 44
ova 169, 172–3
ovaries 171, 172–3
  hormones 23, 105
oviduct 23, 171, 172–3
oxygen
  alveoli 73
  blood cells 25, 26

burning 71
circulation 22, 94, 96–7
diffusion 27
epidermis 34
exercise 76
exhaled air 74
haemoglobin 94–5
heart 98
pulmonary vessels 95
respiration 23, 57, 70, 72
supply 69
transport 102
yawning 75

P

Pacini, Filippo 33
Pacini's endings 33, 34, 164
pain 34, 135, 136, 164
palate 88
palmar blood vessels 97
pancreas
  digestive system 79, 81, 84–5, 90
  hormones 23, 105, 106–7
pancreatic duct 107
papillae
  dermis 34
  tongue 161
Pasteur, Louis 170–1
patella 46
pectoralis muscle 22, 59, 65
pelvis 46
  kidney 108
penis 23
perception 115
periosteum 49
peripheral nervous system 119
peristalsis 57
  swallowing 88–9
permanent teeth 86
peroneal nerve 119
personality 117, 126
perspiration 34, 112

phalanges 47
pharynx
  digestive system
    84–5
  respiratory system 72
  swallowing 88
phlegm, Hippocrates
  94
phosphorous, bones
  45, 48
photo-fit faces 19
physiology 13, 104
pigment, skin 36
pineal gland 118
pinnae 152
pituitary gland 23,
  106–7, 126
placenta 173
plantar nerves 119
plasma, blood 103
platelets 102–3
Plato 70, 116
platysma muscle 56
pons 117, 126
popliteal artery 100–1
pores, membranes 27
prefrontal cortex 127,
  128–9
pregnancy 172
premolars 86, 88
premotor cortex 127
pressure sensors
  136–7, 164, 166
  balance 156
  nerve ending 34
Priestley, Joseph 71
primates 12
proprioceptors 137,
  146–7
proteases 90
proteins 14–15
  blood plasma 103
  bone 43
  cell membrane 28,
    81
  clotting 102–3
  collagen 45, 48
  diet 80, 82–3
  digestion 90–1
  haemoglobin 94–5
  histones 176
  keratin 40
  myofibrils 57
  ribosomes 27
  skin 32, 37

puberty 169, 171, 174
pulmonary circulation
  96
  arteries 72, 95, 97,
    98
  veins 72, 95, 97, 98
pulp cavity 87
pulse 95, 100–1
pupils 138–9, 140
  reflex 121

Q

quadriceps muscle 22,
  59
quadruplets 171

R

radial artery 97, 101
radial nerve 119
radius 46–7, 52
reactions 115, 117,
  122–3, 124
rectum 23, 85
rectus muscles, eye
  138
red blood cells 26, 93,
  102–3
  production 170
  van Leeuwenhoek
    172
red marrow 45
reflexes 118, 120–1
  iris 140
  swallowing 88
renal blood vessels 97,
  108
reproduction 23, 169,
  170, 172–3
respiration, cellular
  57, 70–1, 72
respiratory system 23,
  69, 70–1, 72, 158
  moisture 74
retina 135, 136–7,
  138–9, 140, 142
  blind spot 148
  blood vessels 149
Rhesus blood system
  102

ribosomes 27
ribs
  breathing 23, 72–3,
    77
  intercostal muscles
    72
  nerves 119
  skeleton 22, 43, 44,
    46
rod cells 136–7, 142,
  149
Röntgen, Wilhelm 47
root, tooth 87
rooting reflex 120
roughage 81
Ruffini's ending 164
Rufus of Ephesus 46

S

saliva 80
  chewing 88
  digestive system
    84–5
  taste 160
  teeth 86–7
salivary glands 81, 88,
  90
saphenous vein 97
sartorius muscle 59
scalp, hair 35
scapula 52
sciatic nerve 119
sclera 138–9, 148
scrotum 171
sebaceous glands 32,
  34, 37
sebum 34, 37
secretin 106
semicircular canals
  152, 156–7
semi-permeable
  membrane 28
sense organs 135, 136
  brain 115
  nervous system 118
  skull 46
senses 23, 135, 136–7
sensors, skin 32–3,
  touch 164–5, 166
sensory cells 118–19
sensory centres 127,
  136

sensory memory 127,
  128–9
sensory nerves 121,
  122–3, 136
  reactions 123
septum, heart 94–5
sexual development
  107
sexual intercourse
  170–1, 172
sexual maturity 170
sexual organs 23, 171
shin-bone 22, 46
shivering 104, 113
short-sight 141
short-term memory
  127, 128, 130–1
shoulder blade 52
sinew 56
skeletal muscles 55,
  56–7, 58–9, 65
  voluntary control
    118
skeleton 22, 43, 44–5,
  46–7
  figure 16–17
  muscles 55
  strength 48
skin 31, 32–3, 34–5,
  36
  balance 156
  cancer 36
  collagen 45
  fingerprints 38–9
  hair and nails 40–1
  hand 66
  integumentary
    system 22
  sensors 32–3, 123,
    164–5, 166
  vitamin D 81
skull 45, 46
  bones 43
  Neanderthal human
    12
slow-twitch muscles
  65
small intestine
  absorption 85, 90
  digestive system 23,
    79, 80
  enzymes 81, 85
  hormones 106–7
smell 158–9
  centre 117, 158

sensory system 135,
  136–7
smooth muscle 57,
  58–9
  autonomic control
    118
  peristalsis 89
sneezing 75
sodium
  bones 45
  nerve signals 81
solution 25
somato-sensory cortex
  117, 123, 127
sound waves 135,
  136, 152, 154
space sickness 156
speech 71, 161
  cortex 127
sperm
  cells 13, 26
  chromosomes 176
  reproduction 23,
    169, 170–1, 172
spinal cord
  brain 126
  nervous system 23,
    116–17, 118–19
  reactions 123
  reflexes 120–1
spine 45
splenius capitis
  muscle 59
spongy bone 44–5, 49
spontaneous
  generation 170–1
stamina 21, 64–5
stapedius 56
starches, digestion
  90
Starling, Ernest 106
Stensen, Niels 56
stepping reflex 120
stereoscopic vision
  144
sternocleidomastoid
  muscle 59
sternum 22, 45, 46
stimulus, reactions
  122
St. Martin, Alexis 91
stomach
  blood vessels 97
  digestion 79, 80,
    90–1

digestive system 23, 84–5
enzymes 81
hormones 105
smooth muscle 57, 58–9
swallowing 88
stretch sensors
  balance 156
  co-ordination 146–7
  reflexes 121, 137
striated (striped) muscle 57
subclavian blood vessels 97
subcutaneous fat 32, 34, 36
sugars
  blood 103, 104
  digestion 81, 90
  transport 102
sulphur 15
sunburn 36
superior vena cava 97
swallowing 88–9, 118
Swammerdam, Jan 57
sweat
  glands 32–3, 34, 112
  skin 31, 32–3, 37, 38
  temperature control 112
  water balance 104, 110–11
synapses 28, 119
  memories 128
synovial fluid 45, 51
systemic circulation 96
systems, of the body 14, 22

T

taste 160–1, 162–3
  and smell 158
  buds 137, 160–1, 162
  centre 117, 162
  sensory system 135, 136–7
tears 138
teeth 86–7, 88
  calcium 81

digestive system 23, 80, 84–5, 90
temperature
  breathing 75
  control 22, 33, 112–13
  internal environment 102
  sensors 164, 166
temporalis muscle 61
tendons
  collagen 45
  hand 66
  muscles 56, 58–9, 60–1
  stretch receptors 121, 137, 156
testes 23, 170–1, 172
  endocrine system 23, 105
testosterone 107
thalamus 126
Thiéry's figure 151
thigh bone 22, 44, 46, 48
thirst 105, 111, 116, 126
thought 117, 126–7
three-dimensional vision 144–5
throat
  digestive system 84–5
  respiratory system 70, 72
  swallowing 88
  taste 161
thrombocytes 103
thymus gland 23
thyroid gland 23
thyroxine 105
tibia 22, 46, 52
  arteries 97
  nerves 119
tibialis anterior muscle 59
tissues 14
  bone 48
  muscle 57
toenails 32
tongue 136–7, 160–1
  chewing 88
  digestive system 84–5
  rolling 177

torso 16
touch 164–5, 166–7
  centre 117, 121
  hand 66
  mouth 162
  sensory system 119, 136–7
  skin 22, 31, 32–3, 34
trabecular bone 44
trachea
  coughing 75
  respiratory system 23, 70, 72
  swallowing 88–9
transfusion, blood 102
transitional epithelium 108–9
trapezius muscle 59, 61
triceps muscles 57, 62–3
twins 19
tympanic membrane 152

U

ulna 46–7, 52
  artery 97
  nerve 119
umbilical cord 173
urea 102, 104, 108–9, 111
ureters 23, 108–9
urethra 23, 108
urinary system 23, 104, 108, 110
urine 23, 108–9
uterus 23, 170, 172

V

vagina 23
valves
  heart 95, 98–9
  veins 95, 96–7
van Leeuwenhoek, Antony 13, 24, 172
vas deferens 23
veins 22, 94–5
  heart 98

pulmonary 72
  structure 96–7
vena cava 98
ventricles
  brain 116–17, 126
  heart 94, 98–9
vertebrae 46, 116
  nerves 119
Vesalius, Andreas 13, 22
  blood 95
  muscles 56
  skin 32
villi 79, 84, 85
Virchow, Rudolf 170
visual centres 138
visual cortex 127, 145
visual pathways 145
visual-spatial scratchpad 129
visual tricks 150–1
vitamins 81, 82
  blood transport 102
  foods 83
  skin production, vitamin D 33
  storage 70
vitreous humour 139
vocal cords 71
  adolescence 107
  coughing 75
voice 154
voice-box 71, 72, 89
Volta, Alessandro 117
voluntary actions 118
voluntary muscle 57, 58–9
von Helmholtz, Hermann 137, 139

W

wastes 108–9
  blood transport 93, 102
  carbon dioxide 72, 74
  digestive system 23
  urinary system 23
  water loss 111
water 15, 110–11
  blood plasma 103

bone 44
  cells 25, 28
  reabsorption 81, 85
  vapour 74–5
Watson, James 13, 176
white blood cells 26, 69, 102–3
windpipe 23, 72, 88
wisdom teeth 86
womb 23, 169, 170–1, 172–3, 174
wrist
  bones 47, 52
  pulse 101
writing, learning 132

X Y Z

X-rays, discovery 47

yawning 75
yellow marrow 45
yellow spot 139, 142
Young, Thomas 137

zona pellucida 172
zygomaticus muscle 61

Acknowledgments

STEVE PARKER would like to thank Roger, Bryn, Mukul, Christina, Emily, and the team at Dorling Kindersley for their dedication, hard work, attention to detail, and good humour; Jane for her continuing support; Alan and Martin for being human guinea-pigs; and Jim Cameron for his long-lasting inspiration.

■ DORLING KINDERSLEY would like to thank Tina Brazil, Jeanette Cossar, Fiona Courtenay-Thompson, Neil Lockley, and Des Reid for editorial assistance; Sarah Brigham for design assistance; Richard Walker and Dr Frances Williams for checking the text; all of the staff and pupils at John Perryn Primary School, East Acton, London; Caroline Brooke and Christine Rista for picture research; Jane Parker for the index; Lyn Rutherford for preparing the meal on page 162.

■ PICTURE CREDITS

t top; b bottom; l left; r right; c centre

Allsport: 21cr; / Mike Hewitt 54–55
Archiv für Kunst und Geschichte Berlin: 175 cbr, 175c
Australian Overseas Information Service, London: 12cr
Clive Barda, London: 107bl
Biophoto Associates: 47tr, 47cr, 47br, 103c
Bridgeman: / National Gallery, London 175br, 176cr; / Philip Mould Historical Portraits Ltd 176tr; / Prado, Madrid 176crr
British Museum: 11tr
Bruce Coleman: / Fred Bruemmer 113tc; / Stephen Krasemann 113tl
Comstock: 10–11
Mary Evans Picture Library: 13tl, 22tr, 58tr, 70b, 102cr, 110tr, 171br, 172tr, 176bl, 176br
Chris Fairclough: 128cl
Giraudon: / Munich Pinothek 175cra
Robert Harding Picture Library: 56r, 171bl
Hulton Deutsch Collection: 17tl, 21c
Image Bank: / Brett Fromer 25br; / John Kelly 20cl
Mansell Collection: 16bl, 47tc, 91tr, 96t, 104r, 118tr, 139br
Ruth Midgley: 31
National Library of Medicine: 172bl
National Medical Slide Bank 168–169
Nature Photographers: / Craig Cooper: 89bl
Richard Neave: 46bl, 46bcl, 46bc
Pinsharp 3–d Graphics / Jim Sharp: 144br
SPL: 87bl, 95tr, 134–135; / Michael Abbëy 40tl; / Department of Clinical Cytogenetics, Adden Brookes Hospital, Cambridge 176cll; / Biophoto Associates 176cl; / Dr. Goran Bredberg 134–135; / Dr Jeremy Burgess 26tr, 32l, 34tr; / CNRI 45tl, 91cr, 92–93, 103cl, 103tl, 114–115, 126br; / A.B. Dowsett 102br; / Don Fawsett 58tl; Fawcett / Hirokawa / Heuser 85cl; / Professor C. Ferland / CNRI 71tr, 71br; / Astrid and Hans Friedler Michler 107tl, 119br; / Manfred Kage 42–43, 68–69; / Francis Leroy / Biocosmos 25tl, 94bl; / Will and Deni McIntyre 167br; / P. Motta / Department of Anatomy, University of La Sapienza, Rome 136tr, 161tl, 161tc, 161tr; / Professor P.M. Motta and J. Van Blerkom 172br; / NASA 156bl; / NIBSC 103cr; / David Parker 13cr; / David Scharf 78–79; / Sheila Terry 30–31; / Giani Tortoli 159bl; / Jeremy Trew 24cr; / U.S. Department of Energy 14tr
Tony Stone Images: 66c, 122bl, 174cl; / Thomas Brase 117br; / Paul Chesley 117bl; / Keith Wood 81br
UK Crown / Aspley Ltd (E-Fit photograph) 19tr
Warren Anatomical Medical School Museum, Harvard: 126tr
The Wellcome Institute Library, London: 28tr, 106tr, 173bl
Dr. Robert Youngson: 139bl
Zefa: / H. Sochurek: 112tl

■ ILLUSTRATIONS

Karen Cochran: 22b, 23
Mick Gillah: 27t, 34b, 46r, 59t, 85t, 97c, 98b, 108b, 119l, 139t, 152b
Tony Graham: 27t, 34b, 46r, 59t, 72b, 85t, 87t, 97c, 98b, 119l, 126bl, 139
Selwyn Hutchinson: 22b, 23t, 23b, 72b, 106b, 126bl
Kevin Jones Associates: 108b, 152b
John Temperton: 14b, 15b, 16br, 18b, 26b, 39t, 34bl, 49r, 42bl, 57br, 57tr, 58bl, 60b, 61tl, 73tr, 84tr, 86b, 88br, 89c, 95bl, 97b, 99t, 103b, 109t, 111br, 119tr, 121tl, 123tr, 127t, 127bc, 128tr, 138bl, 138tr, 140cr, 141tr, 142tr, 145t, 148tr, 157tr, 164bl, 173t, 173bl, 179br, 180bl, 181tl, 182tl, 183bl, 184bl, 185t
Bryn Walls: 25bl, 27br, 28cr, 29br, 51b, 90br, 91br, 102bl, 103t, 106b, 111t, 129l, 103bl, 103br, 164br, 173c, 177b

■ MODEL MAKERS

David Donkin: 2b, 6tr, 7cl, 7br, 33b, 41, 67, 124, 125, 127br, 143, 146
Christina Betts: 2cr, 3b, 6bl, 53, 77b, 131, 153, 165
Bill Gordon Models: 115

■ MODELS

Roohi Ahmed, Saima Ahmed, Huda Ismail Ali, Charlene Allen, Karen Banton, Jayne Basterfield, Stephen Baverstock, Christina Betts, Nadine Biddulph, Christopher Birch, Jermaine Bowes, Gavin Browning, Rebecca Bunting, Thomas Bunting, Charmaine Dale, Leo Dudley, Lisa Ganpot, Philip Gilderdale, Jassy Gill, Rikki Hassan, Patora Ho, Phillip Hyde, Camay Jones, Chantelle Joseph, Selina Jules, Goran Kanlic, Davina Kirwan, Michelle Kunzi, Joanna Lagou, Jacqui Lamb, Sarah Lillicrap, Majuran Manohasandra, Joanna Mason, Marrion Murray, Bushra Murza, Sophia Nawaz, Megan Norwood, Jennifer Oatway, Aaron O'Connor, Ian O'Herhily, Philip Ormerod, Najad Osman, Richard Palmer, Hetan Patel, Mukul Patel, Priti Patel, David Pluck, Yasmeen Rahim, James Rasmussen, Ashley Rodwell, Kathleen Rooney, Wayne Saunders, Robina Sakhi, Lisa Scanlon, Samantha Schneider, Sobia Shah, Elham Sharoudi, Oliver Stobbart, Nadeem Syed, Jay Tan, Roger Tritton, Aidan Walls, Bryn Walls, Rosie Walls, Ahmed Warsama, John Whall, Lorraine Williams

■ SPECIAL PHOTOGRAPHY

Geoff Dann: 2, 3, 5, 6, 20, 35, 36, 37, 55, 58, 61, 73, 76, 96, 100, 105, 109, 120, 121, 124, 125, 136, 138, 145, 146, 153, 154, 155, 158, 159, 160, 162, 165
Tim Ridley: 2, 3, 5, 7, 18, 19, 27, 32, 33, 38, 39, 41, 57, 58, 75, 80, 86, 95, 101, 104, 112, 123, 138, 140, 141, 143, 167
Dave Rudkin: 1, 2, 3, 4, 5, 6, 7, 8, 9, 13, 15, 17, 21, 28, 29, 34, 37, 44, 45, 48, 49, 50, 51, 52, 53, 56, 60, 61, 64, 65, 66, 67, 72, 73, 74, 75, 76, 77, 80, 81, 82, 83, 84, 85, 87, 88, 89, 90, 91, 96, 100, 101, 105, 107, 108, 110, 111, 112, 113, 116, 117, 118, 121, 122, 127, 128, 129, 130, 131, 132, 133, 137, 142, 144, 147, 148, 149, 150, 151, 155, 156, 157, 161, 162, 163, 164, 166, 167, 171, 174, 175, 177, 178
Spike Walker (Microworld Services): 13, 24, 29, 33, 34, 35, 36, 40, 48, 56, 57, 59, 81, 105, 107, 108, 110, 137, 170, 172

Geoff Brightling: 105; Jane Burton: 111; Andy Crawford: 116, 120, 137, 174; Philip Dowell: 87; Andreas von Einsiedel: 101; Steve Gorton: 99, 144; Frank Greenaway: 95; Peter Hayman: 37; Dave King: 12, 20, 24, 43, 44, 45, 69, 94, 127, 163; Cyril Laubscher: 117; Bill Ling: 170; David Murray: 163; Steven Oliver: 25; Brian Pitkin: 71; Tim Shepard at Oxford Scientific Films: 80; Chris Stevens: 20; Harry Taylor: 82; Jeff Veitch: 44; Jerry Young: 20, 33, 101, 127, 136